Elementary

♡Japanese♡

To Download or Stream Audio Recordings:

1. You must have an internet connection.

2. Type the URL below into your web browser.

https://www.tuttlepublishing.com/elementary-japanese-volume-1-audio-and-pdf

For support email us at info@tuttlepublishing.com.

Elementary
Japanese

VOLUME ONE

BY YOKO HASEGAWA, Ph.D.

with

Wakae Kambara | Noriko Komatsu

Yasuko Konno Baker | Kayo Nonaka | Chika Shibahara

Miwako Tomizuka | Kimiaki Yamaguchi

TUTTLE Publishing

Tokyo | Rutland, Vermont | Singapore

"Books to Span the East and West"

Tuttle Publishing was founded in 1832 in the small New England town of Rutland, Vermont [USA]. Our core values remain as strong today as they were then—to publish best-in-class books which bring people together one page at a time. In 1948, we established a publishing office in Japan—and Tuttle is now a leader in publishing English-language books about the arts, languages and cultures of Asia. The world has become a much smaller place today and Asia's economic and cultural influence has grown. Yet the need for meaningful dialogue and information about this diverse region has never been greater. Over the past seven decades, Tuttle has published thousands of books on subjects ranging from martial arts and paper crafts to language learning and literature—and our talented authors, illustrators, designers and photographers have won many prestigious awards. We welcome you to explore the wealth of information available on Asia at **www.tuttlepublishing.com**.

Published by Tuttle Publishing, an imprint of Periplus Editions (HK) Ltd.

www.tuttlepublishing.com

Copyright © 2005 by Yoko Hasegawa
Cover photo © Christopher Futcher, IStockphoto

LCC Card Number: 2003110213
ISBN 978-4-8053-1368-8

Distributed by:

North America, Latin America & Europe
Tuttle Publishing
364 Innovation Drive, North Clarendon, VT 05759-9436 U.S.A.
Tel: 1 (802) 773 8930; Fax: 1 (802) 773 6993
info@tuttlepublishing.com
www.tuttlepublishing.com

Japan
Tuttle Publishing
Yaekari Building, 3rd Floor 5-4-12 Osaki,
Shinagawa-ku Tokyo 141-0032
Tel: (81) 3 5437 0171; Fax: (81) 3 5437 0755
sales@tuttle.co.jp
www.tuttle.co.jp

Asia Pacific
Berkeley Books Pte. Ltd.
3 Kallang Sector #04-01, Singapore 349278
Tel: (65) 6741 2178; Fax: (65) 6741 2179
inquiries@periplus.com.sg
www.tuttlepublishing.com

27 26 25 24 23 22   10 9 8 7 6   2201TP
Printed in Singapore

TUTTLE PUBLISHING® is a registered trademark of Tuttle Publishing, a division of Periplus Editions (HK) Ltd.

– Contents –

Lesson 4   しゅうまつのプラン **Weekend Plans**

Lesson 7   山本さんのアパートで At Yamamoto-san's Apartment

Lesson 8   かぞく Family

Lesson 9   レストランで At a Restaurant

Lesson 10   図書館 The Library

Lesson 11   ジャパンクラブで **At the Japan Club**

コールさんの前にすわっている人はだれですか

Who's the person sitting in front of Cole-san? 219

Lesson 12   買い物 **Shopping**

あまい物が少しほしいですね **We want something sweet, right?** 247

Lesson 13   手紙 **A Letter**

会えるのを楽しみにしています

Lesson 14   冬休みのけいかく **Winter-Break Plans**

– Preface –

Elementary Japanese is designed for people beginning their study of the Japanese language at the basic level. Because of its ample grammatical explanation, it can also serve as a grammatical reference. It is suitable for college courses as well as individual study. It consists of 27 lessons: 14 in Volume I and 13 in Volume II. One possibility is to cover Volume I in the first semester, and Volume II in the second semester, using the first week of the second semester to review Volume I.

Lessons typically contain:

   (i)   A dialog

   (ii)   Usage notes

   (iii) Grammar notes

   (iv) Exercises

   (v)   New kanji (Chinese characters) and explanation

   (vi) Kanji review exercises

   (vii) New vocabulary

(i)   The dialog is the core of each lesson as it contains all of the grammatical constructions to be studied in that lesson.

(ii)   Usage notes elaborate dialog expressions and include social and/or pragmatic explanations, e.g. politeness.

(iii) Grammar notes are linguistically oriented, although technical terms are avoided as much as possible. They attempt to explain the rationale behind grammatical constructions and their usage, rather than introducing them as mere facts. Historical changes and morphological processes, e.g. sequential voicing, are occasionally mentioned, making explanations more readable and comprehensible. Whenever appropriate, Japanese and equivalent English expressions are compared and contrasted, enabling students to utilize their already acquired knowledge of language use.

(iv) The exercises evolved from extending and expanding the materials developed in the Japanese Language Program at the University of California, Berkeley during several recent decades. Virtually all exercises emulate actual uses of the language rather than imposing mechanical drills. They are designed primarily for use in classroom activities, emphasizing interaction among students. They can also be used for self-testing at the end of each lesson, in which case, the user is advised to play two (or more) roles if necessary.

(v)   The study of kanji (ideographic Chinese characters) is one of the greatest obstacles in learning Japanese; acquisition of more than 1,000 kanji is needed to read Japanese texts, e.g, newspaper articles. While introducing a total of 313 basic kanji, *Elementary Japanese* explains the fundamental differences between ideographic (primarily representing ideas) and phonographic (representing sounds, e.g. English) writing systems.

(vi)   This textbook considers that the acquisition of kanji is of pivotal importance to any effective Japanese language program; it therefore provides additional kanji exercises.

(vii)   In addition to a vocabulary list for each lesson, comprehensive vocabulary lists (both Japanese-to-English and English-to-Japanese) are provided as appendices.

Cultural information and proverbs are interspersed. The importance of inclusion of contemporary interests and the continuing need for sex/gender neutrality in concepts, words, and images are recognized.

Abundant and innovative uses of illustrations and visual aids are provided throughout *Elementary Japanese*. The dialogs employ comic strip format, a method that enables learning sentences strongly associated with actual daily life situations. When a grammatical particle or a kanji radical is introduced, it is signaled by a clear visual marking, enabling students to locate relevant paragraphs quickly and at the point of need. The dialogs are illustrated by Neil Cohn; other drawings are by Neil Cohn, Yoko Katagiri, Joyce Nojima, Natsuko Shibata Perera, Virginia Tse, and Hiromi Nishida Urayama.

Upon completing the activities provided in *Elementary Japanese*, students can expect to be able to

(a)   describe themselves, their families and friends,

(b)   talk about daily events, using basic vocabulary and grammatical constructions,

(c)   understand conversations on those topics as well as classroom instructions,

(d)   read and write short, simple compositions.

Many people have helped with *Elementary Japanese* and its accompanying online audio recordings over the last ten years of its creation. Acknowledgement is due to our colleagues and students at the University of California, Berkeley who provided valuable feedback and/or participated in numerous recording sessions. They include Kate Chase, Ramon Escamilla, Momoe Saito Fu, Anthony Higgins, Alex Highsmith, Yoko Katagiri, Seiko Kosaka, Wesley Leonard, David Malinowski, Yasuhiro Omoto, Mischa Park-Doob, Kazumi Yahata-Pettersson, Tatsuo Saile, Keiko Sakatani, Shoichi Tamura, Angela Tiao, Masayoshi Tomizuka, and Hiromi Nishida Urayama. We appreciate the generous support of the Berkeley Language Center, where all audio materials were recorded. The recording engineer was Gina Hotta. Special thanks go to Flavia Hodges and Doreen Ng of Tuttle Publishing Company for bringing this work to publication.

This project was supported in part by grants from the Department of East Asian Languages and Cultures and the Center for Japanese Studies at the University of California, Berkeley.

Yoko Hasegawa
Berkeley, California

Useful Expressions

おはようございます
Good morning

1a   Daily Expressions

A   In the Morning

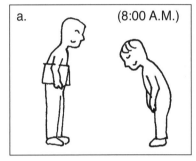

がくせい:	おはようございます。
gakusei	Ohayō gozaimasu.
student	*Good morning.*

せんせい:	おはようございます。
sensei	Ohayō gozaimasu.
teacher	*Good morning.*

がくせい A:	おはよう。
gakusei A	Ohayō.
student A	*Good morning.*

がくせい B:	おはよう。
gakusei B	Ohayō.
student B	*Good morning.*

おはよう is the casual form of おはようございます. It can be used among friends or family members, but not with someone to whom you need to show respect.

B   In the Afternoon

がくせい:	こんにちは。
gakusei	Konnichiwa.
student	*Good day / Hello / Hi.*

せんせい:	こんにちは。
sensei	Konnichiwa.
teacher	*Good day / Hello / Hi.*

The は in こんにちは is the topic marker. The letter は is usually read as [ha], but when used as the topic marker, it is pronounced as [wa] (cf. Lesson 2a). こんにちは is used approximately between 11 A.M. and sundown. There is no polite-casual distinction in this expression. You say こんにちは only when you see someone for the first time in a day. That is, if you have seen the person on that day and said おはようございます or こんにちは and see the person again later, you can still say *Hi* in English, but you cannot use こんにちは again in Japanese.

C   In the Evening

(7:00 P.M.)

がくせい A:	こんばんは。
gakusei A	Konbanwa.
student A	*Good evening.*

がくせい B:	こんばんは。
sensei B	Konbanwa.
teacher B	*Good evening.*

There is no polite-casual distinction. Unlikeこんにちは , you can sayこんばんは if you have already met the person earlier on the same day.

D   Parting

a.

せんせい:	さようなら。
sensei	Sayōnara.
teacher	*Goodbye.*

がくせい A:	さようなら。
gakusei A	Sayōnara.
student A	*Goodbye.*

がくせい B:	しつれいします。
gakusei B	Shitsurei shimasu.
student B	*Goodbye / Excuse me.*

しつれいします literally means "please excuse my rudeness". It is a polite expression and can be used as a substitute for さようなら. To end a telephone conversation, さようなら is rarely used; use しつれいします instead.

がくせい A:	さようなら。		
gakusei A	Sayōnara.		
student A	*Goodbye.*		

がくせい B:	じゃ、またあした。	じゃ	*well then*
gakusei B	Ja, mata ashita.	また	*again*
student B	*See you tomorrow.*	あした	*tomorrow*

またあした, literally "again tomorrow", is a casual expression, so do not use it with a person to whom you need to show respect.

E　　Thanking

がくせい:	どうもありがとうございます。
gakusei	Dōmo arigatō gozaimasu.
student	*Thank you very much.*

せんせい:	どういたしまして。
sensei	Dō itashimashite.
teacher	*You're welcome.*

どうも means "very much". どうもありがとうございます is used when you express your gratitude to someone who has just done something nice for you. どういたしまして is more or less equivalent to "You're welcome" in English. If you say どういたしまして, you are acknowledging that you have done something worthy of thanks. So, on occasions, you might sound arrogant. If you want to avoid this risk, say いいえ "No, (don't mention it)" instead (cf. **F** below).

F　　Apologizing

がくせい:	すみません。
gakusei	Sumimasen.
student	*I'm sorry.*

せんせい:	いいえ。
sensei	Īe.
teacher	*No, (that's okay).*

すみません is an appropriate expression to use when you apologize. In this case, せんせい says いいえ "No" to negate the seriousness of the student's fault.

G   At a Meal

いただきます。　　　　　　ごちそうさま(でした)。

Itadakimasu.　　　　　　Gochisōsama (deshita).

English does not have specific salutations before and after eating, but many cultures do, e.g. *bon appétit* in French. In Japanese いただきます is used at the beginning of a meal, and ごちそうさま at the end. いただきます literally means "I (humbly) receive (this meal)", and ごちそうさま (でした) literally means "(you went to so much trouble) running around (to prepare the meal)", but is used to express simply "Thanks for the treat". ごちそうさまでした is politer than ごちそうさま.

H   At Night

がくせい A:　おやすみ (なさい)。

gakusei A　　　Oyasumi (nasai).

student A　　　*Good night.*

がくせい B:　おやすみ (なさい)。

gakusei B　　　Oyasumi (nasai).

student B　　　*Good night.*

おやすみ is the casual form of おやすみなさい.

1b   Classroom Expressions

Here are convenient sets of expressions to use in classroom:

(1)　せんせい:　いっしょにいってください。　　いっしょに　　　　*together*

　　　sensei　　　Isshoni itte kudasai.　　　　　いってください　　*please say*

　　　teacher　　*Please say it together.*

(2)　せんせい:　もういちどいってください。　　もういちど　　　　*one more time*

　　　　　　　　Mō ichido itte kudasai.

　　　　　　　　Please say it together.

(3)　せんせい：　よくきいてください。　　　　よく　　　　　　　*well*

　　　　　　　　Yoku kiite kudasai.　　　　　きいてください　　*please listen*

　　　　　　　　Please listen (to me) carefully.

(4)　せんせい：　かいてください。

　　　　　　　　Kaite kudasai.

　　　　　　　　Please write it down.

(5)　せんせい：　よんでください。

　　　　　　　　Yonde kudasai.

　　　　　　　　Please read it.

Sentences in (6) and (7) below can be used when you do not understand what your せんせい has said. わかりませんでした is the negative form of わかりました. もういちど means "once more"; おねがいします is a general sentence that is used to make a request.

(6)　せんせい：　わかりましたか↑。　　　　　*Have you understood (it)?*

　　　sensei　　Wakarimashita ka?　　　　　*(≈ Do you understand?*

　　　teacher　　　　　　　　　　　　　　　↑ indicates rising intonation.)

　　　がくせい：　はい、わかりました。　　　　*Yes, I've understood (it).*

　　　gakusei　　Hai, wakarimashita.　　　　*(≈ Yes, I understand.)*

　　　student

(7)　せんせい：　わかりましたか↑。　　　　　*Have you understood (it)?*

　　　　　　　　Wakarimashita ka?　　　　　*(≈ Do you understand?*

　　　がくせい：　わかりませんでした。　　　　*I haven't understood (it).*

　　　　　　　　Wakarimasendeshita.　　　　*(≈ I don't understand.)*

　　　　　　　　もういちどおねがいします。　*Once more, please.*

　　　　　　　　Mō ichido onegai shimasu.

(8)　がくせい：　せんせい、すみません。　　　*Excuse me, Sensei.*

　　　　　　　　Sensei, sumimasen.

　　　　　　　　わかりません。　　　　　　　*I don't understand.*

　　　　　　　　Wakarimasen.

This is another convenient pair of expressions to use when you do not understand what your せんせい has said. すみません means "I'm sorry" or "Excuse me". One major difference between (7) and (8) is that わかりませんでした "I haven't understood" is used in (7), whereas わかりません "I don't understand" is used in (8). As in English, these two expressions are often interchangeable (at least in the sense of "I don't understand"), but わかりませんでした has more specific reference to a particular utterance, while わかりません can be considered more general. In (7), the student says that s/he cannot understand what せんせい has just said (i.e. specific); in (8), the student says that s/he, more generally, could not understand, or does not understand, or does not know (the answer to the question).

1c   Self Introduction

Miller	:	わたしは Jimmy Miller です。	*I'm Jimmy Miller.*
		Watashi wa Jimmy Miller desu.	
		おなまえは↑。	*What's your name?*
		Onamae wa?	
Son	:	わたしは Amy Son です。	*I'm Amy Son.*
		Watashi wa Amy Son desu.	
Miller	:	はじめまして。	*How do you do?*
		Hajimemashite.	
		どうぞよろしく。	*Nice to meet you.*
		Dōzo yoroshiku.	
Son	:	はじめまして。	*How do you do?*
		Hajimemashite.	
		どうぞよろしく。	*Nice to meet you.*
		Dōzo yoroshiku.	

は [wa] in おなまえは marks the topic here. おなまえは literally means "Your name?", but, unlike "Your name?" (which may sound impolite), おなまえは is a polite way to ask the other person's name. Because this is a question, you need to say it with rising intonation, marked by ↑.

はじめまして literally means "(We are meeting) for the first time" and is a very conventional greeting. Like English "How do you do", it can only be used when meeting someone for the first time.

どうぞ means "please", and よろしく literally means "treat things appropriately" or "be nice to me".

Son	:	ごせんもんは↑。	*What's your major?*
		Gosenmon wa?	
Miller	:	にほんごです。	*It's Japanese.*
		Nihongo desu.	

1d   List of College Majors

See Appendix B.

1e   Hiragana Syllabary

Japanese uses four sets of characters: *hiragana*, *katakana*, *kanji*, and *rōmaji* (the Roman alphabet).

Japanese has a very simple sound structure. There are 5 vowels [a, i, u, e, o], 14 simple consonants, and 12 "complex" consonants. There are two syllabaries: hiragana and katakana (the latter will be introduced in Lesson 2). With only a few exceptions, the following charts contain the hiragana characters that are sufficient to represent all Japanese speech sounds. These charts were originally designed by Buddhist clerics in the 9th century, based on the Sanskrit order of consonants and vowels.

Hiragana with Simple Consonants											
	a	i	u	e	o		a	i	u	e	o
	あ	い	う	え	お						
k	か	き	く	け	こ	g	が	ぎ	ぐ	げ	ご
s	さ	し shi	す	せ	そ	z	ざ	じ ji	ず	ぜ	ぞ
t	た	ち chi	つ tsu	て	と	d	だ	ぢ ji	づ zu	で	ど
n	な	に	ぬ	ね	の						
h	は	ひ	ふ fu	へ	ほ	p	ぱ	ぴ	ぷ	ぺ	ぽ
						b	ば	び	ぶ	べ	ぼ
m	ま	み	む	め	も						
y	や		ゆ		よ						
r	ら	り	る	れ	ろ						
w	わ				を o						
n	ん (See (**1f**))										

Pronounce each syllable by taking a consonant from the left column and following it with a vowel from the row above. The first row consists of five vowel sounds. Note that the [s, z, t, d] lines involve some irregularity:

[s+i] → [shi] し   [z+i] → [ji] じ

[t+i] → [chi] ち   [d+i] → [ji] ぢ

[t+u] → [tsu] つ   [d+u] → [zu] づ

Historically, じ and ぢ represented different sounds, and so did ず and づ. In most dialects of modern Japanese, however, じ and ぢ are pronounced as [ji], and ず and づ as [zu]. Usually, じ and ず are used to represent the sounds [ji] and [zu], respectively; ぢ and づ are used when sequential voicing occurs (cf. Lesson 11, **11f**).

Hiragana with Complex Consonants											
	a	i	u	e	o		a	i	u	e	o
ky	きゃ		きゅ		きょ	gy	ぎゃ		ぎゅ		ぎょ
sy [sh]	しゃ		しゅ		しょ	zy [j]	じゃ		じゅ		じょ
ty [ch]	ちゃ		ちゅ		ちょ	dy [j]	ぢゃ		ぢゅ		ぢょ
ny	にゃ		にゅ		にょ						
hy	ひゃ		ひゅ		ひょ	py	ぴゃ		ぴゅ		ぴょ
						by	びゃ		びゅ		びょ
my	みゃ		みゅ		みょ						
ry	りゃ		りゅ		りょ						

Like simple consonants, the [s, z, t, d] lines are irregular:

[s+y] → [sh]   [z+y] → [j]   [t+y] → [ch]   [d+y] → [j]

1f   The Moraic Consonant ん

Japanese consonants always appear with a vowel, e.g. [ka, se, to], etc. The only exception to this rule is [n]. The consonant [n] can occur with a vowel (な, に, ぬ, ね, の) or by itself (ん). ん is called the *moraic nasal,* because it counts as one *mora* (beat).*

ほ**ん**	にほ**ん**ご	せ**ん**せい	こ**ん**にちは
hon	nihongo	sensei	konnichiwa
book	*Japanese*	*teacher*	*Hello*

> * Each ひらがな in the simple-consonant chart above, including ん, counts as a single, approximately equal beat or unit in time. Although written with two ひらがな, those syllables with a complex consonant also count as one beat.

1g Vowel Devoicing

The vowels [i] and [u] are frequently devoiced; i.e., you shape your mouth for [i] or [u], but you do not pronounce it. This *vowel devoicing* occurs when [i] or [u] appears between voiceless consonants or in sentence-final position.

		Pronounced as:
ohayō gozaima**su**	おはようございます	ohayō gozaima**s**
shitsurei shima**su**	しつれいします	**sh**tsurē shima**s**
a**shi**ta	あした	a**sh**ta
dōzo yoro**shiku**	どうぞよろしく	dōzo yoro**shk**

Note that while the vowel loses its voicing, the syllable retains its status as taking up a single mora of time for pronunciation.

1h Long Vowels

In English, making a vowel longer does not change the word's meaning; in casual conversation, you could say "slooooow" to emphasize slowness. In Japanese, by contrast, short and long vowels are contrastive: i.e. if you make a vowel longer, you may change the word. For representing long vowels, the following conventions apply.

(1) Long あ: Add あ.

obasan	おばさん	*aunt, middle-aged woman*
obāsan	おば**あ**さん	*grandmother, elderly woman*

(2) Long い: Add い.

ojisan	おじさん	*uncle, middle-aged man*
ojīsan	おじ**い**さん	*grandfather, elderly man*

(3) Long う: Add う.

| suri | すり | *pickpocket* | sūri | す[う]り | *mathematical principle* |

(4) Long え: In principle, add い.

| eki | えき | *train station* | teki | てき | *enemy* |
| ēki | え[い]き | *energy, spirit* | tēki | て[い]き | *commuter ticket* |

Most of the words that contain the long vowel [ē] are loan words borrowed from Chinese. Although the vowel is pronounced as [ē] in modern Japanese (especially in Tokyo Japanese), it was originally pronounced as [ei]. (Orthography is always more conservative than actual pronunciation.) In extremely careful speech, the vowel can still be uttered as [ei].

A few words require an additional え, instead of い, for [ē]. These words are authentic Japanese words and were historically pronounced with [ē], not [ei].

onēsan	おね[え]さん	*elder sister*
ē	え[え]	*yes*
iidesunē	いいですね[え]	*It's good, isn't it?*

(5) Long お: In principle, add う.

| mo | も | *also* | mō | も[う] | *already* |
| ho | ほ | *sail* | hō | ほ[う] | *law* |

As in the case of the long vowel [ē], the long vowel [ō] is written with another vowel, おう. However, unlike えい, which can be pronounced as [ei], おう is almost always pronounced as [ō].

A small number of words require an additional お, instead of う. Historically, the second お in such a word was either [wo] or [ho].

| ōkii | お[お]きい | *big, large* | kōri | こ[お]り | *ice* |
| tōri | と[お]り | *street* | ōsaka | お[お]さか | *Osaka* |

1i   Long Consonants

Some Japanese words contain a long consonant, which is indicated by placing a small っ before the ひらがな whose consonant sound is lengthened, e.g. ほ[っ]かいどう. In authentic Japanese words, only voiceless consonants can be long, i.e. [p, t, k, s, sh]. In romanization, long consonants are represented by double consonant letters, e.g. Ho[kk]aidō.

This little っ can sometimes be used with a vowel in an interjection to indicate that the vowel is very short and abruptly terminated, e.g. あっ! "Oops", えっ? "What?!".

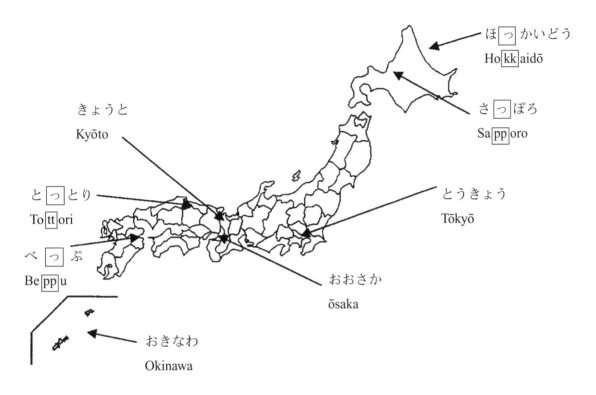

1j　Pitch Accent

Japanese is categorized as a pitch-accent language because some Japanese words are distinguished solely by pitch-pattern differences. Well known examples are はし (High-Low) "chopsticks" and はし (Low-High) "bridge". However, such pairs are not numerous; pitch patterns differ significantly from dialect to dialect, and context almost always resolves the ambiguity. Practically speaking, therefore, pitch accent is the least important aspect of Japanese pronunciation. There are pronunciation dictionaries, but you are encouraged to imitate native speakers as best as you can, rather than trying to fabricate the pronunciation from written notations.

練習問題 Exercises
<ruby>れんしゅうもんだい</ruby>

I.   What would you say in Japanese in the following situations?

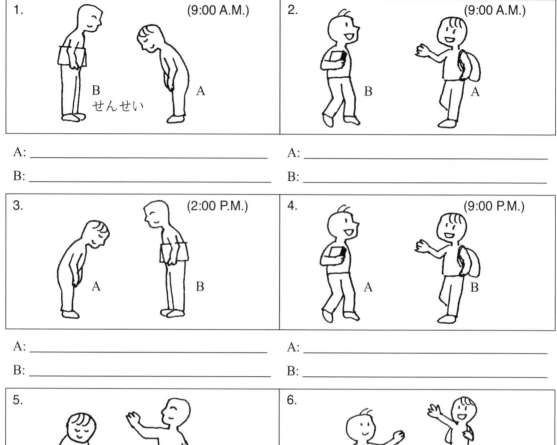

1.   (9:00 A.M.)

B
せんせい   A

A: _____

B: _____

2.   (9:00 A.M.)

B   A

A: _____

B: _____

3.   (2:00 P.M.)

A   B

A: _____

B: _____

4.   (9:00 P.M.)

A   B

A: _____

B: _____

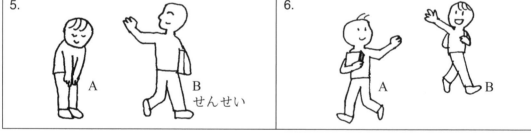

5.

A   B
          せんせい

A: _____

B: _____

6.

A   B

A: _____

B: _____

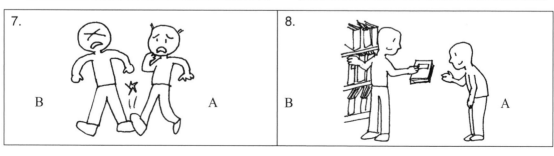

7.

B   A

A: _____

B: _____

8.

B   A

A: _____

B: _____

A: _____   A: _____

B: _____   B: _____

A: _____   A: _____

B: _____   B: _____

A: _____

B: _____

II. Let's read the following words.

1.	うち	*home / house*	10.	だいがく	*university / college*
2.	おおきい	*to be big*	11.	つくえ	*desk*
3.	おかあさん	*mother*	12.	ともだち	*friend*
4.	おとうさん	*father*	13.	にほんご	*Japanese language*
5.	おにいさん	*older brother*	14.	のむ	*to drink*
6.	おねえさん	*older sister*	15.	ひゃく	*one hundred*
7.	しゅみ	*hobby*	16.	ゆめ	*dream*
8.	すし	*sushi*	17.	りょこう	*trip*
9.	せんせい	*teacher*	18.	わたし	*I / me*

III.   Let's read the following words.

1.	いか	*below (quantity)*	いっか	*one family*
2.	もっと	*more*	もと	*formerly*
3.	いち	*one*	いっち	*agreement*
4.	さっき	*thirst for blood*	さき	*ahead*
5.	かき	*persimmon*	かっき	*vigor / energy*
6.	しと	*way of using*	しっと	*jealousy*
7.	べっし	*contempt*	べし	*must ～ (command)*
8.	いっき	*riot*	いき	*breath*
9.	はかい	*destruction*	はっかい	*8th floor*
10.	にっきゅう	*daily wages*	にきゅう	*second level*

新しい語彙 Vocabulary

This textbook's vocabulary, like that in a dictionary, is organized according to the order of the ひらがな chart: あいうえお, かきくけこ, and so forth.

おなまえ	*name (respectful)*	なまえ	*name*
がくせい	*student*	にほんご	*Japanese language*
ごせんもん	*major (respectful)*	ひらがな	*hiragana*
せんせい	*teacher*	わたし	*I / me*
せんもん	*major*		

Self Introduction

わたしのせんもんはけいざいがくです
My major is economics

会話 Dialog

<ruby>会<rt>かい</rt>話<rt>わ</rt></ruby> **Dialog**

1　ミラー　：ここはにほんご１００のクラスですか。

Is this the Japanese 100 class?

　　　ソン　：はい、そうです。

Yes, it is.

2　ミラー　：すみません。これはどなたのほんですか。

Excuse me. Whose book is this?

　　　ソン　：あっ、わたしのです。すみません。

Oops, it's mine. I'm sorry.

3　ミラー　：はじめまして、ジミー・ミラーです。

Nice to meet you. I'm Jimmy Miller.

　　　ソン　：はじめまして、エイミー・ソンです。

Nice to meet you. I'm Amy Son.

4　ミラー　：ソンさんのごせんもんはなんですか。

What's your major, Ms. Son?

5　ソン　：わたしのせんもんはけいざいがくです。ミラーさんは。

My major is economics. What about you, Mr. Miller?

　　　ミラー　：わたしはコンピューターサイエンスです。

Mine is computer science.

6　ソン　：そうですか。なんねんせいですか。

I see. What year are you?

　　　ミラー　：さんねんせいです。ソンさんは。

I'm a 3rd year student. What about you, Ms. Son?

7　ソン　：わたしはだいがくいんせいです。

I'm a graduate student.

　　　ミラー　：そうですか。だいがくいんせいですか。

Oh, you're a graduate student.

8　ミラー　：あのかたもにほんごのがくせいですか。

Is she (that person) a student in our Japanese class, too?

9　ソン　　：いいえ、あのかたはいしかわせんせいです。わたしたちのにほんごの
　　　　　　　せんせいです。

　　　　　No, she's Ishikawa-sensei. (She's) our Japanese teacher.

　　ミラー　：あ、そうですか。

　　　　　Oh, is that so?

使い方 Usage

2　すみません (formal) or すいません (less formal) means "Excuse me" or "I'm sorry", depending on the context. In Mr. Miller's utterance, it is understood as "Excuse me", whereas in Ms. Son's utterance, "I'm sorry" is a more natural interpretation.

The small っ here indicates that あ is short and abruptly ended. あっ is similar to English "Oops" or "Oh".

4　Generally, the Japanese use the family name, rather than the first (given) name, when they refer to a person. In such a case, さん is added to the family name. さん must not be used when referring to yourself; i.e. わたし はソン さん です is **unacceptable**. さん is similar to "Mr./Ms./Mrs./Miss", but there are no variants according to gender or marital status. In American English, the use of "Mr./Ms./Mrs./Miss" is very formal, but in Japanese, the use of さん is the norm, and not particularly formal or polite. When a person is in your intimate circle, you can use his/her first name with or without さん. Because the use of さん is the norm, i.e. not particularly respectful, when you talk with or about a person to whom you need to show respect, using さん would frequently be considered impolite. Do not use さん with your teacher's name; use せんせい instead. That is, いしかわせんせい is appropriate, but calling her いしかわさん would sound very arrogant.

4, 5　When you refer to the addressee's major or specialization, use ごせんもん to show respect. To refer to your own major or specialization, use せんもん, without ご (cf. Lesson 4, **4c**).

6, 7, 9　In Japanese conversation, the speaker usually pauses between phrases, at which point the addressee inserts such short phrases as ええ "Uh huh", はい "Yes", or あ、そうですか "Oh, I see" to signal his/her attentiveness. English speakers also use such signaling, but Japanese do so much more frequently. Therefore, many Japanese feel uneasy conversing with an English speaker if the addressee just listens to them quietly.

8　Literally, this sentence means "Is that person a student of Japanese, too?".

– Notes on Politeness –

You may wonder why politeness is such a big issue in the learning of Japanese. Are Japanese people politer than others? Perhaps, but not necessarily. Each culture puts significance on some aspects of human behavior, and politeness is very important in Japanese society. When we talk about cultural values, the opposite of politeness is casualness rather than impoliteness (no culture values impoliteness). Both are desirable characteristics, so there is a dilemma. Polite expressions are necessarily deferent, or standoffish, and they may sound unfriendly. Casual expressions are friendly but could sound discourteous. Each speaker in each society must select a balance between the two. American society puts more value on casualness, Japanese society on politeness. As an introductory textbook, this book generally teaches polite (but not super polite) expressions, with occasional remarks on casual speech.

文法 Grammar
<small>ぶんぽう</small>

2a	**X は Y です**	**"X is Y"**
2b	**X は Y ではありません／じゃありません**	**"X is not Y"**
2c	**Questions**	
2d	**Personal Pronouns**	
2e	**NOUN の NOUN**	
2f	**こ・そ・あ Demonstratives; ど Interrogatives**	
2g	**も**	**"also"**
2h	**Katakana Syllabary**	

2a   X は Y です   "X is Y"

| わたし あのかた これ | は | ソン せんせい ほん | です。 | *I'm Son.* *That person is a teacher.* *This is a book.* |

は (pronounced, but not written, as わ) is a topic marker. This pattern literally means, "As for X, it is Y" or "Speaking of X, it is Y". Although X is frequently the subject of the sentence, it need not be, e.g.:

わたしはコンピューターサイエンスです。
Speaking of myself, (my major) is Computer Science.

2b　X は Y ではありません／じゃありません　　"X is not Y"

The negative form of ～です is ～ではありません (formal) or ～じゃありません (less formal).

ミラーさんはさんねんせいです。　　　　*Mr. Miller is a 3rd-year student.*

ミラーさんはよねんせい $\left\{ \begin{array}{l} \text{ではありません} \\ \text{じゃありません} \end{array} \right\}$ 。　　*Mr. Miller is not a 4th-year student.*

2c　Questions

Forming a Yes-No question in Japanese is straightforward: add か to the end of the sentence.

ソンさんはがくせいです。　　　　→　　　ソンさんはがくせいです か 。

Ms. Son is a student.　　　　　　　　　　*Is Ms. Son a student?*

これはボールペンです。　　　　→　　　これはボールペンです か 。

This is a ballpoint pen.　　　　　　　　　*Is this a ballpoint pen?*

Questions with a WH-word (e.g. those corresponding to *who*, *what*, *where*, etc.) maintain the same word order as regular sentences.

あのひとは ミラーさん です。　　　　→　　　あのひとは だれ ですか。

That person is Mr. Miller.　　　　　　　　*(Lit.) That person is who?*

　　　　　　　　　　　　　　　　　　　　Who is that person?

あのかたは いしかわせんせい です。　→　　　あのかたは どなた ですか。

That person (respectful) is Ishikawa-sensei.　*(Lit.) That person is who?*

　　　　　　　　　　　　　　　　　　　　Who is that person? (respectful)

これは しんぶん です。　　　　→　　　これは なん ですか。

This is a newspaper.　　　　　　　　　　*(Lit.) This is what? What's this?*

これはじしょですか。　　　　　　　　　*Is this a dictionary?*

はい、これはじしょです。　　　　　　　*Yes, this is a dictionary.*

これはざっしですか。　　　　　　　　　*Is this a magazine?*

いいえ、これはざっしではありません。　*No, this is not a magazine.*

テキストです。　　　　　　　　　　　　*It's a textbook.*

これはえんぴつですか。ペンですか。　　*Is this a pencil? Or a pen?*

これはえんぴつです。　　　　　　　　　*This is a pencil.*

Strictly speaking, か is not a question marker; rather, it indicates that some information is missing in the speaker's knowledge (in the case of a question), or new information has just been acquired and, therefore, has not been fully incorporated into the speaker's knowledge system yet, e.g. あ、そうです か. The latter case is equivalent to "Oh, I see" or "Oh, is that so?" in English. Generally, as in English, questions are uttered with rising intonation at the end, whereas statements end with falling intonation. That is, in a question, か is pronounced with rising intonation, while with newly acquired information, か is pronounced with falling intonation:

あのかたはどなたですか↑。
(Lit.) That person is who?
あのかたはいしかわせんせいです。
That person is Ishikawa-sensei.
あ、そうですか↓。
Oh, I see.

Students sometimes forget to add か and just say そうです instead. そうです means "That's correct/right" and cannot be used to signal your attentiveness.

2d   Personal Pronouns

わたし	*1st-Person Singular*	あなたたち	*2nd-Person Plural*
わたしたち	*1st-Person Plural*	だれ	*Who*
あなた	*2nd-Person Singular*		*Interrogative Pronoun*

Although Japanese has あなた "you", the use of this pronoun is highly discouraged. If you use it, you may sound arrogant. Instead, use the addressee's family name or title whenever possible, e.g. ソンさんのごせんもんはなんですか "Ms. Son, what's (your) major?", せんせいのごせんもんはなんですか "Sensei, what's (your) specialty?".

You can use the addressee's first name if s/he is your close friend. If you do not know the addressee's name, you can simply leave out the subject entirely. English is believed to have a rigid requirement that the subject of a sentence be present in each sentence. But if the subject is *you*, it is almost always obvious and unnecessary. If you have cookies in your hand, *Want some?* is sufficient; in fact, the complete sentence *Do you want some of these cookies?* would often sound unnatural. Likewise, がくせいですか "Student?" is more natural than using a "complete" sentence in Japanese.

The use of わたし does not make your speech impolite, but here, again, it is unnecessary most of the time. If you use わたし whenever you refer to yourself, your speech will sound like *Me, me, me!*

There are 3rd-person pronouns in Japanese, but their usage is very different from English. You will learn them later, but until then, if necessary, use あのひと or あのかた (cf. **2f**).

だれ "who" is an interrogative (question) pronoun.

2e　NOUN の NOUN

 When a noun modifies another noun, の is inserted between them.

わたし の しゃしん	*my photograph (photograph of mine)*
ソンさん の えんぴつ	*Ms. Son's pencil*
だいがく の りょう	*college dorm (dorm of a college)*
にねんせい の テキスト	*second-year textbook*
だいがくせい の ミラーさん	*Mr. Miller, who is a college student*
バークレー の がくせい	*Berkeley student (student at UC Berkeley)*
わたしたち の にほんご の せんせい	*our Japanese teacher*
ニューヨーク の アパート	*New York apartment*
	(Apartment in New York)

The second noun in this construction can be omitted when it is easily identifiable.

これはソンさんのじしょですか。	*Is this your dictionary, Ms. Son?*
はい、わたし の です。	*Yes, it's mine.*
あれはにほんのくるまですか。	*Is that a Japanese car?*
はい、にほん の です。	*Yes, it's Japanese.*

2f   こ・そ・あ Demonstratives; ど Interrogatives

The こ series demonstratives indicate nearness to the speaker, those in the そ series indicate nearness to the addressee, and those in the あ series indicate nearness to neither.

a. これはペンです。

This is a pen.

b. それはコンピューターです。

That is a computer.

c. あれはアパートです。

That over there is an apartment building.

d. ここはにほんごのクラスです。

This place is a Japanese classroom.

e. そこはとしょかんです。

That place is a library.

f. あそこはサンフランシスコです。

That place over there is San Francisco.

g. このがくせいはいちねんせいです。

This student is a 1st-year (student).

h. そのじしょはわたしのです。

That dictionary is mine.

i. あのおんなのひとはウォンさんです。あのおとこのかたは、はやしせんせいです。

That woman over there is Ms. Wong. That man (respectful) over there is Hayashi-sensei.

Customarily, WH-interrogative words are included in this group of vocabulary and learned together; they are called the ど series.

ミラーさんは どの ひとですか。   *(Lit.) Mr. Miller is which person?*

いしかわせんせいは どの かたですか。   *(Lit.) Ishikawa-sensei is which person?*
    (respectful)

けいざいがくのほんはどれですか。   *(Lit.) The economics book is which?*

けいざいがくのほんはこれです。   *The economics book is this.*

ソンさんのアパートはどこですか。   *(Lit.) Son-san's apartment is where?*

ソンさんのアパートはあそこです。   *Son-san's apartment is that place over there.*

	こ	そ	あ	ど
Thing	これ	それ	あれ	どれ
Place	ここ	そこ	あそこ	どこ
+ NOUN (thing)	この X	その X	あの X	どの X
+ ひと (person)	このひと	そのひと	あのひと	どのひと
+ かた (person) (respectful)	このかた	そのかた	あのかた	どのかた

2g　も　"also"

When the *predicates* (verbs, adjectives, NOUN + です) of two sentences are identical, the は of the second sentence is replaced by も, e.g. (2) and (4) below.

(1)　ミラーさんはがくせいです。   *Mr. Miller is a student.*

(2)　ソンさん も がくせいです。   *Ms. Son is also a student.*

(3)　ミラーさんはせんせいじゃありません。   *Mr. Miller isn't a teacher.*

(4)　ソンさん も せんせいじゃありません。   *Ms. Son isn't a teacher either.*

Sentences (1)-(2) and (3)-(4) can be combined into single sentences (も must be repeated):

(5)　ミラーさん も ソンさん も がくせ
　　いです。   *Both Mr. Miller and Ms. Son are students.*

(6)　ミラーさん も ソンさん も せんせいじ
　　ゃありません。   *Neither Mr. Miller nor Ms. Son is a teacher.*

2h   Katakana Syllabary

カタカナ is another syllabary used to represent Japanese speech sounds. Both ひらがな and カタカナ were created from かんじ (Chinese characters, to be introduced in Lesson 3). While ひらがな derives from the simplification of cursive writing of かんじ, カタカナ derives from the modification of some part(s) of かんじ. So, ひらがな involve rounded angles, but カタカナ have more straight lines.

	a	i	u	e	o		a	i	u	e	o
	ア	イ	ウ	エ	オ						
k	カ	キ	ク	ケ	コ	g	ガ	ギ	グ	ゲ	ゴ
s	サ	シ shi	ス	セ	ソ	z	ザ	ジ ji	ズ	ゼ	ゾ
t	タ	チ chi	ツ tsu	テ	ト	d	ダ	ヂ ji	ヅ zu	デ	ド
n	ナ	ニ	ヌ	ネ	ノ						
h	ハ	ヒ	フ fu	ヘ	ホ	p	パ	ピ	プ	ペ	ポ
						b	バ	ビ	ブ	ベ	ボ
m	マ	ミ	ム	メ	モ						
y	ヤ		ユ		ヨ						
r	ラ	リ	ル	レ	ロ						
w	ワ				ヲ						
n	ン (cf. (**1f**))										

Katakana with Simple Consonants

	a	i	u	e	o		a	i	u	e	o
ky	キャ		キュ		キョ	gy	ギャ		ギュ		ギョ
sy [sh]	シャ		シュ		ショ	zy [j]	シャ		シュ		ショ
ty [ch]	チャ		チュ		チョ	dy [j]	ヂャ		ヂュ		ヂョ
ny	ニャ		ニュ		ニョ						
hy	ヒャ		ヒュ		ヒョ	py	ピャ		ピュ		ピョ
						by	ビャ		ビュ		ビョ
my	ミャ		ミュ		ミョ						
ry	リャ		リュ		リョ						

カタカナ is used to represent foreign words (other than Chinese) and onomatopoeic (sound symbolic) words, e.g. *bow-wow*, and can be used in a similar manner to italics in English. Japanese has borrowed many words from foreign languages (e.g. Chinese, Dutch, French, German, Portuguese), but in recent years the overwhelming majority of loan words have been from English.

Identification of カタカナ words is challenging, especially for English speakers. In fact, many advanced learners of Japanese feel that reading カタカナ is more difficult than かんじ. This is due to the difference in Japanese and English sound systems: Japanese has a much simpler sound system than English. So, when Japanese borrows English words, it must "tailor" the sounds to suit its own sound system. The results of such tailoring may sound completely different from the original words. (Conversely, if you pronounce *karaoke* in English, no Japanese person would understand it.) Once you have become familiar with the Japanese sound system, try to pronounce English words with only those sounds available to Japanese. For example, *apple* is represented in カタカナ as アップル [appuru]. If you compare this representation with other possibilities, e.g. [epuru, āpuri, appu] etc., you will find that アップル makes more sense.

In this section, we provide general guidelines to the カタカナ representation of English words. Do not get overwhelmed; you do not have to memorize all of them at once. Later, as need arises, consult this section.

A   Syllable Structure

In Japanese, all consonants, except for ン, must be followed by a vowel in order to form a syllable. By contrast, most other languages do not have this constraint. For example, English allows 3 consonants to appear in a row, e.g. *strike*. In order to represent *strike* in カタカナ, we need to insert a vowel after the [s] and [t] (and [k] as well). The default vowel for such an adjustment is [u]. But if we put a [u] after [t] or [d], the consonant changes. (Recall that the [t] and [d] lines in ひらがな are たち つ てと and だぢ づ でど.) So, after a [t] or [d], an [o] is inserted, instead of [u]. Thus, *strike* becomes ストライク. (The vowel [u] is added after the [k] because, although the letter *e* appears last in spelling, there is no vowel sound following the [k] in pronunciation.)

```
s     t     ri    k     e
      ↑     ↑           ↑
      u     o           u
ス    ト    ライ   ク
```

In some older loan words, [i], rather than [u], was added after a [k], e.g. ケーキ "cake", ジャッキ "jack (to jack up)", ステーキ "steak", デッキ "deck". In fact, *strike* is written in two ways: one with [u], ストライク, meaning a "strike in a baseball game", and the other with [i], ストライキ, meaning a "labor strike".

B   Vowels

When an English word is borrowed, all English vowels must be categorized into one of the five Japanese vowels.

Some English vowels are inherently longer than others. Compare *live* and *leave*, for example. They have different vowel qualities, but to the Japanese ear, both sound like [i]. On the other hand, because the Japanese language makes a distinction between short and long vowels, native speakers are particularly sensitive to length differences. If they hear a vowel as being long, the word is represented as containing a long vowel. Long vowels are written with the symbol "ー" inserted after the syllable.

[i], as in *heal*, is perceived by the Japanese as a long [i].

アイスク リー ム	ス キー	ス ニー カー	チー ズ
aisukurīmu	sukī	sunīkā	chīzu
ice cream	*ski*	*sneaker*	*cheese*

[ɪ], as in *hill*, is perceived as a short [i].

テレ[ビ]

terebi
television

テ[ニ]ス

tenisu
tennis

[ミ]ルク

miruku
milk

[ピ]アノ

piano
piano

[eɪ], as in *hail*, is perceived as a long [e] or, less frequently, as [ei].

[ケ]ーキ

kēki
cake

[テ]ーブル

tēburu
table

エア[メ]ール

eamēru
airmail

[レイ]ンコート

reinkooto
raincoat

[ɛ], as in *bell*, is perceived as a short [e].

ブ[レ]ッド

bureddo
bread

[ペ]ン

pen
pen

[テ]スト

tesuto
test

[デ]スク

desuku
desk

[æ], as in *hat*, is perceived as a short [a].

[ア]ップル

appuru
apple

[カ]メラ

kamera
camera

[バ]ッグ

baggu
bag

プ[ラ]ン

puran
plan

[ɑ], as in *not*, is perceived as a short [o] or, less frequently, as a long [o].

[コ]ーヒー

kōhī
coffee

[ポ]ット

potto
pot

ロ[ボ]ット

robotto
robot

[ゴ]ルフ

gorufu
golf

[oʊ], as in *old*, is perceived as a long [o].

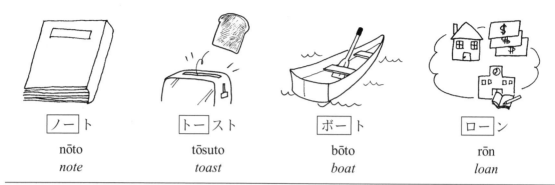

ノート	トースト	ボート	ローン
nōto	tōsuto	bōto	rōn
note	*toast*	*boat*	*loan*

[ʊ], as in *good*, is perceived as a short [u].

インプット	クッキー	ブック	ブッシュ
inputto	kukkī	bukku	busshu
input	*cookie*	*book*	*bush*

[u], as in *moon*, is perceived as a long [u].

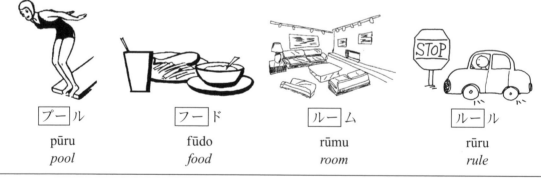

プール	フード	ルーム	ルール
pūru	fūdo	rūmu	rūru
pool	*food*	*room*	*rule*

[ə], as in *hut*, is perceived as a short [a]; however, if [ə] is represented in English spelling by [o], it may be written as [o] in カタカナ as well, e.g. コンピューター.

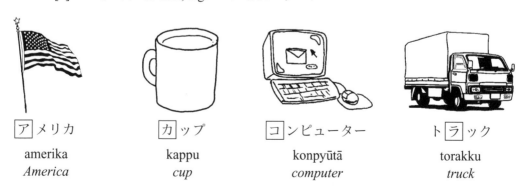

アメリカ	カップ	コンピューター	トラック
amerika	kappu	konpyūtā	torakku
America	*cup*	*computer*	*truck*

[aɪ], as in *ice*, is perceived as a combination of [a] and [i].

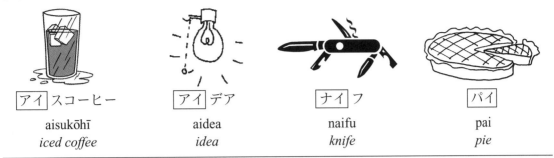

アイ スコーヒー	アイ デア	ナイ フ	パイ
aisukōhī	aidea	naifu	pai
iced coffee	*idea*	*knife*	*pie*

[aʊ], as in *how*, is perceived as a combination of [a] and [u].

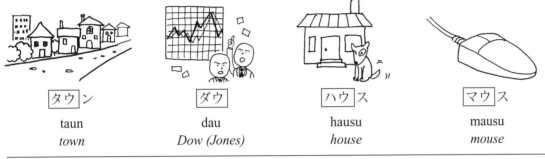

タウ ン	ダウ	ハウ ス	マウ ス
taun	dau	hausu	mausu
town	*Dow (Jones)*	*house*	*mouse*

The sequence of a vowel and an [r] is perceived as the corresponding long vowel. The sounds in English *bird* and *bard* are represented by the same symbols in カタカナ: both would be written and pronounced バード.

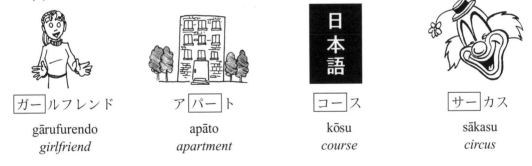

ガー ルフレンド	ア パー ト	コー ス	サー カス
gārufurendo	apāto	kōsu	sākasu
girlfriend	*apartment*	*course*	*circus*

C   [f]

[f] by itself or with a [ʊ, u] is perceived as [hu] and represented as フ, because this has the most "[f]-like" sound of the syllables in this series. [f] with other vowels is written as フ plus the following vowel in a small letter.

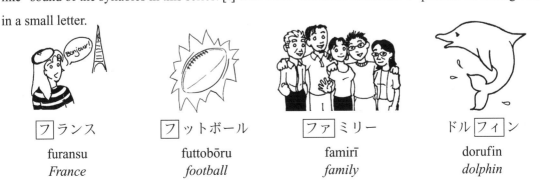

フ ランス	フ ットボール	ファ ミリー	ドル フィ ン
furansu	futtobōru	famirī	dorufin
France	*football*	*family*	*dolphin*

フィルム
firumu
film

フェリー
ferī
ferry (boat)

カリフォルニア
kariforunia
California

D　[l] and [r]

[l] and [r] are perceived as an [r].

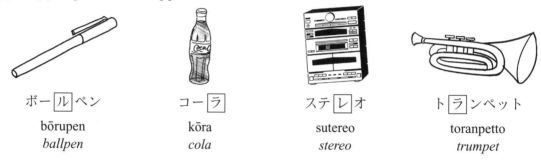

ボールペン
bōrupen
ballpen

コーラ
kōra
cola

ステレオ
sutereo
stereo

トランペット
toranpetto
trumpet

E　[t] and [d]

In the authentic Japanese sound system, [t + i] becomes チ [chi], [d + i] becomes ジ [ji], and [t + u] becomes ツ [tsu].

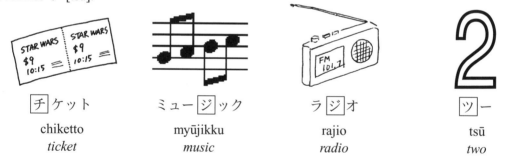

チケット
chiketto
ticket

ミュージック
myūjikku
music

ラジオ
rajio
radio

ツー
tsū
two

However, an increasing number of Japanese speakers pronounce [ti] and [di] in the same way as English speakers do. This new pronunciation can be represented in カタカナ as ティ and ディ, respectively. Some Japanese write [tu] as トゥ, but this notational convention is not yet widely used.

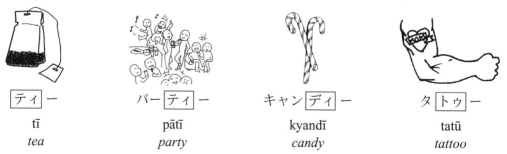

ティー
tī
tea

パーティー
pātī
party

キャンディー
kyandī
candy

タトゥー
tatū
tattoo

F　[th]

The initial consonants in *thank* and *this* are perceived as [s] and [z], respectively, although in a small number of words the voiceless [th] is represented as [t].

シ アター
shiatā
theater

ス リー
surī
three

マ ザー
mazā
mother

サ ンキュー
sankyū
thank you

アロマ テ ラピー
aromaterapī
aromatherapy

エス テ ティック
esutetikku
aesthetic

G　[she, je, che]

The [she, je, che] sounds do not occur in authentic Japanese words, but can be represented in カタカナ as シェ , ジェ , and チェ, respectively.

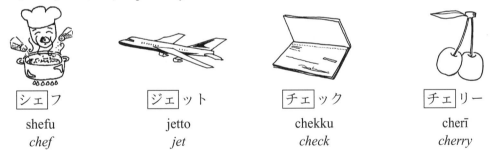

シェ フ
shefu
chef

ジェ ット
jetto
jet

チェ ック
chekku
check

チェ リー
cherī
cherry

H　や , ゆ , よ

Some English sounds are like those represented in ひらがな with a small や , ゆ , よ , and they are represented as such in カタカナ .

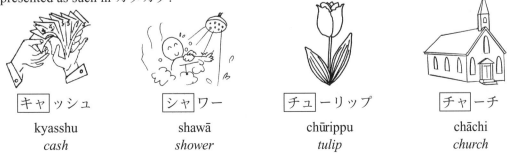

キャ ッシュ
kyasshu
cash

シャ ワー
shawā
shower

チュ ーリップ
chūrippu
tulip

チャ ーチ
chāchi
church

I   [v]

[v] is normally written as [b]. Some Japanese want to make a distinction between [v] and [b] by writing the former as ヴ plus a vowel in a small letter.

アイ ビー   ベ ジタブル   ヴァ イオリン or バ イオリン

aibī   bejitaburu   vaiorin or baiorin
ivy   *vegetable*   *violin*

J   [ye]

Both in ひらがな and カタカナ, [y] occurs only with [a, u, o]. The syllable [ye] can be written as イエ.

イェーツ   *Yates*   イェール   *Yale*
イェルサレム   *Jerusalem*   イェロー   *yellow*

K   [w]

In ひらがな, [w] can occur only with [a], but in カタカナ, other combinations are possible: [w] is represented as ウ, and the following vowel in a small letter.

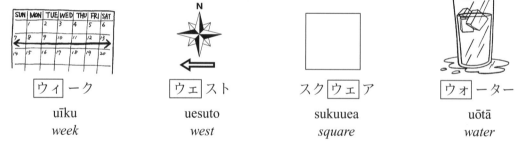

ウィ ーク   ウェ スト   スク ウェ ア   ウォ ーター

uīku   uesuto   sukuuea   uōtā
week   *west*   *square*   *water*

L   Long Consonants

Like in ひらがな, long consonants are represented by a small ッ appearing before the consonant, making the consonant sound sharp and clipped. When an English syllable ends with a stop [p, b, t, d, k, g] or a strong voiceless fricative [s, sh], the Japanese perceive the final consonant as being long and tend to insert a ッ.

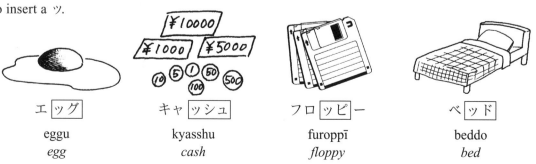

エ ッグ   キャ ッシュ   フロ ッピー   ベ ッド

eggu   kyasshu   furoppī   beddo
egg   *cash*   *floppy*   *bed*

The following words commonly occur with or without a small ッ.

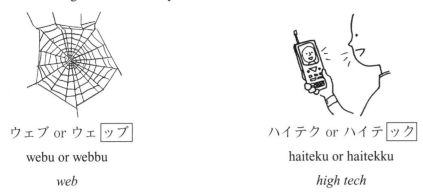

ウェブ or ウェ ッブ

webu or webbu

web

ハイテク or ハイテック

haiteku or haitekku

high tech

練 習 問題 Exercises

I.　　Practice conversations with your partner, using これ／それ／あれ／どれ.

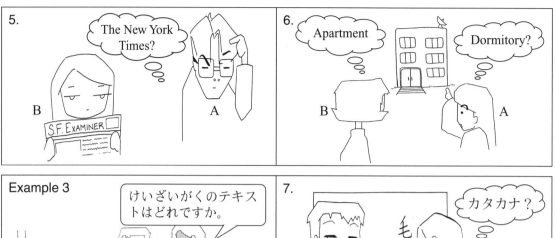

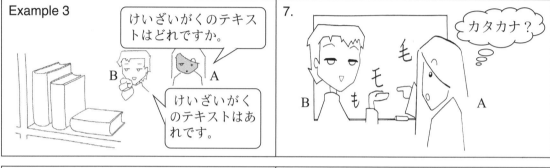

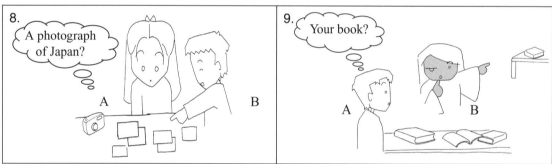

II.   Let's find out about your partner. Interview your partner using his／her name in the blank.

1. ＿＿＿＿＿＿＿＿＿＿＿＿＿＿＿＿ さんはなんねんせいですか。

2. ＿＿＿＿＿＿＿＿＿＿＿＿＿＿＿＿ さんのごせんもんはなんですか。

3. ＿＿＿＿＿＿＿＿＿＿＿＿＿＿＿＿ さんのせんせいはどなたですか。

III.   Practice the following conversations with your partner; use この／その／あの／どの.

A: ＿＿＿＿＿＿＿ ビルはとしょかんですか。

B: いいえ、(このビルは) としょかんじゃあ
     りません。(このビルは) りょうです。

A: としょかんは ＿＿＿＿＿＿＿ ビルですか。

B: としょかんは ＿＿＿＿＿＿＿ ビルです。

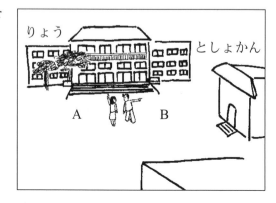

IV.　Look at the photograph and practice with your partner.

　　A:　このかたはどなたですか。

　　B:　＿＿＿＿＿＿かたは＿＿＿＿＿＿＿＿です。

Bring your own picture and practice more.

　　A:　このかたはどなたですか。

　　B:　＿＿＿＿＿＿かたは＿＿＿＿＿＿＿＿です。

　　A:　＿＿＿＿＿＿ひとはだれですか。

　　B:　＿＿＿＿＿＿ひとは＿＿＿＿＿＿＿です。

V.　Following the example below, practice with your
　　own book, textbook, pencils, etc.

　　A:　これは｛どなた／だれ｝のほんですか。

　　B:　それはわたしのです。

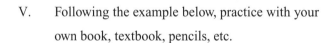

VI.　Reading practice

　　こんにちは。はじめまして。わたしはブラウンです。きょうとだいがくのがくせいです。さんねんせいです。せんもんはコンピューターサイエンスです。

　　あのおとこのひとはすずきさんです。すずきさんのせんもんはえいごです。すずきさんはだいがくせいじゃありません。だいがくいんせいです。

○ (Correct/True) ですか。× (Incorrect/False) ですか。

1.　（　　）すずきさんはだいがくせいです。

2.　（　　）ブラウンさんはいちねんせいです。

3.　（　　）ブラウンさんはニューヨークのだいがくのがくせいです。

4.　（　　）すずきさんのせんもんはにほんごじゃありません。

新しい語彙 Vocabulary

～たち	(plural indicator for people)		しんぶん	newspaper
あそこ	place over there		そこ	there
あなた	you		それ	that one
アパート	apartment		だいがく	college, university
あれ	that one, those ones		だいがくいんせい	graduate student
いちねんせい	1st-year student		だいがくせい	undergraduate student
えいご	English		だれ	who
えんぴつ	pencil		テキスト	textbook
おとこ	male		どこ	where
おんな	female		としょかん	library
かた	person (respectful)		どなた	who (respectful)
カタカナ	katakana		どれ	which one
クラス	class		なん	what
くるま	car		なんねんせい	what-year student
けいざいがく	economics		にねんせい	2nd-year student
ここ	here		ひと	person
これ	this one		ビル	building
コンピューター	computer		ペン	pen
サイエンス	science		ボールペン	ballpoint pen
ざっし	magazine		ほん	book
さんねんせい	3rd-year student		よねんせい	4th-year student
じしょ	dictionary		りょう	dormitory
しゃしん	photograph		わたしたち	we

なまえ (Mostly proper nouns)

いしかわ	*Ishikawa*		ソン	*Son*
ウォン	*Wong*		タイムズ	*Times*
エイミー	*Amy*		にほん	*Japan*
エグザミナー	*Examiner*		ニューヨーク	*New York*
きょうと	*Kyoto*		バークレー	*Berkeley*
サンフランシスコ	*San Francisco*		ブラウン	*Brown*
ジミー	*Jimmy*		ミラー	*Miller*

Places

だいがくのちかくにゆうびんきょくがあります
There's a post office near campus

会話 Dialog

1　ミラー　：ソンさん、このだいがくににほんごのとしょかんがありますか。

(Lit.) Son-san, is there a special library for Japanese books at this university?

Son-san, does this university have a special library for Japanese books?

　　　ソン　　：ええ、ありますよ。

Yes, there is / Yes, it does.

2　ミラー　：どこにありますか。

Where is it?

　　　ソン　　：にほんごプログラムのビルのとなりにあります。

It's next to the building where the Japanese Program office is.

3　ミラー　：あのう、にほんごプログラムのビルはどれですか。

Ummm, which one is the Japanese Program office?

　　　ソン　　：あのビルです。

That building.

4　ミラー　：あ、そうですか。だいがくにゆうびんきょくもありますか。

Oh, I see. Is there a post office on campus, too?

5　ソン　　：いいえ、ありません。でも、ゆうびんきょくはだいがくのちかくにありますよ。

No, there isn't. But there's one near campus.

6　ミラー　：そうですか。ありがとうございます。

I see. Thank you.

　　　ソン　　：あっ、あそこにこやまさんがいます。こやまさんはわたしのルームメートです。

Oh, that's Koyama-san over there. She's my roommate.

7　ミラー　：どのひとですか。

Which person is she?

8　ソン　　：あのおんなのひとです。

That woman over there.

　　　ミラー　：ああ、あのひとですか。

Oh, that person.

<ruby>使<rt>つか</rt></ruby>い<ruby>方<rt>かた</rt></ruby> Usage

1   にほんごのとしょかん literally means a "library of the Japanese language".

ええ↓ is less formal and gentler than はい "yes".

3   あのう is equivalent to "Ummm ..." or "Well, ~". It indicates that the speaker has something to say, but is hesitant to say it for some reason. あのう can also be used to cut in on a conversation. In general, it allows the speaker to sound less direct, and therefore more polite.

5   でも means "but/however". It's a casual expression—a more formal one is けれども.

6   あっ in this sentence expresses surprise.

8   ああ↓ conveys the same meaning as あ in あ、そうですか.

<ruby>文法<rt>ぶんぽう</rt></ruby> Grammar

3a	**Existential Verbs**
3b	**Topic Marker** は
3c	**Location Marker** に
3d	なにか／だれか／どなたか／どこかに **+ Affirmative Predicate**
	なにも／だれも／どなたも／どこにも **+ Negative Predicate**
3e	**NOUN1** と **NOUN2** **(NOUN1 and NOUN2)**
3f	**Final Particle** よ
3g	**Numbers**

3a   Existential Verbs

LOCATION	に	SUBJECT	が	あります／います／いらっしゃいます
SUBJECT	は	LOCATION	に	あります／います／いらっしゃいます

あります is used when the subject is a thing; います when it is a human, animal, etc. The location is marked with に. The use of いらっしゃいます is necessary when you are supposed to show respect to the person referred to by the subject.

(1)   つくえのうえ に ほん が あります。   *(Lit.) On the desk there is a book.*
                                                    There is a book on the desk.

(2)   ほん は つくえのうえ に あります。   *The book is on the desk.*

Although both sentences can be used to depict the same physical situation, they are not interchangeable. (2) cannot be used unless you believe that the addressee already knows which book you're talking about.

Note that Japanese does not have different nouns or verbs for singular and plural entities. So, (1) and (2) can also mean "There are books on the desk" and "The books are on the desk", respectively.

The negative form of 〜ます is 〜ません. Note that the negative counterpart of 〜に〜 $\boxed{が}$ あります is 〜に〜 $\boxed{は}$ ありません. This use of は will be explained in Lesson 6, **6h**.

(3)　ソン　　：　ミラーさんのへやにラジオ $\boxed{が}$ ありますか。
　　　ミラー　：　いいえ、わたしのへやにラジオ $\boxed{は}$ あり $\boxed{ません}$ 。

(4)　ソン　　：　ノートはつくえのうえにありますか。
　　　ミラー　：　いいえ、ノートはつくえのうえにあり $\boxed{ません}$ 。

(5)　ソン　　：　いしかわせんせいはオフィスにいらっしゃいますか。
　　　ミラー　：　いいえ、いしかわせんせいはオフィスにいらっしゃい $\boxed{ません}$ 。

3b　Topic Marker は

は　In grammar classes we were told that the subject is the person or thing that we are talking about. However, the *topic* is also an entity that we are talking about. Are they the same? Well, frequently, but not always. The subject is a notion that directly relates to the *predicate* (remember, the predicate usually consists of a VERB, ADJECTIVE, or NOUN + です). Generally, when there is a predicate, there is a subject. Topic, on the other hand, is a broader notion. We can talk about the topic of a sentence or paragraph, or even of a book. Frequently, the topic appears as the subject, but not always: in sentences like *Fish, I hate*, the topic *fish* is the direct object of the predicate *hate*.

は is the topic marker, which can mark the subject only when the referred entity is known by both the speaker and the addressee. つくえのうえにほんがあります "There is a book on the desk" can be uttered if there is a book on the desk, but ほん $\boxed{は}$ つくえのうえにあります "The book is on the desk" is meaningful only when the addressee knows which book you are talking about. Because the topic needs to be identifiable by both the speaker and addressee, WH-interrogative words cannot appear as a topic. That is, だれ $\boxed{は}$ いますか "Who's there?" is unnatural in Japanese; you must say だれ $\boxed{が}$ いますか.

3c   Location Marker に

 に is used with a word of location to indicate that a certain thing or person exists in that place. The location word can be a proper name or a relational word such as *top of*, *under*, *in front of*, *behind*, *next to*, etc.

(1)   ヨセミテはカリフォルニア に あります.   *Yosemite is (located) in California.*

(2)   おてあらいはオフィスのとなり に あります.   *The restroom is next to the office.*

(3)   いしかわせんせいはソンさんのとなり に
       いらっしゃいます.   *Ishikawa-sensei is next to Son-san.*

Xのうえに
on (the top of) X, above X

いぬはつくえのうえにいます。
The dog is on the desk.

Xのしたに
below X, under X

いぬはつくえのしたにいます。
The dog is under the desk.

Xのまえに
in front of X

いぬはねこのまえにいます。
The dog is in front of the cat.

Xのうしろに
behind X

いぬはねこのうしろにいます。
The dog is behind the cat.

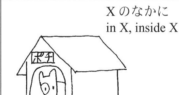

Xのなかに
in X, inside X

いぬはいぬごやのなかにい
ます。
*The dog is {in/inside} the
doghouse.*

Xのちかくに
near X

いぬはいぬごやのちかくに
います。
The dog is near the doghouse.

Xのとなりに
Xのよこに
next to X,
beside X

いぬはねこの{となり／よこ}にいます。
The dog is {next to/beside} the cat.

「Xのとなりに」 "next to X" and「Xのよこに」"be-side X" are similar in meaning and thus sometimes interchangeable. However, while「Xのよこに」can be used for a broad range of objects, the use of「Xのとなりに」is very limited. In「XのとなりにYがあります」, both X and Y are similar entities of cultural or personal significance: e.g. people, animals, houses, countries, facilities, furniture, visual symbols (pictures, letters／characters, articles, books).

3d　なにか／だれか／どなたか／どこかに + Affirmative Predicate
　　　なにも／だれも／どなたも／どこにも + Negative Predicate

なにか	something	なにも	anything
だれか	someone	だれも	anyone
どなたか	someone (respectful)	どなたも	anyone (respectful)

With なにか／だれか／どなたか, the use of が is optional; with なにも／だれも／どなたも, が **must not be used**.

(1)　ベッドのうえに なにか （が）ありますか。

Is there something on the bed?

はい、ベッドのうえにてがみがあります。

Yes, there's a letter on the bed.

いいえ、ベッドのうえに なにも ありません。

(Lit.) No, there isn't anything on the bed.

No, there's nothing on the bed.

(2)　きょうしつのそとに だれか （が）いますか。

(Lit.) Is there someone outside the classroom?

Is anyone outside the classroom?

はい、きょうしつのそとにソンさんがいます。

Yes, Son-san is outside the classroom.

いいえ、きょうしつのそとに だれも いません。

(Lit.) No, there isn't anyone outside the classroom.

No, there's no one outside the classroom.

(3)　きょうしつに どなたか （が）いらっしゃいますか。

(Lit.) Is there someone in the classroom? (respectful)

Is anyone in the classroom? (respectful)

はい、きょうしつにいしかわせんせいがいらっしゃいます。

(Lit.) Yes, there is Ishikawa-sensei in the classroom. (respectful)

Yes, Ishikawa-sensei is in the classroom. (respectful)

いいえ、きょうしつに どなたも いらっしゃいません。

(Lit.) No, there isn't anyone in the classroom. (respectful)

No, there's no one in the classroom. (respectful)

| どこかに | *somewhere* | どこにも | *anywhere* |

Note that with どこ, に occurs **after** か, but it occurs **before** も.

(4) どこかに にほんごのほんがありますか。

Are there Japanese books somewhere?

はい、としょかんににほんごのほんがあります。

Yes, there are Japanese books in the library.

いいえ、 どこにも ありません。

(Lit.) No, there are none anywhere.

No, there aren't any Japanese books here.

This construction is very different from English, so literal translations result in ungrammatical or unnatural sentences. In order to make natural English translations, you need to supply some specific location, e.g. *Are there any Japanese books somewhere on campus?*, *There aren't any on campus.*

(5) にほんごのほんはどこにありますか。

Where are Japanese books?

Where can I find Japanese books?

にほんごのほんはつくえのうえにあります。

(The) Japanese books are on the desk.

にほんごのほんは どこにも ありません。

(Lit.) Japanese books aren't anywhere (not on campus, in the library, etc).

(6) いしかわせんせいはどこにいらっしゃいますか。

Where is Ishikawa-sensei?

いしかわせんせいはきょうしつにいらっしゃいます。

Ishikawa-sensei's in the classroom.

いしかわせんせいは どこにも いらっしゃいません。

Ishikawa-sensei isn't anywhere (on campus, in the building, etc.)

Note that なに／だれ／どなた／どこ are WH-interrogative words, whereas なにか／だれか／どなたか／どこかに／なにも／だれも／どなたも／どこにも are not.

(7) つくえのうえに なに がありますか。

What *'s on the desk?*

つくえのうえにかばんがあります。

There's a briefcase on the desk.

(8)　つくえのうえに　なにか　ありますか。

Is there *something* *on the desk?*

はい、つくえのうえにかばんがあります。

Yes, there's a briefcase on the desk.

いいえ、つくえのうえに　なにも　ありません。

No, there isn't *anything* *on the desk.*

No, there's nothing on the desk.

3e　NOUN1 と NOUN2　　(NOUN1 and NOUN2)

 When you talk about two entities, X and Y, と is used. When more than two nouns are mentioned, と may be repeated as in つくえのうえにペン　と　しゃしん　と　じしょがあ ります. と cannot be used when X and Y are not nouns; you will learn other expressions corresponding to the English *and* shortly.

3f　Final Particle よ

 よ is one of the *sentence-final particles* that frequently appear in conversation. よ can be added when you supply new information.

ミラー　：ソンさん、このだいがくににほんごのとしょかんがありますか。

　　　　　(Lit.) Son-san, is there a special library for Japanese books at this university?

　　　　　Son-san, does this university have a special library for Japanese books?

ソン　　：ええ、あります　よ　。

　　　　　Yes, there is / Yes, it does.

In this exchange, ソンさん could have said ええ、あります without changing the meaning, but the use of よ adds more attentiveness to ミラーさん. On some occasions, よ may sound extremely assertive or imposing, i.e. *I tell you!*. Because such a subtle difference is context dependent, you are advised to use よ with great care. Pronounce よ with slightly rising intonation and never put stress on it.

3g　Numbers

1	一	いち
2	二	に
3	三	さん

4	四	し／よん
5	五	ご
6	六	ろく

7	七	しち／なな
8	八	はち
9	九	く／きゅう
10	十	じゅう
11	十一	じゅういち
12	十二	じゅうに
13	十三	じゅうさん
14	十四	じゅうし／じゅうよん
15	十五	じゅうご
16	十六	じゅうろく
17	十七	じゅうしち／じゅうなな
18	十八	じゅうはち

19	十九	じゅうく／じゅうきゅう
20	二十	にじゅう
21	二十一	にじゅういち
100	百	ひゃく
101	百一	ひゃくいち
111	百十一	ひゃくじゅういち
1000	千	せん
1001	千一	せんいち
1011	千十一	せんじゅういち
1111	千百十一	せんひゃくじゅういち
2222	二千二百二十二	にせんにひゃくにじゅうに

練習問題 Exercises
れんしゅうもんだい

I.　　Look at the picture of Young-san's room. Following the example, ask whether certain things are in the room. Use the vocabulary you have learned.

Example

Q:　ヤングさんのへやにコンピューターがありますか。

A:　はい、あります。

Q:　ヤングさんのへやにソファーがありますか。

A:　いいえ、ありません。

II.　　Tell your partner where the things are.

Example　テーブルのうえにしんぶんとほんがあります。

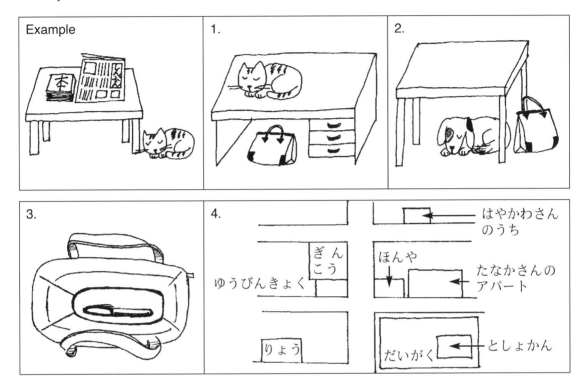

III.　　This is Kimura-san's room. Tell your partner where the given entities are.

Example

A:　きむらさんのアパートにとけいがありますか。

B:　はい、あります。

A:　とけいはどこにありますか。

B:　とけいはつくえのうえにあります。

IV.   This is Son-san's apartment building.
       Find out where each tenant lives.

Example 1

Q: ソンさんのアパートの
      うえにだれかいますか。

A: はい、います。

Q: だれがいますか。

A: ヤングさんがいます。

Example 2

Q: ヤングさんのアパートの
      うえにだれかいますか。

A: いいえ、だれもいません。

V.   Look at the pictures below and practice the dialog as shown in the example.

Example

A: どこかににほんごのほんがありますか。

B: ええ、ありますよ。

A: （にほんごのほんは）どこにありますか。

B: （にほんごのほんは）としょかんにありますよ。

A: あ、そうですか。

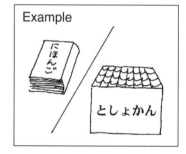

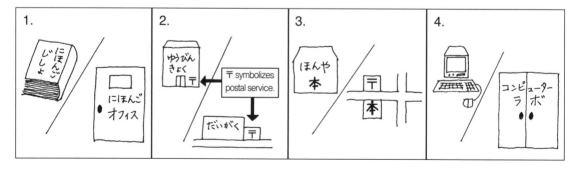

VI.   Reading practice

　　パクさんはがくせいです。シカゴだいがくのよねんせいです。せんもんはけいざいがくです。パクさんのアパートはだいがくのちかくにあります。パクさんのアパートのまえにほんやがあります。ほんやのとなりにゆうびんきょくがあります。ぎんこうはアパートのちかくにありません。

○ですか。×ですか。

1.　(　　)パクさんはシカゴだいがくのせんせいです。
2.　(　　)パクさんのせんもんはにほんごじゃありません。
3.　(　　)パクさんのアパートはぎんこうのちかくにあります。
4.　(　　)ほんやはパクさんのアパートのまえにあります。

かんじ　Introduction to the Ideographic Writing System

かんじ literally means "characters of the Han dynasty of ancient China (206 BC – 220 AD)". Recording a language with かんじ is fundamentally different from writing with the Roman alphabet, ひらがな, or カタカナ. These three scripts record the *sounds* of the language and are called *phonographic* (phono = sound). In かんじ writing, ideas, rather than sounds, are recorded, so we refer to it as an *ideographic* writing system (ideo = idea). Each かんじ is associated with some string of sounds in a particular language, but this sound association is secondary.

Some かんじ are *pictographs* (picto = picture), pictorial representations of what they refer to.

Both phonographic and ideographic writing systems have their own advantages and disadvantages.

	Phonographic Writing System	**Ideographic Writing System**
1.	Records sounds e.g. ひらがな, カタカナ, alphabet	Records meanings e.g. かんじ, numerals
2.	Small set of symbols	Large number of symbols
3.	Language dependent	Language independent
4.	More processing time	Less processing time

(1)　Most languages make limited use of ideographic writing, namely numerals. Symbols like *1, 2, 3*, etc. are pronounced differently from language to language, but we know what they mean, regardless of their pronunciation. Even within English, the character *2* is pronounced differently in *2* and *2nd*, but the idea remains constant.

(2)　Each language uses a fairly small number of sounds out of all possible sounds that humans can produce. So if you record such selected speech sounds, you need a small set of symbols. By contrast, the ideas that humans can create are limitless. So if you record ideas directly, you need an infinite number of symbols—which is, of course, impossible. In かんじ writing, a compromise is made: each character represents a group of ideas, rather than a specific idea. Even so, the number of かんじ necessary for recording Japanese is much larger than ひらがな or カタカナ. The Japanese Government has established a set of commonly used 1,945 かんじ, which can appear in official documents, newspapers, magazines, etc. Naturally, some かんじ are used more frequently than others. If you learn 500 basic かんじ, you can recognize about 75% of all occurrences of かんじ; if you know 1,000, your recognition rate rises to approximately 90%. In this textbook, you will learn a little more than 300.

(3) Ideographic writing has an advantage over phonographic writing. As exemplified by numerals, ideographs are language independent. In phonographic writing, a string of symbols like *two* is meaningless unless you know the language, whereas the symbol *2* conveys its meaning without knowledge of the language. With some ingenuity, you can record English using かんじ.

(4) The greatest advantage of ideographic writing is its fast processing time. Compare, for example, *fifty three thousand six hundred ninety one* and *53,691*. Similarly, 二千二百二十二 is faster to comprehend than にせんにひゃくにじゅうに. While English uses ideographs in only a limited domain, Japanese uses them extensively.

2	
Ainu	*tu*
Arabic	*ithna:n*
Dyirbal	*bulay*
Finnish	*kaksi*
Hebrew	*shtayim*
Hindi	*do*
Korean	*tul*
Mandarin	*er*
Mongolian	*xoyor*
Navajo	*naaki*
Portuguese	*dois*
Swahili	*mbili*
Tagalog	*dalawá*
Tibetan	*nyee*
Turkish	*iki*

新しい漢字 New Kanji

いち 一	に 二	さん 三	し・よん 四	ご 五	ろく 六	しち・なな 七	はち 八	きゅう・く 九	じゅう 十	ひゃく 百	せん 千

一	一											
いち	*one*											
二	一	二										
に	*two*											
三	一	二	三									
さん	*three*											

四	一	口	匹	四	四				
し・よん・よ	*four*								
五	一	丁	五	五					
ご	*five*								
六	丶	亠	六	六					
ろく	*six*								
七	一	七							
しち・なな	*seven*								
八	ノ	八							
はち	*eight*								
九	ノ	九							
く・きゅう	*nine*								
十	一	十							
じゅう	*ten*								
百	一	丆	丆	百	百	百			
ひゃく	*hundred*								
千	丿	二	千						
せん	*thousand*								

新しい語彙 Vocabulary

あたら・ご・い

あります	to exist (things)
いす	chair
一 (いち)	one

いぬ	dog
いぬごや	doghouse
います	to exist (people, animals)

いらっしゃいます	to exist (respectful)		とけい	watch, clock
うえ	on, above		どこかに	somewhere
うしろ	back, behind		どこにも	anywhere
うち	house		どなたか	someone (respectful)
おてあらい	toilet, lavatory		どなたも	anyone (respectful)
オフィス	office		となり	next to
かばん	briefcase		なか	inside
カメラ	camera		なに	what
九 (きゅう・く)	nine		なにか	something
きょうしつ	classroom		なにも	anything
ぎんこう	bank		二 (に)	two
五 (ご)	five		ねこ	cat
三 (さん)	three		ノート	notebook
四 (し・よん)	four		八 (はち)	eight
した	beneath, under, below		百 (ひゃく)	hundred
七 (しち・なな)	seven		プログラム	program
十 (じゅう)	ten		ベッド	bed
千 (せん)	thousand		へや	room
そと	outside		ほんや	bookstore
ソファー	sofa		まえ	front
だれか	someone		ゆうびんきょく	post office
だれも	anyone		よこ	side
ちかく	vicinity		ラジオ	radio
つくえ	desk		ルームメート	roommate
テーブル	table		六 (ろく)	six
てがみ	letter			

なまえ (Mostly proper nouns)

カリフォルニア	*California*	やまだ	*Yamada*
きむら	*Kimura*	ヤング	*Young*
シカゴ	*Chicago*	ヨセミテ	*Yosemite*
ドイル	*Doyle*	リン	*Lin*
パク	*Pak*	ワトソン	*Watson*
ホームズ	*Holmes*		

しゅうまつのプラン
Weekend Plans

しゅうまつに何をしますか
What are you doing this weekend?

会話 Dialog

1　ソン　：ミラーさん、いま、うちへかえりますか。

Miller-san, are you going home now?

2　ミラー：いえ、かえりません。ジムでうんどうします。ソンさんも何かしますか。

No, not yet. I'm going to (go) exercise at the gym. Are you going to do something, too, Son-san?

3　ソン　：はい、わたしはこれからこやまさんとテニスをします。ミラーさんはしゅうまつ、何をしますか。

Yes, I'm going to play tennis with Koyama-san. (By the way,) what are you doing this weekend?

4　ミラー：あした、としょかんでしゅくだいをします。でも、日曜日にサンフランシスコへいきます。

I'm going to do homework at the library tomorrow. But on Sunday I'm going to San Francisco.

5　ソン　：へえ、サンフランシスコですか。何でいきますか。

Oh, (you're going to) San Francisco? How will you get (go) there?

　　ミラー：でんしゃでここからサンフランシスコのダウンタウンまでいきます。そして、ダウンタウンからバスで日本まちへいきます。

I'll take a train from here to San Francisco downtown. Then, I'll take a bus to Japantown.

6　ソン　：日本まちで何をしますか。

What are you going to do in Japantown?

　　ミラー：かいものをします。それから、えいがをみます。

I'm going to go shopping and then see a movie.

　　ソン　：わあ、いいですね。

Wow, that's great.

7　ミラー：ソンさんも、いっしょにいきますか。日本ごのクラスのウォンさんもジョーンズさんもいきますよ。

Will you come with me? Wong-san and Jones-san from Japanese class are also coming.

　　ソン　：ええっ、いいですか。

Oh, would that be alright?

8   ミラー　：ええ、いいですよ。いっしょにいきましょう。

　　　　　　Sure, that's fine. Let's go there together.

　　　ソン　　：何時<ruby>なんじ</ruby>にあいましょうか。

　　　　　　What time shall we meet?

9   ミラー　：一時にえきであいましょう。

　　　　　　Let's get together (meet) at one o'clock at the station.

　　　ソン　　：はい、わかりました。じゃ、たのしみにしています。

　　　　　　All right. Well then, I look forward to it.

使い方 Usage
<ruby>つか</ruby><ruby>かた</ruby>

1   かえります means "go back to the place considered to be one's territory", e.g. his / her home, country, or place of employment. It is slightly different from "return", which does not include the notion of territory. For example, if you go to Japan, you can say *I'll return some day*, but you cannot use かえります if Japan is not your home country.

2   いえ is a casual form of いいえ.

5   へえ↑ is used to indicate admiration or amazement.

そして means "and then". It is used at the beginning of a sentence, rather than conjoining two clauses.

6   それから "and after that" is similar to そして, but the sequentiality of the two events is emphasized more. This phrase also appears sentence-initially.

わあ↑ is an exclamation expressing admiration, *Wow!* (へえ↑ can also be used here).

7   ええっ↑ is another exclamation expressing surprise. This is uttered with rising intonation with an abrupt ending, as opposed to ええ↓ "yes", which has falling intonation.

Both いいですか↑ "Is it okay / fine / alright?" and いいですよ↑ "That's okay / fine / alright" are pronounced in rising intonation. If いいですよ is uttered with falling intonation, the conveyed nuance will be "*I don't care*".

9   じゃ is a casual form of それでは "well then / in that case".

たのしみにしています means "I look forward to ~". The expected event in this case has already been introduced in the conversation, i.e. going to San Francisco with Miller-san and others.

文法 Grammar

4a　Verb Conjugation: Pre-ますフォーム

The verb form that appears before ます, e.g. たべ , is called the "*Pre-ますフォーム*", and the Pre-ますフォーム combined with ます, e.g. たべます, is called the " ますフォーム " in this textbook.

The ますフォーム is used in polite speech (as opposed to plain speech, which will be learned in Lesson 6) to indicate present states (e.g. います, あります, いらっしゃいます) or future or habitual activities.

A　Present

いしかわせんせいは、いま、どこにいらっしゃいますか。

Where is Ishikawa-sensei now?

いしかわせんせいは、いま、オフィスにいらっしゃいます。

Ishikawa-sensei is in her office now.

B　Future

しゅうまつ、何をしますか。　　　　*What are you going to do this weekend?*

しゅうまつ、シカゴへいきます。　　*I'm going to Chicago this weekend.*

C　Habitual

りょうでしんぶんをよみますか。

Do you read newspapers in (your) dorm?

いいえ、としょかんでしんぶんをよみます。

No, I read newspapers in the library.

4b   Object Marker を

 Verbs like たべます／のみます／よみます require two entities: the subject and the direct object. This type of verb is called *transitive* (see Lesson 10, **10d** for further explanation). The subject is marked by は or が, and the direct object by を (pronounced as お).

わたしはコーヒー を のみます。	*I drink coffee.*
わたしはしんぶん を よみます。	*I read newspapers.*
わたしは（お）すし を たべます。	*I eat sushi.*
ミラーさんはテレビ を みます。	*Miller-san watches TV.*
わたしはコーラ は のみません。	*I don't drink cola.*
わたしはざっし は よみません。	*I don't read magazines.*

Like ～に～ が あります vs. ～に～ は ありません (Lesson 3, **3a**), を becomes は in negative statements. See Lesson 6, **6h** for further explanation.

When 何 か "something" or 何も "anything (in a negative clause)" appears as the direct object, を is not used:

○ 何か のみますか。	*(Lit.) Will you drink something?*
✕ 何かを のみますか。	*Would you like something to drink?*
○ いいえ、 何も のみません。	*No, I won't drink anything.*
✕ いいえ、 何もを のみません。	

4c   Beautifiers お and ご

 お in おすし is categorized as a *prefix* because it appears before a word. This use of お is slightly different from お in おなまえ. In the case of おな

まえ, お indicates the speaker's respect to the person for whom おなまえ is used. So, you use なまえ without お for yourself. In the case of おすし, お "beautifies" すし, indicating its cultural significance. Unlike おなまえ, you can use お for your own すし, e.g. わたしのおすし. Certain nouns are commonly beautified with お, e.g. おかね "money", おこめ "uncooked rice", and おちゃ "tea". The words すし, かね, こめ, and ちゃ can be used without お, but, if you do so, your speech conveys that you do not value these entities much. Another common prefix with the same function is ご, e.g. ごはん "cooked rice, meal". (Unlike こめ, はん by itself without ご is not used.) Here, again, ご is slightly different from that in ごせんもん. For your own major, you need to use せんもん, but you can use ごはん for your own meal, わたしのごはん. お is generally used with native Japanese words, and ご with loan words from Chinese. お and ご are not used with loan words that are borrowed from European languages.

Female speakers use お more frequently than male speakers do, and some female speakers overuse it, e.g. おビール "beer". In this textbook, if a word is commonly used both with and without お, the お is put in parentheses.

4d　で : Location Marker for Action Verbs

Both (1) and (2) below express the same location, namely としょかん .

(1)　としょかん に 日本のしんぶんがあります。
There are Japanese newspapers in the library.

(2)　としょかん で 日本のしんぶんをよみます。 *I read Japanese newspapers in the library.*

としょかん is marked with に in (1), whereas it is marked with で in (2). This variation is due to the different nature of the verbs: あります／います／いらっしゃいます commonly denote *states* (or existence), whereas あいます／します／たべます／のみます／よみます denote *activities*. When you express an activity or event, you need to use で to indicate its location, as in (3) and (4):

(3)　としょかん で べんきょうをします。　　*I study in the library.*

(4)　えき で あいます。　　*We'll meet at the station.*

4e　Instrument Marker で　　　"by means of"

いしかわせんせいはペン で てがみをかきます。
Ishikawa-sensei writes letters with a pen.

はし で たべます。　　　　　　　　*I eat with chopsticks.*
こやまさんは日本ご で てがみをかきます。　*Koyama-san writes letters in Japanese.*
ひこうき で 日本へいきます。　　　　*I'll go to Japan by airplane.*

でんしゃ で きょうとへいきますか。　　*Are you going to Kyoto by train?*
いいえ、くるま で （きょうとへ）いきます。　*No, I'll go (to Kyoto) by car.*

If you walk somewhere, you need あるいて "by walking"/"on foot".

じてんしゃでだいがくへきますか。   *Do you come to the University by bike?*

いいえ、 あるいて (だいがくへ) きます。   *(Lit.) No, I come (to the University) on foot.*

No, I walk (to the University).

4f   Direction / Goal Marker へ・に

  When someone/something moves from one place to another, へ (pronounced as え) is used to mark the direction or goal. に is also used in this situation as a goal marker; they are interchangeable with movement verbs.

ニューヨーク $\left\{\begin{array}{c}へ\\に\end{array}\right\}$ いきます。   *I'm going to New York.*

ともだちはカリフォルニア $\left\{\begin{array}{c}へ\\に\end{array}\right\}$ きます。   *My friend is coming to California.*

うち $\left\{\begin{array}{c}へ\\に\end{array}\right\}$ かえります。   *I'm going home.*

Unlike を with 何か or 何も (cf. 4b), へ and に do not drop when they co-occur with どこ／どこか.

○ あした、どこか $\left\{\begin{array}{c}へ\\に\end{array}\right\}$ いきますか。   *Are you going somewhere tomorrow?*

○ いいえ、どこ $\left\{\begin{array}{c}へ\\に\end{array}\right\}$ もいきません。   *No, I'm not going anywhere.*

× いいえ、どこも $\left\{\begin{array}{c}へ\\に\end{array}\right\}$ いきません。

4g   Time Marker に

 に marks a point in time.

九時に うちでばんごはんをたべます。   *I'm having dinner at home at 9.*

いつ、えいがをみますか。   *When are you going to see a movie? /*

When do you watch movies?

日曜日に えいがをみます。   *I'm going to see a movie on Sunday.*

Generally, with relative time expressions (e.g. きょう, あした), に is not used. (Lesson 13, **13e** provides a list of relative time expressions.) しゅうまつ can be used with or without に.

○ あした、スーパーでかいものをします。

　I'm going to shop at the supermarket tomorrow.

× あした に 、スーパーでかいものをします。

○ しゅうまつ、デパートへいきます。

　I'm going to a department store (this) weekend.

○ しゅうまつ に 、デパートへいきます。

4h　と "with"; ひとりで "by oneself"

 と frequently occurs with いっしょに "together".

わたしは土曜日<ruby>土曜日<rt>どようび</rt></ruby>にこやまさん と テニスをします。

　I'm playing tennis with Koyama-san on Saturday.

ソンさんはしゅうまつ、ミラーさん といっしょに 日本まちへいきます。

Son-san is going to Japantown with Miller-san this weekend.

If a person does something by him/herself, ひとりで (ひとり "one person" + で "by") is used.

だれといっしょにいきますか。　　　　　*Who are you going with?*

ひとりで いきます。　　　　　　　　*I'm going by myself.*

4i　A から B まで　　"from A to B; from A as far as B"

 から indicates the starting point, and まで the end point. This expression can be used for both time and space.

ソンさんはきょう、二時 から 三時半<ruby>半<rt>はん</rt></ruby> まで テニスをします。

Son-san is going to play tennis from two until half past three today.

日本ごのクラスは何時 から 何時 まで ですか。

From what time to what time is Japanese class?

日本ごのクラスは九時 から 十時 まで です。

Japanese class is from 9 to 10 o'clock.

わたしはここ から ダウンタウン まで でんしゃでいきます。

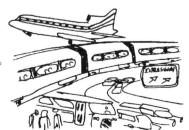

I'm going from here to downtown by train.

バスはダウンタウン から 日本まち まで いきます。

The bus goes from downtown to Japantown.

4j   Pre-ますフォーム + ましょう   "Let's do ~"
Pre-ますフォーム + ましょうか   "Shall we do ~?"

This symbol indicates the appropriate verb conjugation.

The Pre-ますフォーム can also be used with verb endings other than ます.

何かたべ ましょう 。   *Let's eat something.*

いっしょにいき ましょう 。   *Let's go together.*

わたしのアパートでビールをのみ ましょう 。

Let's drink beer at my apartment.

Like English "let's do ~", 〜ましょう may sound highly assertive on some occasions. The use of the question form 〜ましょうか "shall we ~?" makes the proposal softer than 〜ましょう.

おちゃをのみ ましょうか 。   *Shall we drink tea?*

はい、のみましょう。   *Yes, let's drink (some).*

はい、そうしましょう。   *Yes, let's (do so).*

いえ、ちょっと……。   *Hmmm ... no ... (I don't really want any right now ...)*

4k   Verbal Nouns

Some nouns can form a verb with します. Such nouns are called *verbal nouns*.

うんどう *exercise*

かいもの *shopping*

べんきょう *study*

They can be used with or without を: e.g. べんきょう を します or べんきょうします. If you add the direct object, e.g. にほんご, you cannot use two を in a single clause. Instead, you need to say:

○ にほんご を べんきょうします。   *I study Japanese.*

○ にほんご の べんきょう を します。   *(Lit.) I do the study of Japanese.*

✗ にほんご を べんきょう を します。   *I engage in the study of Japanese.*

When a verb is borrowed from a foreign language, it is treated as a verbal noun.

コピー (を) します。   *to copy*

テキストをコピーします。   *I'll copy the textbook.*

4l　Final Particle ね

 Like よ (Lesson 3, **3f**), ね can appear in sentence-final position. Its function is at times similar to the English tag question:

わあ、いいです ね ↑。　　　　　　　*Wow, that's nice, isn't it?*

あした、としょかんへいきます ね ↑。　*You're going to the library tomorrow, aren't you?*

そうですか and そうですね appear frequently in Japanese conversation.

(1)　そうですか。(Used when you've just acquired new information, corresponding to the English "Is that so?／Really?／Oh, yeah?".)

　　　ソン　　　：　ミラーさんはしゅうまつに何をしますか。
　　　ミラー　　：　日曜日にデパートへいきます。
　　　ソン　　　：　へえ、そうですか↓。

(2)　そうですね。(Used when you agree with the preceding statement.)

　　　ミラー　　：　一時にあいましょうか。
　　　ソン　　　：　そうですね↑。一時にあいましょう。

4m　Days of the week

げつようび 月曜日 *Monday*	かようび 火曜日 *Tuesday*	すいようび 水曜日 *Wednesday*	もくようび 木曜日 *Thursday*
きんようび 金曜日 *Friday*	どようび 土曜日 *Saturday*	にちようび 日曜日 *Sunday*	なんようび 何曜日 *what day of the week*

4n　Time

As mentioned in Lesson 1g, the vowels [i] and [u] are normally devoiced when they occur between voiceless consonants. So when 一 (ich i), 六 (rok u), 八 (hach i) are combined with 分 (fun), they are devoiced. This process creates a succession of voiceless consonants [ich-fun, rok-fun, hach-fun]. In Japanese, when two voiceless consonants are next to each other, some modification may apply. In this case, the final consonant of the numerals disappears and the [f] in 分 becomes a long [p], resulting in いっぷん, ろっぷん, and はっぷん. Note that 三分 (さんぷん) and 何分 (なんぷん) are exceptions.

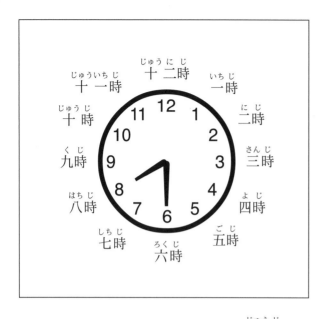

<table>
<tr><td>いっぷん
一分</td><td>じっぷん
十分</td></tr>
<tr><td>に ふん
二分</td><td>にじっぷん
二十分</td></tr>
<tr><td>さんぷん
三分</td><td>さんじっぷん
三十分</td></tr>
<tr><td>よんぷん
四分</td><td>よんじっぷん
四十分</td></tr>
<tr><td>ご ふん
五分</td><td>ごじっぷん
五十分</td></tr>
<tr><td>ろっぷん
六分</td><td>ろくじっぷん
六十分</td></tr>
<tr><td>なな ふん
七分</td><td>なん じ
何時</td></tr>
<tr><td>はっぷん・はちふん
八分・八分</td><td>なんぷん
何分</td></tr>
<tr><td>きゅうふん
九 分</td><td></td></tr>
</table>

十 is usually pronounced as じゅう, e.g. 十時, but when followed by a word that begins with a voiceless consonant, it is pronounced as じっ, e.g. 第十課. This irregularity is due to historical changes in the Japanese language. However, most Japanese nowadays pronounce 第十課 as だい じゅ っか. Like 一分, 六分, 八分, when the second word begins with an [h], the [h] becomes a long [p], i.e. 十分 (じっぷん／じゅっぷん).

いま、何時 (何分) ですか。	*What time is it now?*
いま、十時八分です。	*It's 8 minutes after 10 now.*
九時半です。	*It's half past 9.*
何時にあいましょうか。	*What time shall we meet?*
いつあいましょうか。	*When shall we meet?*
八時にあいましょう。	*Let's meet at 8.*
ごご八時ですか。	*8 P.M.?*
いいえ、ごぜん八時です。	*No, 8 A.M.*

練習問題 Exercises
_{れんしゅうもんだい}

I.　The following pictures show what いのうえさん does regularly. Following the example, talk about いのうえさん's activities.

れい

Q:　いのうえさんは何をしますか。

A:　（いのうえさんは）<u>コーヒーをのみます</u>。

1.	2.	3.	4.
			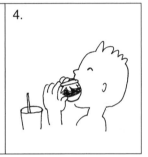

II.　Look at the pictures and interview your partner as shown in the example.

れい

Q:　Bさんは<u>ひるごはんをたべます</u>か。

A:　はい、（わたしはひるごはんを）<u>たべます</u>。

　　(or) いいえ、（わたしはひるごはんは）<u>たべません</u>。

れい	1.	2.	3.

4.	5.	6.	7.

III.　　Practice the following conversation with your partner, using the activities listed below.

れい

A:　Bさん、きょう、<u>しゅくだいをします</u>か。

B:　ええ、きょう、<u>しゅくだいをします</u>。

A:　いっしょに<u>しましょう</u>か。

B:　ええ、いいですね。

A:　どこで<u>しましょう</u>か。

B:　<u>としょかん</u>で<u>しましょう</u>。何時にあいましょうか。

A:　<u>四時</u>にあいましょう。

B:　はい、じゃあ、<u>四時</u>に<u>としょかん</u>であいましょう。

1. うんどうします	3.	ひるごはんをたべます
2. えいがをみます	4.	かいものをします

IV.　　Ask and tell the time.

れい

Q:　いま、何時ですか。

A:　いま、<u>十時</u>です。

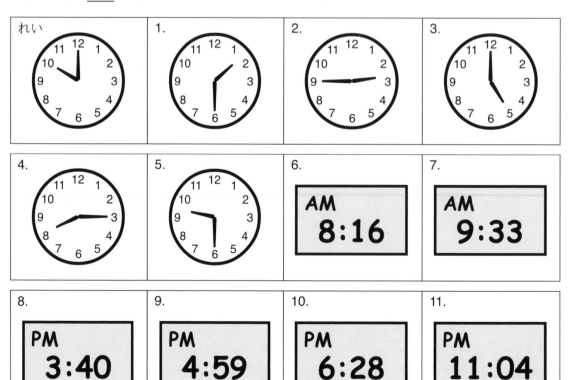

V. The pictures below show what いのうえさん will do tomorrow. Practice the conversation as shown in the example.

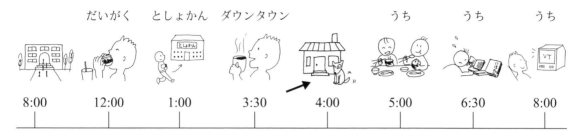

だいがく　　としょかん　ダウンタウン　　　　　　うち　　　　うち　　　　うち

8:00　　12:00　　1:00　　3:30　　4:00　　5:00　　6:30　　8:00

れい

Q: いのうえさんはあした、<u>ひるごはんをたべますか</u>。

A: はい、いのうえさんはあした、<u>ひるごはんをたべます</u>。

Q: <u>どこで</u> (ひるごはんを) たべますか。

A: <u>だいがくで</u> (ひるごはんを) たべます。

Q: <u>何時に</u> (ひるごはんを) たべますか。

A: <u>十二時に</u> (ひるごはんを) たべます。

VI. Ask your partner appropriate questions and complete the chart.

れい

A: Bさんはきょう、何かべんきょうしますか。

B: はい、します。

A: 何をべんきょうしますか。

B: 日本ごをべんきょうします。

A: どこでべんきょうしますか。

B: としょかんでべんきょうします。

A: だれかといっしょにべんきょうしますか。

B: はい、ともだちと (いっしょに) べんきょうします。

	何を	どこで	だれと
きょう、何かべんきょうしますか。			
土曜日に何かみますか。			
しゅうまつ、何かよみますか。			

VII.   The pictures show some of いのうえさん's activities and how she does them. Some information is missing in each picture, but your partner has the missing information. Ask your partner and find out how いのうえさん does each activity.

れい

A: いのうえさんは何で<u>だいがくへきますか</u>。

B: (いのうえさんは)<u>バスでだいがくへきます</u>。

れい

A: いのうえさんは何で<u>だいがくへきますか</u>。

B: (いのうえさんは)<u>バスでだいがくへきます</u>。

VIII.   Practice telling time using から and まで.

1.   Use the following information.

れい 1

ゆうびんきょくは月曜日から金曜日までです。

れい2

Q: でんしゃはリッチモンドからどこまでいきますか。

A: でんしゃはリッチモンドからフリーモントまでいきます。

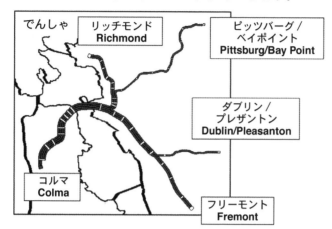

2. Continue practicing, using information about your own schedule, work, shopping, etc.

IX. A travel agency is offering a bus tour, *A Week in California*. It starts in San Diego and ends in San Francisco. The schedule is partially shown in the map, and partially in the table. Ask your partner to complete the itinerary.

れい

B: 日曜日にどこからどこまでいきますか。

A: 日曜日にサンディエゴからパームスプリングスまでいきます。

日曜日	
月曜日	パームスプリングス *Palm Springs*　→　ロサンゼルス *Los Angeles*
火曜日	
水曜日	モントレー *Monterey*　→　ヨセミテ *Yosemite*
木曜日	
金曜日	タホ *Tahoe*　→　サクラメント *Sacramento*
土曜日	サクラメント *Sacramento*　→　サンフランシスコ *San Francisco*

X.　Tell your partner what いのうえさん will do next week.

れい

いのうえさんは<u>月曜日</u>にダウンタウンで<u>えいがをみます</u>。

XI.　The following pictures show what やまださん will do tomorrow. Your partner has missing information, so ask him/her and find out やまださん's activities.

れい

B:　やまださんはあした、十二時半から二時まで何をしますか。

A:　やまださんはあした、十二時半から二時までとしょかんでべんきょうします。

A:

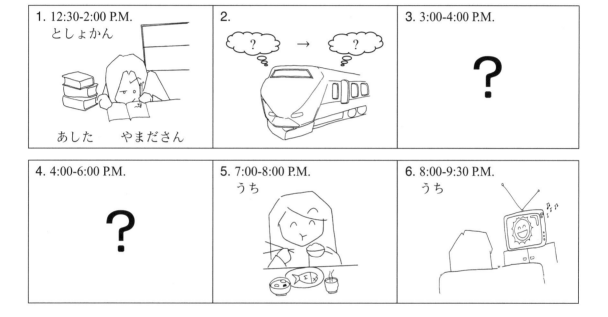

B:

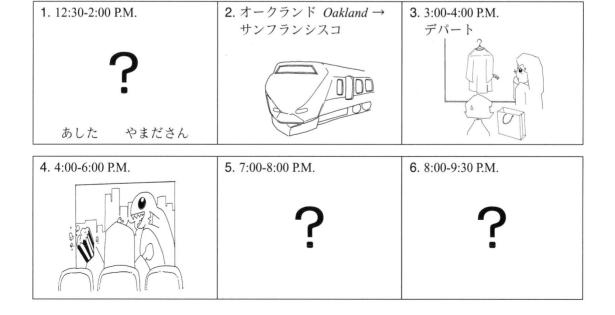

XII.   しんかんせんはどこからどこまでいきますか。

れい 1

Q: しんかんせん ❶ は博多からどこまでいきますか。

A: （しんかんせん ❶ は）博多から新大阪までいきます。

れい 2

Q: しんかんせん ❶ はどこから新大阪までいきますか。

A: （しんかんせん ❶ は）博多から新大阪までいきます。

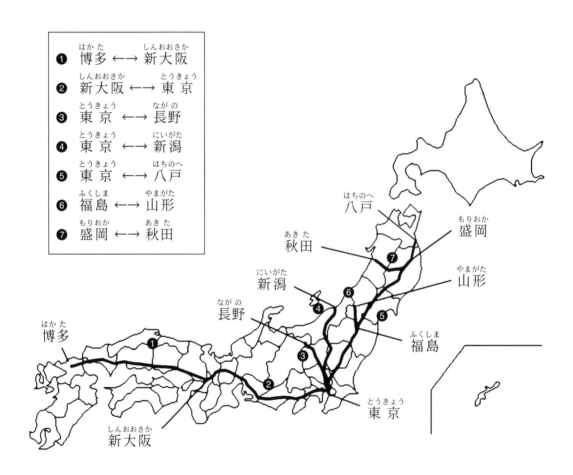

XIII. よみましょう。

わたしはキムです。 	わたしはだいがくの三ねんせいです。 	月曜日から金曜日まで、わたしは九時にだいがくへいきます。クラスは一時までです。 	それから、ともだちとだいがくのカフェテリアでひるごはんをたべます。 
そして、二時から五時までひとりでとしょかんでべんきょうします。 	しゅうまつ、わたしはラウールさんといっしょにかいものをします。 	そして、ジムでうんどうをします。 	

〇 ですか。× ですか。

1. （　　）キムさんはだいがくせいです。
2. （　　）キムさんは月曜日から金曜日までだいがくへいきます。
3. （　　）キムさんはひとりでだいがくのカフェテリアでひるごはんをたべます。
4. （　　）キムさんは一時から二時までともだちととしょかんでべんきょうします。
5. （　　）キムさんはしゅうまつ、ひとりでかいものをします。

新しい漢字 New Kanji

～時 じ	何 なに・なん	何か なに	何も なに	日本 にほん	半 はん	～分　日 ふん・ぶん　にち
曜日 ようび	月曜日 げつようび	火曜日 かようび	水曜日 すいようび	木曜日 もくようび	金曜日 きんようび	土曜日 どようび
何時 なんじ	何分 なんぶん	何曜日 なんようび				

The Days of the Week

Japanese names for the days of the week are based on the ancient Chinese calendar, whose idea originated in Mesopotamian astrology. In addition to the sun and moon, they include the five "basic elements": *fire* 火, *water* 水, *wood* 木, *metal* 金, and *earth* 土.

日	l	冂	日	日					
に・にち・び	*sun/day:* 日本 (にほん) *Japan (sun origin),* 日曜日 *Sunday (the day of the sun)*								
本	一	十	才	木	本				
ほん	*origin:* 日本 (にほん) *Japan (sun origin)*								
何	ノ	イ	仁	仁	佢	佢	何		
なに・なん	*what:* 何 is read as なに when it stands by itself or in 何か and 何も. When the following particle is に or で, both readings of なに and なん are possible. When it is combined with another word, it is almost always read as なん, e.g. 何時, 何分, 何曜日.								
時	l	冂	日	日	日一	日十	昨	昨	時	時
じ	*time:* Many かんじ are made of combinations of simpler かんじ, and each かんじ represents a group of ideas, rather than the pronunciation of a word (cf. Lesson 3). 時 appears in words related to the notion of time. For it to contain 日 "sun" is reasonable because ancient people conceived time according to the movement of the sun.								
分	ノ	八	分	分					
ふん・ぷん	*minutes:* 一分 (いっぷん) *one minute,* 二分 (にふん) *two minutes*								
半	丶	ソ	丷	半	半				
はん	*half*								
曜	l	冂	日	日	日ㄱ	日ㄱ	日ㅋ	日ㅋㄱ	日ㅋㅋ	日ㅋㅋ
	昭ㅋㅋ	暉ㅋ	暉ㅋ	暉	曜	曜	曜	曜		
よう	Although this かんじ is rarely used other than in the days of the week, it represents all celestial objects: the sun, moon, and stars. Like 時, it contains 日.								

月	ノ	刀	月	月					
げつ	*moon:* 月曜日 *Monday (the day of the moon)*								
火	丶	丷	少	火					
か	*fire:* 火曜日 *Tuesday (the day of fire)*								
水	亅	刀	水	水					
すい	*water:* 水曜日 *Wednesday (the day of water)*								
木	一	十	才	木					
もく	*wood/tree:* 木曜日 *Thursday (the day of wood)*								
金	ノ	人	스	今	全	全	金	金	
きん	*metal/gold:* 金曜日 *Friday (the day of metal)*								
土	一	十	土						
ど	*earth:* 土曜日 *Saturday (the day of the earth)*								

漢字の復習 Review
<ruby>漢<rt>かん</rt></ruby><ruby>字<rt>じ</rt></ruby>の<ruby>復<rt>ふく</rt></ruby><ruby>習<rt>しゅう</rt></ruby>

よみましょう。

1. 日本ごのクラスは月曜日から金曜日までです。
2. ミラーさんはしゅうまつ、何をしますか。
3. わたしは水曜日に二時から四時十五分までテニスをします。
4. ゆうびんきょくは八時半から五時までです。
5. 日曜日にヨセミテへいきます。

新しい語彙 Vocabulary

(します) means that the word is a verbal noun.

X 時	X o'clock	コーラ	cola
X 分	X minute(s)	これから	now, from now on
あいます	to meet	ごご	P.M, afternoon
あさごはん	breakfast	ごぜん	A.M, morning
あした	tomorrow	ごはん	cooked rice, meal
あるいて	on foot	コピー (します)	copy
いきます	to go	じてんしゃ	bicycle
いつ	when	します	to do
いま	now	ジム	gymnasium
うんどう (します)	exercise	しゅうまつ	weekend
えいが	movie	しゅくだい	homework
えき	station	水曜日	Wednesday
おちゃ	tea	スーパー	supermarket
かいもの (します)	shopping	(お) すし	sushi
かえります	to go home	そして	and then
かきます	to write	それから	after that
カフェテリア	cafeteria	ダウンタウン	downtown
火曜日	Tuesday	たべます	to eat
きます	to come	テニス	tennis
きょう	today	デパート	department store
金曜日	Friday	でも	but
月曜日	Monday	テレビ	TV
コーヒー	coffee	でんしゃ	train

ともだち	friend		ひこうき	airplane
土曜日 (どようび)	Saturday		ひるごはん	lunch
日曜日 (にちようび)	Sunday		プラン	plan
日本まち (にほん)	Japantown		べんきょう (します)	study
のみます	to drink		まち	town, city
(お)はし	chopsticks		みます	to see, watch
バス	bus		木曜日 (もくようび)	Thursday
半 (はん)	half		よみます	to read
ばんごはん	dinner, supper		れい	example
ビール	beer			

なまえ (Mostly proper nouns)

キム	Kim		しんかんせん	Japanese bullet train
ジョーンズ	Jones		ラウール	Raoul

ソンさんのアパートで
At Son-san's Apartment

今日、何をしましたか
What did you do today?

会話 Dialog
かいわ

1 ソン　：ただいま。
I'm home.

小山　：おかえりなさい。
こやま
Welcome back.

2 ソン　：ああ、つかれました。
Oh, I'm so tired.

小山　：今日、何をしましたか。
What did you do today?

3 ソン　：ミラーさんたちとサンフランシスコへ行きました。そして、日本まちでえい
い
がをみました。それから、かいものをしました。
I went to San Francisco with Miller-san and the others. We saw a movie in Japantown.
And we did some shopping.

4 小山　：何をかいましたか。
What did you buy?

ソン　：本やCDなどをかいました。
ほん
Books and CDs and stuff.

5 小山　：そうですか。チャイナタウンにも行きましたか。
I see. Did you go to Chinatown too?

ソン　：いいえ、行きませんでした。
No, we didn't.

6 小山　：もう、ばんごはんをたべましたか。
Have you eaten dinner already?

ソン　：はい、日本まちで日本りょうりをたべました。
Yes, we had Japanese food in Japantown.

7 小山　：そうですか。いいですねえ。あっ、もう十時ですね。私はねます。
わたし
Oh yeah? That's good. Oh, it's already 10 o'clock. I'm going to bed now.

ソン　：どうしてですか。
Why?

8   小山 ：明日のあさ、八時からとしょかんでしゅくだいをするつもりですから。

I plan to do some homework at the library tomorrow morning, starting at 8 o'clock.

　　　　ソン ：たいへんですね。何のしゅくだいですか。

That's tough, isn't it. What homework?

　　　　小山 ：けいざいがくです。

Economics.

9   ソン ：そうですか。つかれましたから、私ももうすぐねるつもりです。

I see. I'm tired, so I'm going to bed soon, too.

　　　　小山 ：じゃ、おやすみなさい。

Okay, good night.

　　　　ソン ：おやすみなさい。

Good night.

使い方 Usage

1   When you come home or come back to a place that can be considered your territory, e.g. your office, you say ただいま "I'm home / back" to your family members or colleagues. The addressees are supposed to say おかえりなさい "welcome back".

7   もう is frequently used to indicate "already", as in あ、もう十時ですね, cf. (5i). But when it is used with the non-past tense, it can mean "now", e.g. 私はもうねます "I'm going to bed now", もうかえります "I'm going home now". When もう appears in もうすぐ "soon", it forms a softer version of すぐ "immediately".

8   たいへん originally meant "big change". Today, it is used to mean that the situation is serious, difficult, awful, a pain in the neck, a big hassle, etc.

9   You say おやすみなさい "good night" when you go to bed, or when you part from someone late at night.

文法 Grammar

<ruby>文法<rt>ぶんぽう</rt></ruby>

5a	Object Marker に	
5b	Past Tense (Polite Speech)	
5c	Verb Conjugation: Dictionary フォーム	
5d	Dictionary フォーム + つもりです	"I intend/plan to do ~"
5e	X は Y があります	"X has Y"
5f	CLAUSE1 から CLAUSE2	"Because C1, C2; C1, so C2"
5g	どうしてですか	"Why is/was it so?"
5h	NOUN1 や NOUN2 など	"NOUN1 and NOUN2, among other things"
5i	もう "already"; まだ "yet"	
5j	Months of the Year	

5a　Object Marker に

In Lesson 4, we studied the object marker を. A small number of Japanese verbs take に as the object marker. These verbs imply directionality and include the verbs corresponding to English *meet*, *climb*, *ride*, etc.

ソンさんはともだち に あいます。　　　*Son-san is going to meet her friend.*

5b　Past Tense (Polite Speech)

Making the past tense form of a verb to be used in polite speech is simple: change ～ます to ～ました.

私は明日、ミラーさんにあいます。　　*I'm meeting Miller-san tomorrow.*
私は昨日、ミラーさんにあい ました 。　*I met Miller-san yesterday.*

私は<ruby>昨日<rt>きのう</rt></ruby>

The past tense form of ～です is ～でした.

今日は水曜日です。　　　　　　　　*Today is Wednesday.*
昨日は火曜日 でした 。　　　　　　*Yesterday was Tuesday.*

The negative of ～ました is ～ませんでした, and the negative of ～でした is ～ではありませんでした or ～じゃありませんでした.

昨日のばん、ステーキをたべましたか。
Did you eat steak last evening?
いいえ、昨日のばん、ステーキはたべ ませんでした 。
No, I didn't eat steak last evening.

そのじしょは20ドルでしたか。

Was that dictionary $20?

いいえ、このじしょは20ドル $\left\{ \begin{array}{l} ではありませんでした \\ じゃありませんでした \end{array} \right\}$ 。50ドルでした。

No, this dictionary wasn't $20. It was $50.

5c   Verb Conjugation: Dictionary フォーム

Japanese verbs have more forms than English, but less irregularity. Although the Pre-ますフォーム is the most versatile and you hear/see it frequently, it is useless if you want to look a verb up in a dictionary. Dictionaries use the form that has been considered the most basic in traditional Japanese grammar. Let us call this form the *Dictionary* フォーム.

Pre-ます フォーム	Dictionary フォーム	Gloss	Pre-ます フォーム	Dictionary フォーム	Gloss
あい（ます） ai-	あう au	meet	い（ます） i-	いる iru	be, exist
あり（ます） ari-	ある aru	be, exist	おき（ます） oki-	おきる okiru	get up
行き（ます） iki-	行く iku	go	み（ます） mi-	みる miru	see, watch
かえり（ます） kaeri-	かえる kaeru	go home	おしえ（ます） oshie-	おしえる oshieru	teach
かき（ます） kaki-	かく kaku	write	たべ（ます） tabe-	たべる taberu	eat
きき（ます） kiki-	きく kiku	listen, hear	ね（ます） ne-	ねる neru	go to bed
のみ（ます） nomi-	のむ nomu	drink	来（ます） ki-	来る kuru	come
よみ（ます） yomi-	よむ yomu	read	し（ます） shi-	する suru	do

As you can see in this table, the Pre-ますフォーム ends with either the vowel *i* or *e*. When ending with *e*, add る to make the Dictionary フォーム, e.g. たべる, ねる. Those verbs are called (*e*-ending) る-*verbs*. Approximately 10% of Japanese verbs are of this type.

$$\boxed{たべます \rightarrow たべる}$$

There are two types of verbs whose Pre-ますフォーム ends with *i*. In one, you need to drop *i* and add *u*; such verbs are called う-*verbs*. More than 80% of Japanese verbs are う-*verbs*, e.g. あう, かく.

わ	ら	や	ま	は	な	た	さ	か	あ
	り		み	ひ	に	ち	し	き	い
	る	ゆ	む	ふ	ぬ	つ	す	く	う
	れ		め	へ	ね	て	せ	け	え
を	ろ	よ	も	ほ	の	と	そ	こ	お

あいます → あう

かきます → かく

Some of the *i*-ending verbs are る-verbs; in order to create the Dictionary フォーム, you simply add る to the Pre- ますフォーム, e.g. いる, みる.

います → いる

Approximately 10% of the verbs are *i*-ending る-verbs. Therefore, for each *i*-ending verb, you need to remember whether it's an う-verb or る-verb.

いらっしゃいます is an う-verb, but it exhibits irregularity here because of a historical change; it was originally pronounced as いらっしゃ り ます. Therefore, its Dictionary フォーム is いらっしゃ る, **not** いらっしゃ う.

Japanese has only two genuine irregular verbs: きます and します. Their Dictionary フォーム are く る and する, respectively.

To recapitulate:

(1) Japanese verbs are categorized into う-verbs, る-verbs, and two irregular verbs, くる and する.

(2) The Pre- ますフォーム of う-verbs ends with *i*.

(3) The Pre- ますフォーム of る-verbs ends with either *i* or *e*.

(4) う-verbs: to make the Dictionary フォーム, drop the final vowel *i* of the Pre- ますフォーム and add *u*.

(5) る-verbs: to make the Dictionary フォーム, add る to the Pre- ますフォーム.

Conversely, you can make the Pre- ますフォーム from the Dictionary フォーム. If the Dictionary フォーム ends with る, drop る; if it ends with (a consonant +) *u*, change *u* to *i*. The only exception so far is かえる. かえる is an う-verb whose final consonant happens to be *r*. So, when you change *i* of its Pre- ますフォーム to *u*, it turns out to be る and かえる looks like a る-verb.

Unlike the Pre- ますフォーム, which requires some ending like ます to make a sentence, the Dictionary フォーム can be used by itself. Both the ますフォーム and Dictionary フォーム indicate that the event has not taken place, or has not yet come to reality. Therefore, we refer to these forms as being in the *non-past tense*.

The use of ます makes speech polite, whereas the use of the Dictionary フォーム alone makes speech plain, casual, and possibly impolite. Japanese people use casual speech when they talk with friends or family members. Do not use casual speech with someone to whom you need to show respect. In casual speech, particles such as を are frequently omitted.

A:	この本をよみますか↑。	*Are you going to read this book? (Polite)*
B:	はい、よみます。	*Yes, I am. (Polite)*
C:	この本(を)よむ↑？	*Are you going to read this book? (Plain)*
D:	うん、よむ。	*Yes, I am. (Plain)*

5d   Dictionary フォーム + つもりです   "I intend / plan to do ~"

 Use this construction to express your own intention; do not use it with a 3rd-person subject—describing someone else's intentions is considered presumptuous in Japanese society. In a question, you can use this construction to ask the addressee's intention only if the addressee is psychologically close to you, e.g. your family member or friend. Do not use it if the addressee is someone who is **not** psychologically close to you, and/or someone to whom you need to show respect.

When the Dictionary フォーム is used with つもりです, the speech is not considered plain or impolite because です in つもりです adds politeness. The rule of thumb in human communication is "Be polite" unless you are certain that informality is more desirable. If you are too polite, you just look ridiculous or standoffish, but if you are impolite, you may suffer serious consequences.

You will learn how to express "I intend/plan not to do ~" in Lesson 6. Until then, use the Pre-ます フォーム + ません when you want to provide a negative answer.

私は明日、六時に おきる つもりです。	*I intend to get up at 6 o'clock tomorrow.*
私は日本でえいごを おしえる つもりです。	*I plan to teach English in Japan.*
アメリカぶんがくのクラスをとりますか。	*Are you going to take an American literature class?*
はい、 とる つもりです。	*Yes, I plan to take it.*
いいえ、とりません。	*No, I'm not going to take it.*
今日、ゆうびんきょくへ行きますか。	*Are you going to the post office today?*
はい、 行く つもりです。	*Yes, I plan to go.*
いいえ、行きません。	*No, I'm not going.*

5e　X は Y があります　　"X has Y"

We learned in Lesson 3 that 「X に Y があります」 means "there is Y in / at X". When 「Person ＋ は」 appears, instead of 「Place ＋ に」, the sentence means "person X has Y". When the Y is an activity rather than a thing, the sentence usually contains a time expression.

私 は じてんしゃ が あります。　　*I have a bicycle.*
私 は 明日、テスト が あります。　　*I have a test tomorrow.*
チェンさん は くるま は ありません。　　*Chen-san doesn't have a car.*

5f　CLAUSE1 から CLAUSE2　　"Because C1, C2; C1, so C2"

Note that から attaches to the end of the first clause.

つかれましたから 、私はもうすぐねるつもりです。
I'm tired, so I intend to go to bed soon.
明日テストがありますから 、こんばん、十二時までべんきょうするつもりです。
Because I have a test tomorrow, I plan to study until midnight tonight.

You can present the two clauses in the reversed order by using two sentences. If you do so, the second sentence is understood as an afterthought.

こんばん、十二時までべんきょうするつもりです。 明日テストがありますから 。
I plan to study until midnight tonight ... because I have a test tomorrow.

5g　どうしてですか　　"Why is / was it so?"

「どうして "why" ＋ ですか」 can be used to request a reason. Like English *Why?*, this expression can be interpreted as criticism or a challenge, so use it carefully. To answer a どうして question, use ～から.

こんばん、十二時までべんきょうします。　　*I'm going to study until midnight tonight.*
どうして ですか↑。　　*Why is it so?*
明日テストがあります から 。　　*Because I have a test tomorrow.*

ひるごはんをたべましたか。　　*Have you eaten lunch? /*
　　Did you eat lunch?

いいえ、ひるごはんはたべませんでした。　　*No, I haven't eaten lunch /*
　　No, I didn't eat lunch.

どうして ですか↑。　　*(Lit.) Why is it so? / Why not?*
クラスがありました から 。　　*Because I had a class.*

5h   NOUN1 や NOUN2 など   "NOUN1 and NOUN2, among other things"

In Lesson 3, we studied one way to conjoin nouns: つくえの上にペン と 本 と じしょがあります. If there are more than three nouns, listing all of them is cumbersome. You can use「Noun や Noun など」for partial listing. The use of など is optional.

私はデパートでとけい や カメラ など をかいました。

I bought a watch and a camera, among other things, at the department store.

ミラーさんはビール や ワイン や さけ など をのみます。

Miller-san drinks beer, wine, sake, and so forth.

ソンさんはそのレストランでてんぷら や とんかつをたべました。

Son-san ate tempura, pork cutlet, and so forth at that restaurant.

5i   もう "already"; まだ "yet"

もう appears in an affirmative sentence, meaning some event has already occurred. まだ is similar to English "yet" or "still"; it frequently, but not necessarily, appears in a negative sentence and means that some expected event has not yet occurred. When responding to もう 〜か "already 〜?", use まだです for now, because "X has/have not done 〜" requires a different construction in Japanese, which will be studied in Lesson 26.

もう 十一時ですね。	*It's already 11 o'clock, isn't it?*
はい、 もう 十一時です。	*Yes, it's already 11.*
いいえ、 まだ です。	*No, not yet.*
もう 、ひるごはんをたべましたか。	*Have you already eaten lunch?*
はい、 もう たべました。	*Yes, I have.*
いいえ、 まだ です。	*(Lit.) No, still (haven't eaten lunch).*
	No, not yet.
バスは もう 来ましたか。	*Has the bus already come (and gone)?*
いいえ、 まだ です。	*(Lit.) No, still (hasn't come) / No, not yet.*

5j Months of the Year

一月 *January*
二月 *February*
三月 *March*
四月 *April*
五月 *May*
六月 *June*
七月 *July*

八月 *August*
九月 *September*
十月 *October*
十一月 *November*
十二月 *December*
何月 *what month*

練習問題 Exercises

I.　Using the keys provided below, ask your partner what s/he did.

れい

Q:　Xさんは昨日、日本ごをべんきょうしましたか。

A:　はい、(私は昨日、日本ごを) べんきょうしました。

(or) いいえ、(私は昨日、日本ごは) べんきょうし

ませんでした。

1. 昨日
2. 火曜日
3. 昨日

4. せんしゅう
5. せんしゅうの月曜日
6. 金曜日

II.   Ask your classmate about his/her plans. Answer the questions using つもり.

れい

Q:　今日、何かよみますか。

A:　はい、よむつもりです。

Q:　何をよみますか。

A:　しんぶんをよむつもりです。

1.　しゅうまつどこかへ行きますか。

2.　日曜日に何かべんきょうしますか。

3.　こんばん何かしますか。

III.　やまださんは昨日、何をしましたか。ききましょう。

れい

B:　やまださんは昨日、十二時半から二時まで何をしましたか。

A:　（やまださんは昨日、十二時半から二時まで）としょかんでべんきょうしました。

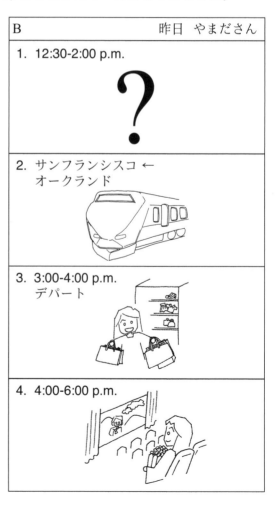

A　　　　　　　　　　昨日　やまださん	B　　　　　　　　　　昨日　やまださん
1.　12:30-2:00 p.m. 　　としょかん	1.　12:30-2:00 p.m. 　　？
2.	2.　サンフランシスコ ← 　　オークランド
3.　3:00-4:00 p.m. 　　？	3.　3:00-4:00 p.m. 　　デパート
4.　4:00-6:00 p.m. 　　？	4.　4:00-6:00 p.m.

5. 7:00-8:00 p.m. うち 	5. 7:00-8:00 p.m. **?**
6. 8:00-9:30 p.m. うち	6. 8:00-9:30 p.m. **?**

IV.　Let's play Bingo. Find out who intends to do each activity.

れい

Q:　日曜日にマクドナルドでハンバーガーをたべますか。

A:　はい、(日曜日にマクドナルドでハンバーガーを) たべ るつもりです。

　　(or) いいえ、(日曜日にマクドナルドでハンバーガーは) たべません。

マクドナルド

1. 日曜日 デパート ＄90 _____ さん	2. 明日 タホ 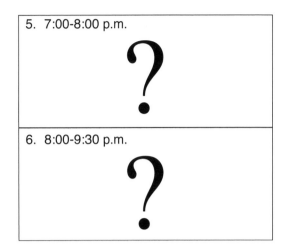 _____ さん	3. 土曜日 ダウンタウン _____ さん
4. 今(いま) としょかん  _____ さん	5. 今日 カフェテリア  _____ さん	6. 日曜日 チャイナタウン  _____ さん
7. 明日 としょかん  _____ さん	8. 今日 うち 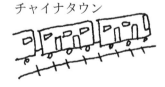 _____ さん	9. 土曜日 レストラン  _____ さん

V.   Look at the pictures and ask your partner as in the example.

れい

Q: X さんは<u>くるま</u>がありますか。

A: はい、（私は<u>くるま</u>が）あります。(or) いいえ、（私は<u>くるま</u>は）ありません。

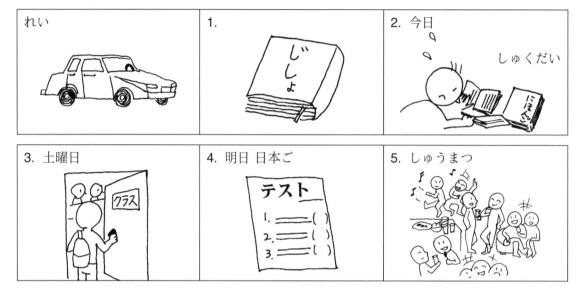

VI.   Select one sentence from each box and connect them with から.

Box A

1. 明日は土曜日です。
2. テニスをしました。
3. 明日、テストがあります。
4. 明日、ミラーさんがうちに来ます。
5. 日本にともだちがいます。

Box B

a. 十二月に日本へ行きます。
b. 日本りょうりをつくります。
c. つかれました。
d. だいがくへ来ません。
e. テキストをよみます。

VII.   Using the sentences you have created in VI, converse with your classmate as demonstrated below.

れい

A: 私は明日、だいがくへ来ません。

B: どうしてですか。

A: 明日は土曜日ですから。

VIII.   Ask your partner (B さん) the following questions. Your partner will answer with 〜や〜など or 〜や〜.

れい

A: B さんはデパートで何をかいますか。

B: 私はかばんやカメラやじしょなどをかいます。

A:　Bさんは何をよみますか。

B:　私はしんぶんやざっしなどをよむつもりです。

1.　Bさんのへやに何がありますか。

2.　Bさんは昨日どこへ行きましたか。

3.　Bさんは日本りょうりのレストランで何をたべますか。

4.　Bさんはパーティーで何をのみますか。

5.　Bさんはしゅうまつどこかへ行きますか。

6.　Bさんは日曜日に何かべんきょうしますか。

IX.　Look at the pictures and practice a conversation as in the example.

れい

A:　もうひるごはんをたべましたか。

B:　はい、もうたべました。 (or) いいえ、まだです。

X.   よみましょう。

○ ですか。×ですか。

1. (）このひとは昨日、二時から四時までとしょかんにいました。
2. (）このひとはあるいてうちへかえりました。
3. (）このひとはうちでハンバーガーをつくりました。
4. (）このひとはルームメートとてんぷらをたべました。
5. (）このひとはビールをのみました。

新しい漢字 New Kanji

Reading 漢字

Japanese borrowed from Chinese not only 漢字 but also many words (and concepts). 学生 "student", for example, is such a borrowing, and so is 先生 "teacher". The loan words from Chinese are called *Sino-Japanese words*. In 漢字 writing, ideas are frequently decomposed and represented by a combination of characters. The notion of student is represented as 学 "to learn/study" + 生 "life" (= learning/studying person), and the notion of teacher as 先 "preceding" + 生 "life" (= preceding person). In Sino-Japanese words, the pronunciation of each 漢字 is very consistent: 生 is read as せい in both 学生 and 先生.

The notion of tomorrow is represented in Chinese as 明 "shining" + 日 "day" (or 明 + 天 "heaven"). As explained in Lesson 3, 漢字 are ideographs and, therefore, language independent. That is, you can write 明日 and read it as [tomorrow]. When you do so, it is not meaningful to consider that 明 is read as [to] and 日 as [morrow]. Rather, 明日 as a whole is assigned the sound value [tomorrow]. This is an illustration of how ancient Japanese people adapted 漢字 to represent their language. The Japanese word for *tomorrow* was あした, so people wrote 明日 and read it as あした. Like the English example of [tomorrow], it is not the case that the reading of 明 is あ, and the reading of 日 is した; rather, 明日 as a whole is read as あした. When Japanese people borrowed the 漢字「明日」, they also borrowed the Chinese word for *tomorrow*, which was close to the sound みょうにち. Thus, 明日 has two readings: the native reading of あした and the Sino-Japanese reading of みょうにち.

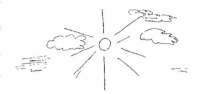

The status of Sino-Japanese words in the Japanese language is similar to that of Latinate words in English (e.g. *appreciate* vis-à-vis *thank*, *obtain* vis-à-vis *get*); they generally sound more formal and sophisticated. The native Japanese reading is called 訓読み "the explanatory/instructional reading", and the Sino-Japanese reading is called 音読み "the sound/phonetic reading". From this point, 訓読み will be written in ひらがな, and 音読み in カタカナ in 漢字 tables. (In normal writing, ひらがな is used for **both** 訓読み and 音読み.)

明	丨	冂	冃	日	町	明	明	明	
	shining/clearness/brightness: 明日（あした）*tomorrow (shining day)*								
行 い（く）	丿	彳	彳	彳	行	行			
	to go								
今 いま	丿	人	今	今					
	current time: 今（いま）*now,* 今日（きょう）*today (current day)*								
上 うえ	丨	上	上						
	up/above/top								

学	丶	丷	丷	丷	丷	学	学		
ガク	*study:* 学生 *student (studying person)*								
生	ノ	㇒	牛	牛	生				
セイ	*life:* 先生 *teacher (preceding person),* 学生 *student (studying person)*								
月	ノ	刀	月	月					
ゲツ・ガツ	*moon:* 月曜日 *Monday (moon day),* 何月 *what month of the year*								
昨	丨	冂	日	日	日	昨	昨	昨	
past: 昨日（きのう）*yesterday (last day)*									
来	一	𠃍	冖	二	平	来	来		
き（ます）・く（る）	*to come*								
小	亅	小	小						
こ	*small:* 小山 *Koyama*								
山	丨	凵	山						
やま	*mountain:* 小山 *Koyama*								
下	一	丁	下						
した	*down / below*								
先	ノ	㇒	牛	生	歨	先			
セン	*preceding:* 先生 *teacher (preceding person)*								
本	一	十	才	木	本				
ホン	*origin:* 本 *book (origin of knowledge),* 日本 *Japan (sun origin)*								
私	㇒	二	千	千	禾	私	私		
わたし	*I / me*								

漢字の復習 Review

I.　よみましょう。

1.　小山さんはきょうとだいがくの学生です。
2.　ソンさんは昨日、としょかんで先生にあいました。
3.　これは私の本ではありません。
4.　十二月に日本からともだちが来ます。
5.　土曜日に日本まちへ行くつもりです。

II.　While most 漢字 have more than one reading, some 漢字 have an unusually large number of readings. 日 is one such 漢字. Let's read the following words. Write the reading of 日 or the whole word in each blank.

1.　日曜日　2.　昨日　3.　今日　4.　明日　5.　日本
　　（　）よう（　）　　（　　）　　（　　）　　（　　）　　（　）ほん

新しい語彙 Vocabulary

From now on the dictionary form of verbs will be listed.

ウ：う -verb　　　ル：る -verb　　　I：Irregular verb

あさ		morning
一月		January
おきる	ル	to wake / get up
おしえる	ル	to teach
かう	ウ	to buy
きく	ウ	to listen, ask
昨日		yesterday
九月		September
五月		May
こんばん		this evening

（お）さけ	alcoholic drink, Japanese sake
三月	March
四月	April
七月	July
十一月	November
十月	October
十二月	December
ジョギング（する）	jogging
すぐ	immediately, soon

ステーキ		steak	二月		February
せんしゅう		last week	日本りょうり		Japanese cuisine
たいへん		tough	ねる	ル	to go to bed
たくさん		a lot, many	八月		August
チャイナタウン		Chinatown	ばん		evening
つかれる	ル	to get tired	ハンバーガー		hamburger
つくる	ウ	to make	ぶんがく		literature
つもり		intention	まだ		(not) yet
テスト（する）		test, examination	もうすぐ		soon
てんぷら		tempura	りょうり（する）		cuisine, cooking
どうして		why	レストラン		restaurant
とる	ウ	to take	六月		June
ドル		dollar	ワイン		wine
とんかつ		pork cutlet			

なまえ (Mostly proper nouns)

アメリカ	America	チェン	Chen
オークランド	Oakland	マクドナルド	McDonald's
タホ	Tahoe		

第六課 LESSON 6

中間しけん
ちゅうかん
Midterm Examination

明日、中間しけんがあるんです
I have a midterm exam tomorrow

会話
かいわ

1 ソン　　：ミラーさん、今晩、日本のえいがを見に行きませんか。
こんばん　　　　　　　　み

　　　　　　　　(Lit.) Miller-san, wouldn't you like to go to see a Japanese movie this evening?

　　　　　　　　Miller-san, would you like to go see a Japanese movie tonight?

　　　　ミラー：ざんねんですが、今晩、行くことはできません。

　　　　　　　　Sorry, but I can't go out tonight.

2 ソン　　：そうですか。今晩も、ジムでうんどうをするんですか。

　　　　　　　　Oh, are you going to go exercise at the gym again tonight?

　　　　ミラー：いえ、今晩はしないつもりです。明日、中間しけんがあるんです。ですから、
　　　　　　　　としょかんでふくしゅうをするつもりです。

　　　　　　　　No, not tonight. I have a midterm exam tomorrow. So, I plan to review at the library.

3 ソン　　：へえ、もう中間しけんですか。たいへんですね。何のしけんですか。

　　　　　　　　A midterm exam already? That's tough, isn't it? What's it on?

4 ミラー：すうがくです。

　　　　　　　　Mathematics.

5 ソン　　：そうですか。それじゃ、えいがを見に行くことはできませんね。

　　　　　　　　I see. Well then, you can't go to see a movie, can you?

　　　　ミラー：ええ、すみません。

　　　　　　　　No, sorry.

6 ソン　　：今晩、何時までべんきょうしますか。

　　　　　　　　How late (Until what time) are you going to study tonight?

　　　　ミラー：十二時までするつもりです。

　　　　　　　　I plan to study until midnight.

　　　　ソン　　：それはたいへんですねえ。

　　　　　　　　Sounds like a lot of work.

7 ミラー：でも、土曜日にともだちの山本さんの家へあそびに行きます。山本さんは日
やまもと　　うち
　　　　　　　　本人の留学生です。ソンさんもいっしょに行きませんか。
りゅうがくせい

　　　　　　　　But on Saturday I'm going to visit my friend Yamamoto-san. Yamamoto-san is a foreign student from Japan. Would you like to come too?

8 ソン　　：いいんですか。

　　　　　　　　Is it okay?

9 ミラー：もちろんですよ。いっしょに行きましょう。

　　　　　　　　Of course. Let's go together.

10 ソン　　：じゃ、また土曜日に。しけん、がんばってください。

　　　　　　Okay, see you again on Saturday then. Good luck on your exam.

使い方

1　ざんねんですが "Unfortunately, …／I'm sorry, but …／I regret to say that …" is used when you decline an offer, invitation, etc.

2　ですから can begin a new sentence and mean "So／Therefore". 明日、中間しけんがあるんです。ですから、としょかんでふくしゅうをするつもりです can be combined into one as 明日、中間しけんがありますから、としょかんでふくしゅうをするつもりです.

5　それじゃ is another casual form of それでは "well then／in that case".

8　いいんですか "Is it okay?" is used to confirm the preceding statement. Here, Miller-san has invited Son-san to go to Yamamoto-san's house with him, but Son-san wants to make sure that her participation will not cause any inconvenience.

10　また means "again": また明日 "(see you) again tomorrow", また土曜日に "(see you) again on Saturday".

　　　がんばってください "please do your best" is used when you encourage someone. You can respond to it by saying はい、がんばります.

文法

6a	**Verb Conjugation: Negative フォーム**	
6b	**Plain フォーム vs. Polite フォーム**	
6c	**ないフォーム＋つもりです**	"I intend／plan not to do ～"
6d	**Pre-ますフォーム＋ませんか**	"Won't you do ～?; Would you like to do ～?"
6e	**Pre-ますフォーム＋に＋{ 行く / 来る / かえる }**	"go／come／return in order to do ～"
6f	**Dictionary フォーム＋ことができる**	"can; be able to do ～"
6g	**Plain フォーム＋のです／んです**	"It is the case that ～"
6h	**Negative Scope Marker は**	
6i	**Answers to Negative Yes-No Questions**	
6j	**Nationalities (Examples)**	
6k	**Languages (Examples)**	

6a   Verb Conjugation: Negative フォーム

In this lesson, you will learn a new conjugation called the *Negative* フォーム. This form almost always occurs with ～ない "not", so let us consider「Negativeフォーム＋ない」as a unit and call it the ない フォーム. To create the ないフォーム of う -verbs, drop the final *i* of the Pre- ますフォーム and change it to *a*, and then add ない, e.g. 行き (ik[i]) to 行か (ik[a]) ない.

う -Verbs

わ	ら	や	ま	は	な	た	さ	か	あ
	り		み	ひ	に	ち	し	き	い
	る	ゆ	む	ふ	ぬ	つ	す	く	う
	れ		め	へ	ね	て	せ	け	え
を	ろ	よ	も	ほ	の	と	そ	こ	お

ikimasu   →   ik[a]-nai

行きます   →   行かない

かえ~~り~~ます	→	かえらない	飲み~~ます~~	→	飲まない
kaeri-masu		kaera-nai	nomi-masu		noma-nai

You can also derive the ないフォーム from the Dictionary フォーム by changing the final *u* to *a* and adding ない.

かえ~~る~~	→	かえらない	飲~~む~~	→	飲まない
kaeru		kaera-nai	nomu		noma-nai

If the Pre- ますフォーム ends with *i* without a preceding consonant, the ないフォーム acquires the consonant *w*.

会います	→	会わない	買います	→	買わない
ai-masu		a[w]a-nai	kai-masu		ka[w]a-nai

いらっしゃいます, again, exhibits irregularity if you form the ないフォーム from its Pre-ますフォーム. However, if you derive the ないフォーム from the Dictionary フォーム, the conjugation is regular.

いらっしゃいます	→	いらっしゃらない
irasshai-masu		irassha[r]a-nai
いらっしゃる	→	いらっしゃらない
irassharu		irasshara-nai

The Negative フォーム of a る -verb is identical to its Pre- ますフォーム.

る -Verb:　食べ<ruby>ます<rt>た</rt></ruby>　　→　　食べない

　　　　　見ます　　→　　見ない

　　　　　います　　→　　いない

来る and する (listed below) are irregular because they do not have any invariant part. Note that ある is a regular う-verb, but its ないフォーム exhibits irregularity.

6b　Plain フォーム vs. Polite フォーム

In Lesson 5, **5c**, we learned that the Dictionary フォーム, rather than the ますフォーム, can be used to indicate the non-past tense in an affirmative sentence in plain/casual speech. Likewise, the ないフォーム can be used in a negative sentence in plain/casual speech, rather than the Pre- ますフォーム + ません.

A:　この本をよみますか↑。　　*Are you going to read this book? (Polite)*

B:　いいえ、よみません。　　*No, I am not. (Polite)*

C:　この本 (を) よむ↑ ?　　*Are you going to read this book? (Plain)*

D:　ううん、よまない。　　*No, I'm not. (Plain)*

Frequently, therefore, the Dictionary フォーム and the ないフォーム are grouped together and called the *Plain* フォーム, whereas the Pre-ますフォーム + ます and the Pre-ますフォーム + ません are called the *Polite* フォーム.

Polite フォーム				Plain フォーム	
Non-past		Past		Non-past	
Affirmative	Negative	Affirmative	Negative	Affirm.	Negative
Pre- ます フォーム	Pre- ます フォーム + ません	Pre- ます フォーム + ました	Pre- ますフォーム + ませんでした	Dict. フォーム	ない フォーム
会います	会いません	会いました	会いませんでした	会う	会わない
あります	ありません	ありました	ありませんでした	ある	ない
行きます	行きません	行きました	行きませんでした	行く	行かない
いらっしゃいます	いらっしゃいません	いらっしゃいました	いらっしゃいませんでした	いらっしゃる	いらっしゃらない

買います	買いません	買いました	買いませんでした	買う	買わない
かえります	かえりません	かえりました	かえりませんでした	かえる	かえらない
かきます	かきません	かきました	かきませんでした	かく	かかない
ききます	ききません	ききました	ききませんでした	きく	きかない
つくります	つくりません	つくりました	つくりませんでした	つくる	つくらない
とります	とりません	とりました	とりませんでした	とる	とらない
飲みます	飲みません	飲みました	飲みませんでした	飲む	飲まない
よみます	よみません	よみました	よみませんでした	よむ	よまない
います	いません	いました	いませんでした	いる	いない
おきます	おきません	おきました	おきませんでした	おきる	おきない
見ます	見ません	見ました	見ませんでした	見る	見ない
おしえます	おしえません	おしえました	おしえませんでした	おしえる	おしえない
食べます	食べません	食べました	食べませんでした	食べる	食べない
ねます	ねません	ねました	ねませんでした	ねる	ねない
来ます	来ません	来ました	来ませんでした	来る	来ない
します	しません	しました	しませんでした	する	しない

6c　　ないフォーム + つもりです　　　"I intend / plan not to do~"

In Lesson 5, **5d**, we used the Pre- ますフォーム + ません , e.g. (1b), to supply a negative answer to a question about our future plans. With the ないフォーム, we can now say "I intend/plan not to do ~", e.g. (1c):

(1a)　今日、家にいますか。

Are you going to stay at home today?

(1b)　いいえ、今日、家にいません。

No, I'm not going to stay at home today.

(1c)　いいえ、今日、家に いない つもりです。

(Lit.) No, I plan not to stay home today. / No, I don't plan to stay home today.

(2)　私は何も 買わない つもりです。

(Lit.) I plan not to buy anything. / I don't plan to buy anything.

(3)　私は何も しない つもりです。

(Lit.) I plan not to do anything. / I don't plan to do anything.

(4)　私はなつやすみはどこへも 行かない つもりです。

(Lit.) I plan not to go anywhere during summer vacation.

I don't plan to go anywhere during summer vacation.

6d　Pre-ますフォーム＋ませんか　　　"Won't you do~?; Would you like to do~?"

 ～ませんか can be interpreted as a genuine negative question, e.g. 小山さんはスペイン語をはなしません か "Doesn't Koyama-san speak Spanish?". But more fre-  quently, it is used to make a suggestion or invitation.

そとで はなしませんか 。	*(Lit.) Won't you talk outside?*
	Would you like to talk outside?
あのみせでおちゃを 飲みませんか 。	*(Lit.) Won't you drink some tea at that shop?*
	Would you like to drink some tea at that shop?
はい、飲みましょう。	*Yes, let's drink some.*
はい、そうしましょう。	*Yes, let's do so.*

If you do not wish to accept the invitation, saying it directly, e.g. *No, I don't / won't*, is too blatant. Say:

ちょっと……。	*Well, ... (Literally, 'a little ...')*
またこんど。	*Well, next time ...*

Both ～ませんか and ～ましょう (cf. Lesson 4, **4g**) are frequently used to make a suggestion/invita- tion. But the former sounds less assertive than the latter, so they are not always interchangeable. For example, if the addressee has already agreed to go on the picnic with you, you can say 行きましょう when the time comes. But if you are not certain whether the addressee is willing to go with you, it may be safer to use 行きませんか.

When making a suggestion/invitation, ～ましょうか can be used with a WH-word, but ～ませんか cannot:

○	何を食べましょうか。	*What shall we eat?*
○	どこへ行きましょうか。	*Where shall we go?*

The following can be interpreted only as true negative questions:

×	何を食べませんか。	*What do you not eat?*
×	どこへ行きませんか。	*Where do you not go?*

Because 何か, どこか, etc. are not WH-words, they can appear with both ～ましょうか and ～ませんか：

○　何か食べ {ましょう / ません} か。　　　*Shall we eat something?*

○　どこかへ行き {ましょう / ません} か。　　*Shall we go somewhere?*

6e　Pre-ますフォーム + に + 行く／来る／かえる　　　"go / come / return in order to do~"

私はとしょかんへ べんきょうしに 行きます。

I'm going to the library to study.

おちゃを 飲みに 行きませんか。

(Lit.) Won't we go to drink tea? / Wouldn't you like to go out for tea?

私はキャンパスへテープを かえしに 行くつもりです。

I plan to go to campus to return a tape.

せんしゅうの土曜日にともだちが あそびに 来ました。

(Lit.) A friend came to play Saturday last week.

My friend visited me (my home) last Saturday.

いしかわ先生、しつもんしに 来ました。

Ishikawa-sensei, I've come to ask you some questions.

私は明日、デパートへくつとかさを 買いに 行くつもりです。

I plan to go to a department store tomorrow to buy shoes and an umbrella.

6f　Dictionary フォーム + ことができる　　　"can / be able to do~"

Although this construction can be used to express circumstantial possibility, e.g. (6) below, it generally indicates that one has the ability to do something.

(1)　英語のしんぶんをよむことができますか。

Can you read English newspapers?

はい、英語のしんぶんをよむことができます。

Yes, I can read English newspapers.

(2)　ちゅうごく語をよむことができますか。

Can you read Chinese?

いいえ、ちゅうごく語をよむことはできません。

No, I can't read Chinese.

(3)　日本語のじしょをつかうことができますか。

Can you use a Japanese dictionary?

いいえ、日本語のじしょをつかうことはできません。

No, I can't use a Japanese dictionary.

(4)　何語をはなすことができますか。

What language(s) can you speak?

日本語と英語をはなすことができます。

I can speak Japanese and English.

(5)　ゴルフをすることができますか。

Can you play golf?

はい、すこしゴルフをすることができます。

Yes, I can play golf a little.

(6)　日曜日に私の家へ来ることができますか。

Can you come to my house on Sunday?

すみません、行くことはできません。

(Lit.) Sorry, I can't go (to your house).

Sorry, I can't come (to your house).

6g　Plain フォーム + のです／んです　　"It is the case that~"

Plain

Plain フォーム + のです／んです is used to provide an explanation. 〜のです is formal; 〜んです colloquial. In (4), without 〜んです, the two sentences would be presented as unrelated. It is 〜んです that indicates that the addressee must interpret the second sentence as an explanation. This expression can also be used in the form of a question, 〜のですか／〜んですか, e.g. (3). Here, the question must be interpreted as asking an explanation for the preceding statement, i.e. for why the person cannot go eat sashimi.

(1)　今晩、おさしみを食べに行きませんか。

(Lit.) Wouldn't you like to go eat sashimi this evening?

Would you like to go eat sashimi tonight?

(2)   ざんねんですが、今晩はちょっと……。

Sorry, but ...

(3)   そうですか。今晩もジムでうんどうをする んですか 。

Oh, (is it because) you're going to go exercise at the gym again tonight?

(4)   いえ、今晩はしないつもりです。明日、中間しけんがある んです 。

No, not tonight. (Because) I have a midterm exam tomorrow.

When the predicate is a noun, 〜なのです／〜なんです is used:

(5)   どうして、日本語をはなすことができる んですか 。

How is it that you can speak Japanese?

(6)   私のルームメートは日本人 なんです 。

(Because) My roommate is Japanese.

6h   Negative Scope Marker は

In Lesson 3, we learned that the negative counterpart of 「X に Y が あります」 is 「X に Y は ありません」.

このへやにとけい が ありますか。   *Is there a clock in this room?*

いいえ、このへやにとけい は ありません。   *No, there isn't a clock in this room.*

は is frequently used in negative sentences to indicate what is negated. This use of は is called the *negative scope marker*. The term negative scope means the part of the sentence which is negated. In the following, the negative answers with が or を are grammatical and acceptable, but those with は sound much more natural. In these examples, the focus of negation is highlighted. Note that this は implies a *contrast*, i.e., it implies a positive counterpart to the scope that is negated.

(1)   かんこく語をかくことができますか。

Can you write Korean?

いいえ、かんこく語をかくこと は できません。

No, I can't write Korean (implies that the speaker can do something else with Korean, such as reading).

(2)　はなを買いましたか。

Did you buy some flowers?

いいえ、はな は 買いませんでした。

No, I didn't buy flowers (implies that the speaker bought something else).

(3)　今晩、パーティーに行きませんか。

Wouldn't you like to go to a party this evening?

ざんねんですが、今晩 は 行くことができません。

Unfortunately, I can't go out this evening (implies that the speaker wants to go, but that this evening is inconvenient).

In negative sentences, は *replaces* が and を, e.g. (1)-(2), but は is *added* to other particles, e.g. へ, に, で, と.

(4)　小山さんはふゆやすみにアメリカにいますか。

Will Koyama-san be (stay) in the U.S. during winter break?

いいえ、（小山さんはふゆやすみに）アメリカ には いません。

No, she won't be in the U.S. (She'll be elsewhere.)

(5)　こうえんへ行きましたか。

Did you go to the park?

いいえ、こうえん へは 行きませんでした。

No, I didn't go to the park. (I went somewhere else.)

(6)　ソンさんからおかねをかりるつもりですか。

Do you plan to borrow money from Son-san?

いいえ、ソンさん からは かりないつもりです。

(Lit.) No, I plan not to borrow from Son-san.

No, I don't plan to borrow from Son-san. (I may borrow money from someone else.)

(7)　ソンさんといっしょに行きましたか。

Did you go (there) with Son-san?

いいえ、ソンさん とは 行きませんでした。

No, I didn't go (there) with Son-san. (I went there with someone else.)

(8)　レストランでさかなを食べましたか。

Did you eat fish at the restaurant?

いいえ、レストラン｜では｜食べませんでした。

No, I didn't eat any at a restaurant. (I ate fish somewhere else.)

(9)　くるまで行きましたか。

Did you go there by car?

いいえ、くるま｜では｜行きませんでした。

No, I didn't go by car. (I went there by some other means.)

6i　Answers to Negative Yes-No Questions

In English, the use of *Yes* or *No* in answers to affirmative and negative Yes-No questions remains the same.

(1)　Can you go to see a movie this evening?　　　　(Affirmative Question)

Yes, I can.

No, I can't.

(2)　Can't you go to see a movie this evening?　　　　(Negative Question)

Yes, I can.

No, I can't.

This is because in English *Yes* and *No* usually correspond to the content of the answer: if you can go, you use *Yes*, and if you cannot, you use *No*. In Japanese, by contrast, はい（ええ）and いいえ（いえ）refer to the question, not to the answer. はい（ええ）indicates that the questioner's assumption is correct, and いいえ the opposite.

(3)　ソン　：　そうですか。それじゃ、えいがを見に行くことは｜できません｜ね。

Well then, you can't go to see a movie, can you?

ミラー　：　｜ええ｜、すみません。

(Lit.) That's right. Sorry. / No, sorry.

In this exchange, ミラーさん uses ええ "Yes" to indicate that he cannot go to see a movie. He uses ええ because ソンさん's assumption that he cannot go out is correct. English is also capable of responding to the assumptions of the questioner, e.g. *right*, *sorry*, but not usually with the word *yes*.

(4) としょかんへ行きましたか。 *You went to the library?*

はい、としょかんへ行きました。 *Yes, I went to the library.*

いいえ、としょかんへは行きませんでした。 *No, I didn't go to the library.*

(5) としょかんへ行きませんでしたか。 *You didn't go to the library?*

はい 、としょかんへは行きませんでした。 No , *I didn't go to the library.*

いいえ 、としょかんへ行きました。 Yes , *I went to the library.*

(6) 今晩はジムでうんどうをしないんですか。

You're not going to go exercise at the gym tonight?

はい 、今晩はしないつもりです。明日、中間しけんがあるんです。

No , *I plan not to. (Because) I have a midterm exam tomorrow.*

いいえ 、今晩もするつもりです。

Yes , *I plan to.*

6j   Nationalities (Examples)

アメリカ人	American	ドイツ人	German
カナダ人	Canadian	日本人	Japanese
かんこく人	Korean	フランス人	French
ちゅうごく人	Chinese	メキシコ人	Mexican

6k   Languages (Examples)

英語	English	ドイツ語	German
かんこく語	Korean	日本語	Japanese
スペイン語	Spanish	フランス語	French
ちゅうごく語	Chinese	ロシア語	Russian

<ruby>練<rt>れん</rt>習<rt>しゅう</rt>問<rt>もん</rt>題<rt>だい</rt></ruby>

I.　　Let's practice forming the Negative フォーム.

II.　Using the verbs in Exercise I (6-15), talk with your partner about your plans on weekends.

れい

Q:　しゅうまつ、ダウンタウンへ行きますか。

A:　はい、しゅうまつ、ダウンタウンへ<u>行くつもりです</u>。

　　(or) いいえ、しゅうまつ、ダウンタウンへは<u>行かないつもりです</u>。

III.　Let's invite your classmates to the following activities.

れい

A:　<u>今晩、えいがを見ませんか</u>。

B:　いいですね。

A:　どこで<u>見ましょうか</u>。

B:　<u>ダウンタウンで見ましょう</u>。

IV.　Look at the pictures and tell for what purpose each person is going to that place.

れい

やまださんは<u>としょかんへ本をかえしに</u>行きます。

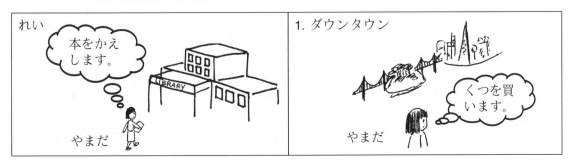

V.　Ask your partner if s/he can do each of the activities mentioned below.

れい

Q:　<u>X さんはスパゲティをつくる</u>ことができますか。

A:　はい、<u>(私は) スパゲティをつくる</u>ことができます。

　　(or) いいえ、<u>(私は) スパゲティをつくる</u>ことはできません。

VI.　You and your partner are going to do each activity below. Following the example, decide when you will get together.

れい

A:　今日、いっしょにしゅくだいをしませんか。

B:　ざんねんですが、今日、しゅくだいをすることはできません。でも、明日、しゅくだいをすることができます。

A:　じゃあ、明日、いっしょにしゅくだいをしましょう。

VII.　Look at the pictures and discover the reasons.

れい

Q:　チェンさんはちゅうごく語をはなすんですか。

A:　ええ、私はちゅうごく人なんです。

VIII.　Read the following dialogues and write はい or いいえ.

1.　A:　としょかんへ行きましたか。

　　　B:　＿＿＿＿＿＿＿＿、行きませんでした。

　　　A:　そうですか。行きませんでしたか。

　　　B:　＿＿＿＿＿＿＿＿、行きませんでした。

2.　A:　明日、何かしますか。

　　　B:　＿＿＿＿＿＿＿＿、明日、としょかんでべんきょうするつもりです。

　　　A:　そうですか。じゃあ、ピクニックに行くことはできませんね。

　　　B:　＿＿＿＿＿＿＿＿、すみません。

3.　A:　山本さんは四ねんせいじゃありませんね。

　　　B:　＿＿＿＿＿＿＿＿、四ねんせいじゃありません。

　　　A:　やまださんも四ねんせいじゃありませんね。

　　　B:　＿＿＿＿＿＿＿＿、四ねんせいです。

4.　A:　りょうのへやにテレビがありますか。

　　　B:　＿＿＿＿＿＿＿＿、ありません。

　　　A:　ラジオもありませんか。

　　　B:　＿＿＿＿＿＿＿＿、ラジオはありますよ。

5.　A:　今日、でんしゃで来ましたか。

　　　B:　＿＿＿＿＿＿＿＿、バスで来ました。

　　　A:　そうですか。昨日もでんしゃで来ませんでしたか。

　　　B:　＿＿＿＿＿＿＿＿、昨日はでんしゃで来ました。

IX.　よみましょう。

私は日本人の留学生です。

アメリカのだいがくはたいへんです。しゅくだいとしけんがたくさんあるんです。

私のせんもんはちゅうごく語です。私は日本人ですから、かんじをかくことができます。でも、ちゅうごく語をはなすことはできません。

走进碑林第一室，这里有石刻的中国古代经》②，共用一百一十四块碑石，两面刻写，大五万字。里，看到这些又高又大的石碑地立在明先生感叹地说："这是世界的一年来，它对中国历史的发展有读书人，不论作事、说话或他看到了唐代书法家颜真直临写他的字帖，今天感到特别亲切。

明日、ちゅうごく語の中間しけんがあります。ですから、今日ジムへは行かないつもりです。

三時から五時までちゅうごく人のルームメートといっしょに家でふくしゅうをするつもりです。

そして、ひとりでとしょかんで十二時までべんきょうするつもりです。

○ ですか。×ですか。

1.　（　　）このひとはアメリカ人です。
2.　（　　）このひとはかんじをかくことはできません。
3.　（　　）このひとは明日、中間しけんがあります。
4.　（　　）このひとは今晩、十二時までルームメートといっしょにふくしゅうします。
5.　（　　）このひとは今晩、としょかんへべんきょうしに行きます。

新しい漢字

会う	家	英語	買う	～語	今晩	～人
食べる	中間	何語	日本語	日本人	飲む	見る
山本	留学生					

おくりがな

Suppose that you need to write with 漢字 (かんじ) the English sentence *I bought a house*. You may write it as 私買家. Although the *a* in *a house* is not represented, it is easily inferable from the context. But what about *bought*? 私買家 could mean *I'll buy a house*, so you need some marker to indicate that the event took place in the past. One possibility is to write 私買 *-ed* 家, where *-ed* marks the past tense. This strategy was

adopted by the Japanese. Keeping the original meaning of 買 "buying", they added inflectional endings in ひらがな. Generally, the 漢字 represents the invariant (unchanging) syllable(s) of the verb or adjective, whereas the variant syllables are written in ひらがな (called おくりがな). This rule applies straightforwardly to う-verbs:

買います	ka⎡imasu⎤		買う	ka⎡u⎤
買いません	ka⎡imasen⎤		買わない	ka⎡wanai⎤
飲みます	no⎡mimasu⎤		飲む	no⎡mu⎤
飲みません	no⎡mimasen⎤		飲まない	no⎡manai⎤

For る-verbs, おくりがな normally begins with the last syllable of the invariant part.

| 食べます | ta⎡bemasu⎤ | | 食べる | ta⎡beru⎤ |
| 食べません | ta⎡bemasen⎤ | | 食べない | ta⎡benai⎤ |

When the invariant part of a る-verb consists of one syllable, おくりがな begins with the second syllable of the word.

| 見ます | mi⎡masu⎤ | | 見る | mi⎡ru⎤ |
| 見ません | mi⎡masen⎤ | | 見ない | mi⎡nai⎤ |

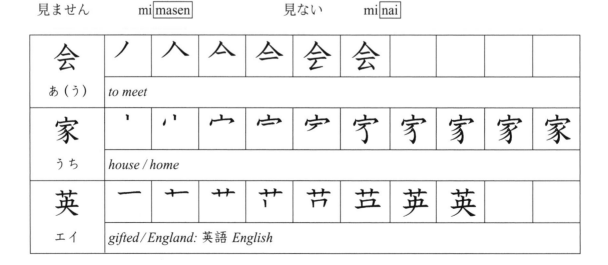

会	ノ	入	스	会	会	会				
あ（う）	*to meet*									
家	丶	宀	宀	宀	宁	宁	冡	家	家	
うち	*house / home*									
英	一	十	艹	艹	苎	苹	英	英		
エイ	*gifted / England:* 英語 *English*									

語	丶	二	二	言	言	言	言	訁	訂	訪
ゴ	語	語	語	語						
	word / language: 日本語 *Japanese,* 英語 *English*									

買	丶	冂	罒	罒	罒	罒	買	買	買	買
か（う）	買	買								
	to buy									

今	ノ	人	𠆢	今						
コン・いま	*current time:* 今 *now,* 今日（きょう）*today,* 今晩 *this evening*									

晩	丨	冂	日	日	日ク	日ク	日ク	昭	昭	
バン	晩	晩								
	evening: 今晩 *this evening*									

人	ノ	人								
ジン	*person:* 日本人 *Japanese (person),* アメリカ人 *American (person)*									

食	ノ	𠆢	𠆢	今	今	슬	食	食	食	
た（べる）	*to eat*									

中	丶	冂	口	中						
チュウ	*center / middle:* 中間 *midterm*									

間	丨	冂	冂	門	門	門	門	門	間	
カン	間	間								
	interval / between: 中間 *midterm*									

本	一	十	才	木	本					
ホン・もと	*origin:* 日本 *Japan (sun origin),* 本 *book (origin of knowledge),* 山本 *Yamamoto*									

飲	ノ	入	今	今	今	今	食	食	食	飲
の (む)	飲	飲								
	to drink (Notice how this かんじ *contains* 食*.)*									
見	一	冂	冂	月	目	貝	見			
み (る)	*to see/look*									
留	ノ	ᄂ	ᄼ	幻	卯	𠄎	留	留	留	
リュウ	*stay:* 留学生 *foreign student*									

漢字の復習
<ruby>漢字<rt>かんじ</rt></ruby>の<ruby>復習<rt>ふくしゅう</rt></ruby>

I.　よみましょう。

1.　木曜日に山本さんといっしょにえいがを見ました。
2.　今晩六時ごろ、私の家へ来ませんか。
3.　いしかわ先生はかんこく語をはなすことができます。
4.　火曜日に日本語の本を買いました。
5.　明日、ソンさんに会うつもりです。

II.　Complete the sentences by selecting an appropriate verb from the following list. The verbs are given in their Dictionary フォーム; you may have to change them to a different form.

会う	行く	買う	来る	食べる	見る

1.　さとうさんはせんしゅうの日曜日に
　　しんかんせんできょうとへ

　　_____。

2.　山本さんは明日ともだちに

　　_____。

3.　A:　今晩いっしょにえいがを

　　　　_____。

　　B:　いいですね。

　　　　_____。

4.　こんどの土曜日にレストランでばんごはんを

　_____。

5.　今、三時です。キムさんは四時に私の家に

　_____。

6.　せんしゅう、日本まちでじしょを　_____。

新しい語彙

〜語	suffix for a language		キャンパス	campus
〜人	suffix for nationality		くつ	shoes
あそぶ　ウ	to play		こうえん	park
アメリカ人	American people		ゴルフ	golf
およぐ　ウ	to swim		こんど	next time, this time
かえす　ウ	to return (something)		さかな	fish
かさ	umbrella		(お)さしみ	raw fish
カナダ人	Canadian people		ざんねん	regrettable, regret
(お)かね	money		しけん	quiz, examination
かりる　ル	to borrow		しつもん (する)	question
かんこく語	Korean language		すうがく	mathematics
かんこく人	Korean people		スキー	ski
がんばる　ウ	to do one's best		すこし	a little

スパゲティ		spaghetti	はなす	ウ	to talk, speak
スペイン語		Spanish language	ピアノ		piano
中間		midterm	ひく	ウ	to play (a stringed instrument)
ちゅうごく語		Chinese language			
ちゅうごく人		Chinese people	ピクニック		picnic
つかう	ウ	to use	ふくしゅう（する）		review
テープ		tape	ふゆやすみ		winter vacation
できる	ル	to be able to	フランス語		French language
ですから		therefore, so	フランス人		French people
ドイツ語		German language	また		again
ドイツ人		German people	（お）みせ		shop, store
なつやすみ		summer vacation	メキシコ人		Mexican people
日本人		Japanese people	もちろん		of course
パーティー		party	留学生		foreign student
はな		flower	ロシア語		Russian language

なまえ

山本	Yamamoto

第七課 LESSON 7

だいなな か (furigana above 第七課)

山本さんのアパートで
At Yamamoto-san's Apartment

きれいなへやですね
What a lovely room!

会話
かい わ

1 ミラー ：山本さんのアパートはここです。

　　　　　　(Lit.) Yamamoto-san's apartment is here.

　　　　　　Here's Yamamoto-san's apartment building.

　　ソン ：わあ、大きいですねえ。

　　　　　　Wow, it's big, isn't it?

　　ミラー ：そうですね。さあ、入りましょう。

　　　　　　Yes, it is. Well, let's go in.

2 山本 ：あっ、ミラーさん。

　　　　　　Oh, Miller-san!

　　ミラー ：山本さん、今晩は。こちらはソンさんです。

　　　　　　Good evening, Yamamoto-san. This is Son-san.

3 ソン ：はじめまして。ソンです。

　　　　　　Nice to meet you. I'm Son.

　　山本 ：はじめまして。山本です。

　　　　　　Nice to meet you. I'm Yamamoto.

4 山本 ：どうぞ。

　　　　　　Please (come this way).

　　ミラーとソン ：はい、しつれいします。

　　　　　　Thank you.

5 ソン ：わあ、きれいなへやですね。

　　　　　　(Lit.) Wow, it's a beautiful room, isn't it?

　　　　　　Wow, what a lovely room!

　　　　　　そして、とてもしずかですね。

　　　　　　And very quiet, too.

　　山本 ：ええ。ここはとてもしずかでいいです。でも、大学からとおくて、ちょっとふべんです。ソンさんの家はどうですか。

　　　　　　Yes, it is very quiet, so it's nice here. But it's far from campus, so it's a little inconvenient. What about your place, Son-san?

6 ソン ：私のアパートはキャンパスのちかくにあります。とてもべんりです。でも、せまくてうるさいですから、家でべんきょうすることはできません。

　　　　　　My apartment is close to campus. (So,) it's quite convenient. But because it's small and noisy, I can't study at home.

ソン　　：となりの家でいつもパーティーがあるんです。

(Lit.) There are always parties next door.

My next-door neighbor is always having parties.

7　山本　　：そうですか。

Is that so?

たいへんですね。

(Lit.) That's terrible, isn't it?

What a pain that must be!

使い方

1　アパート means either an "apartment" or "apartment building". Here, because ミラーさん and ソンさん have not entered the building yet, the latter is the natural translation.

さあ↓ is used when you encourage or urge someone to do something, e.g. さあ、入りましょう "Let's go in／enter".

4　しつれい literally means "rudeness／bad manners". しつれいします is used when you enter another's territory, e.g. home or office. In this case, it means "Excuse me". As you studied in Lesson 1, it can also be used when you part from someone; in such a case, it means "Goodbye". しつれい is a な -adjective (cf. **7b**), e.g. しつれいなひと "rude person".

5　As explained in (**7c**), きれい means "pretty／beautiful" or "clean". In this situation, the former interpretation is more appropriate, although it is not common to describe a room with "pretty／beautiful" in English. You can translate the sentence as "What a nice/lovely room!".

文法

7a	い -**Adjectives**	
7b	な -**Adjectives**	
7c	**Antonyms (Opposite Terms)**	
7d	**Multiple Adjectives**	
7e	は－が **Construction**	
7f	X で Y がある	**"There is Y in／at X"**
7g	**Degree Adverbs**	
7h	が	**"but"**
7i	X はどうですか／いかがですか	**"How is X?"**
7j	X はどんな Y ですか	**"What kind of Y is X?"**
7k	こちら／そちら／あちら	**"this／that direction"**

7a　い -Adjectives

Adjectives are words used to describe someone/something. There are two kinds of adjectives in Japanese: い -*adjectives* and な -*adjectives*.

The Dictionary フォーム of all い -adjectives ends with い, which normally expresses the non-past tense. The part preceding い is called *the stem* of the い-adjective. い-adjectives can be used by themselves, but です is frequently added to make the speech polite.

Polite 大きいです	Plain 大きい	Stem 大きー

山本さんのアパートは広いです。

Yamamoto-san's apartment is spacious.

りょうのへやはうるさいです。

The dorm rooms are noisy.

この大学は古いです。

This college is old.

私の車は安いです。

My car is inexpensive.

あのレストランのりょうりはおいしいです。

That restaurant's food is delicious.

The negative form of い -adjectives can be derived by adding 〜くありません or 〜くないです to the stem. 〜くありません is more formal than 〜くないです.

私の家は広 くありません 。 　　　　*My house/home is not spacious.*

あのみせは高 くありません 。 　　　　*That store is not expensive.*

日本語はむずかし くないです 。 　　　　*Japanese is not difficult.*

When an い -adjective modifies the following noun, the *plain form* (i.e. without です) is used.

このへやは暗いです。 　　　　*This room is dark.*

暗い へや 　　　　*dark room*

このケーキはおいしいです。 　　　　*This cake is delicious.*

おいしい ケーキ 　　　　*delicious cake*

日本語のしゅくだいはやさしいです。 　　　　*Japanese homework assignments are easy.*

やさしい しゅくだい 　　　　*easy homework assignments*

7b　な -Adjective

The second type of adjective is called a な -*adjective*. Most な -adjectives do not end with い; some exceptions are きれい "clean / pretty", ゆうめい "famous" (cf. Lesson 14), とくい "good at" (cf. Lesson 9). な -adjectives are also called *adjectival nouns*, because they exhibit noun-like properties. Unlike い -adjectives, な -adjectives need です to form a sentence.

小山さんのへやは きれいです 。	*Koyama-san's room is clean / beautiful.*
山本さんのアパートは しずかです 。	*Yamamoto-san's apartment is quiet.*
大阪は にぎやかです 。	*Osaka is lively.*

To derive the negative form of な -adjectives, just add 〜ではありません, 〜じゃありません, or 〜じゃないです. 〜ではありません is more formal than 〜じゃありません／〜じゃないです. The は in 〜ではありません is the negative scope marker は (cf. Lesson 6, **6h**).

私のアパートはきれい｛ではありません／じゃありません／じゃないです｝。

As we studied in Lesson 2, regular nouns require の when they modify another noun, e.g. 英語の本 "English book". な -adjectives, which share some characteristics with both い -adjectives and nouns, require な when they modify a noun. Hence the name な -adjectives. The stem (invariant part) of a な -adjective is the な -adjective by itself, without な, e.g. きれい, しずか.

このこうえんはきれいです。	*This park is beautiful.*
きれい な こうえん	*beautiful park*
このへやはしずかです。	*This room is quiet.*
しずか な へや	*quiet room*
このじしょはべんりです。	*This dictionary is convenient.*
べんり な じしょ	*convenient dictionary*

い -adjectives are authentic Japanese adjectives and involve conjugations, e.g. おいしーい → おいしーく. な -adjectives, on the other hand, are like nouns and require です. Consequently, the category of い -adjectives cannot accommodate new or foreign adjectives easily, but the category of な -adjectives can. In fact, most な -adjectives are loan words from Chinese. In recent years, many English words have been borrowed and used as な -adjectives.

エスニックな	*ethnic*		ハンサムな	*handsome*
キュートな	*cute*		フレッシュな	*fresh*
グローバルな	*global*		ヘルシーな	*healthy*
シンプルな	*simple*		ホットな	*hot*
ナチュラルな	*natural*		リッチな	*rich*

7c   Antonyms (Opposite Terms)

Most adjectives have multiple meanings. For example, 高い means "high" in the sense of physical height (tall) or in the sense of a cost (expensive). For physical height, the opposite is ひくい (short), whereas for costs, the opposite is 安い (cheap/inexpensive).

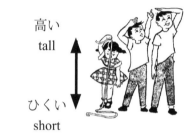

高い
tall

ひくい
short

 Some adjectives describe a characteristic which can be evaluated either positively or negatively. In addition to *inexpensive* vs. *cheap*, a good pair of examples from English is *thrifty* and *stingy*. Similarly, にぎやか and うるさい can be used to describe the same situation. If you enjoy the sounds, you use にぎやか "lively", but if you are annoyed, you want to say うるさい "noisy".

新(あたら)しい
new

古い
old

Still other adjectives have different nuances when they are used to describe a thing, situation, or person. 明るい and 暗い can be used to describe a person and mean "cheerful" and "gloomy", respectively.

大きい
big

小(ちい)さい
small

やさしい is another adjective that has multiple meanings. When it is used for an activity, it means "easy", but when it is used for a person, it means "kind/gentle". Do you see any commonality between these two senses?

高い
expensive

安い
inexpensive

きれい means "pretty/beautiful" or "clean". For the Japanese, these two concepts are very close, if not identical.

明(あか)るい
bright/light

暗い
dark

The following table lists the adjectives you learn in Lesson 7. The antonym of an い-adjective may be a な-adjective, and vice versa. な-adjectives are marked with ⊕ in this table.

$E = MC^2$
むずかしい
difficult

$Y = 2X^2$
やさしい
easy

明るい	*bright, cheerful*	暗い	*dark, gloomy*
新しい	*new*	古い	*old*
いい	*good*		
おいしい	*delicious*	まずい	*not tasty / yucky*
大きい	*big*	小さい	*small*
おもしろい	*interesting*	つまらない	*boring*
きたない	*dirty*	きれい　㋤	*clean / pretty / beautiful*
げんき　㋤	*energetic*		
しずか　㋤	*quiet*	うるさい	*noisy*
しずか　㋤	*quiet*	にぎやか　㋤	*lively*
しんせつ　㋤	*kind*	いじわる　㋤	*mean*
せまい	*narrow, small*	広い	*spacious*
高い	*tall*	ひくい	*low / short (height)*
高い	*expensive*	安い	*cheap / inexpensive*
ちかい	*near*	とおい	*far*
長い	*long*	みじかい	*short (length)*
べんり　㋤	*convenient*	ふべん　㋤	*inconvenient*
まじめ　㋤	*serious*	ふまじめ　㋤	*not serious*
むずかしい	*difficult*	やさしい	*easy*

7d　Multiple Adjectives

In Lesson 3, we learned と to conjoin nouns, e.g. くつ と かばんを買いました. The English *and* can be used to conjoin two words from the same category (and sometimes from different categories), e.g. NOUN + NOUN, VERB + VERB, ADJECTIVE + ADJECTIVE, ADVERB + ADVERB. Unlike English, Japanese lacks an invariant word corresponding to *and*. In order to combine two adjectives, if the first one is an い-adjective, you need to add くて to its stem:

新し い ＋ 明るい　→　新し くて 明るいへや

new and bright room

このへやは新し|くて|明るいです。

This room is new and bright.

古い　＋　しずか　→　古|くて|しずかな家

old and quiet house

この家は古|くて|しずかです。

This house is old and quiet.

日本語のしゅくだいはみじか|くて|やさしいです。

Japanese homework assignments are short and easy.

このレストランのコーヒーは安|くて|おいしいです。でも、ケーキはまずいです。

The coffee at this restaurant is inexpensive and delicious. But their cake is not tasty.

When the first one is a な -adjective, add で to its stem.

しずか　＋　きれい　→　しずか|で|きれいなアパート

quiet and clean apartment

わたしのアパートはしずか|で|きれいです。

My apartment is quiet and clean.

きれい　＋　明るい　→　きれい|で|明るいオフィス

clean and bright office

石川先生のオフィスはきれい|で|明るいです。

Ishikawa-sensei's office is clean and bright.

しずか|で|安いアパートはありませんか。

Aren't there any quiet and inexpensive apartments?

あのレストランは、きれい|で|にぎやかです。

That restaurant is clean and lively.

This construction is similar to English *and*, not to *but*. So like in English, the combined adjectives should match in their positive or negative connotation. That is, if the first adjective is positive, the second one should also be positive, e.g. *delicious* and *inexpensive*. If the first one is negative, so is the second, e.g. *noisy* and *dirty*. Disagreement in such connotations will result in a strange, albeit grammatical, sentence, e.g. *gentle* and *dishonest*. If adjectives do not agree in positive/negative connotations, use the conjunctive が (cf. **7h**) instead.

あのレストランは安いです|が|、きたないです。

That restaurant is inexpensive, but it's dirty.

When the second adjective is judgmental in nature, the first adjective is normally understood as the reason for the judgment.

あのみせは安くてとても　いい　です。

That store is inexpensive, so it's very good.

チェンさんのコンピューターは小さくて　べんり　です。

Chen-san's computer is small, so it's convenient.

としょかんはとおくて　ふべん　です。

The library is far away, so it's inconvenient.

けいざいがくのコースはむずかしくて　たいへん　です。

The economics courses are difficult, so they're challenging (tough to handle).

Note that the opposite order is anomalous:

× 　あのみせはとてもよくて安いです。

　　That store is good and inexpensive.

× 　チェンさんのコンピューターはべんりで小さいです。

　　Chen-san's computer is convenient and small. (If the smallness is not a basis for your judgment of convenience, the sentence will be okay.)

× 　としょかんはふべんでとおいです。

　　The library is inconvenient and far away. (This sentence means that the distance is not a basis for your judgment of inconvenience.)

× 　けいざいがくのコースはたいへんでむずかしいです。

　　The economics courses are challenging and difficult.

　　(The order of たいへん and むずかしい is anomalous here. たいへん is a more general characteristic, whereas むずかしい is a more specific characteristic of the two. If you place a specific description first, it is understood to be a reason for the more general description. But the opposite order does not work.)

7e 　は−が Construction

Having separate markers for the topic and the subject, Japanese permits an interesting construction:

TOPIC は、SUBJECT が ADJECTIVE

(1) 　日本りょうり　は　てんぷら　が　おいしいです。

　　　As for Japanese dishes, tempura is delicious.

(2) 東京は家が高いです。

In Tokyo, houses are expensive.

(3) 山下さんは目が大きいです。

(Lit.) As for Yamashita-san, her eyes are big.

Yamashita-san has big eyes.

Compare (3) with:

(4) 山下さんの目は大きいです。

Yamashita-san's eyes are big.

In (3), we are talking about 山下さん; her eyes being big is one of her characteristics. In (4), on the other hand, we are talking about 山下さん's eyes. (3) is appropriate to answer the question, "What type of a person is 山下さん?", but (4) cannot be used in this situation.

You can combine more than one description of the topic entity.

(5) 山下さんは、目が大きくて、かみが長いです。

(Lit.) As for Yamashita-san, her eyes are big, and her hair is long.

Yamashita-san has big eyes and long hair.

(6) 日本語プログラムは、先生がしんせつで、クラスがにぎやかです。

(Lit.) Regarding the Japanese Program, the teachers are kind, and the classes are lively.

The Japanese Program has kind teachers and lively classes.

7f   X で Y がある   "There is Y in/at X"

In Lesson 3, we studied「X に Y があります」"there is Y in X". When the Y is an activity, rather than a thing, で must be used instead of に to indicate location.

デパートでセールがあります。

There's a sale at the department store.

しゅうまつ、家でパーティーがあります。

There's going to be a party at my house (this) weekend.

明日、大学でデモがあります。

There's going to be a (political) demonstration at the university tomorrow.

7g Degree Adverbs

Adverbs are those words that modify predicates in degree, frequency, etc. There are two types of degree adverbs that often occur with adjectives: one with affirmative sentences, and the other with negative sentences.

A Affirmative Sentences

(1) とても *"very"*

　　このじしょはとてもべんりです。　　　*This dictionary is very convenient.*

　　石川先生はとてもしんせつです。　　　*Ishikawa-sensei is very kind.*

(2) すこし *"a little"*；ちょっと *"a little (colloquial)"*

　　あのみせはすこし高いです。　　　*That store is a little expensive.*

　　日本語はちょっとむずかしいです。　　　*Japanese is a little difficult.*

Like the English a *little*, すこし and ちょっと are more commonly used as hedging expressions (avoiding clear statements), rather than as pure degree adverbs. Because of this hedging function, すこし and ちょっと appear more natural when the predicate has some negative connotation. For example, in

　　日本語のクラスはちょっとつまらないです
　　Japanese class is a little boring,

it is unlikely that the speaker means that his/her Japanese class is less boring than some standard. Rather, the speaker uses ちょっと, or *a little* in English, to soften the statement. Conversely, if you use すこし or ちょっと with a positive adjective, they add a connotation that the positive characteristic may not meet the addressee's expectation.

　　このじしょはちょっとべんりです。　　　*(You may not agree, but) this dictionary is somewhat convenient.*

B Negative Sentences

(1) ぜんぜん *"(not) at all"*

　　この本はぜんぜんおもしろくありません。　　*This book isn't interesting at all.*

　　ひらがなはぜんぜんむずかしくありません。　*Hiragana isn't difficult at all.*

(2) あまり *"(not) very much"*

私のへやはあまり広くありません。   *My room isn't very spacious.*

私はあまりお金^{かね}がありません。   *I don't have much money.*

Note that the *not* part of these adverbs must be expressed by the predicate; that is, ぜんぜん and あまり must occur in a negative sentence.

7h   が   **"but"**

(1) 八時からクラスがあります が 、行かないつもりです。

I have class starting at 8 o'clock, but I plan not to go.

(2) としょかんへ行きました が 、ラボへは行きませんでした。

I went to the library, but I didn't go to the lab.

(3) すみません が 、これはどなたの本ですか。

Excuse me, but whose book is this?

Some instances of が cannot be translated as "but".

(4) 私はソンです が 、石川先生はいらっしゃいますか。

I'm Son. Is Ishikawa-sensei in?

(5) 私は明日、こうえんへ行きます が 、いっしょに行きませんか。

I'm going to the park tomorrow. Won't you come with me?

This use of が is called the *premisal* が because the が-attached clause supplies an introductory statement as a premise. With the premisal が, the second clause is frequently a genuine question, e.g. (4), or an invitation in the form of a question, e.g. (5). Sentence (3) is marginal in terms of the function of が: in its English translation, we can use *but*; however, the function of this *but* deviates from its normal meaning, because there is no clear contrast between *Excuse me* and *whose book is this?* If we had to spell out our motivation for using *but* here, we would say *I know I'm bothering you (so excuse me), but I do so anyway; whose book is this?* Asking questions and making invitations, requests, etc. are always risky; if the addressee does not respond to you as you have expected, you might get hurt. So we know it is safer to provide a good reason for doing something. が is a convenient connective to supply such background information. You will see this function of が throughout the textbook.

7i　Xはどうですか／いかがですか　　"How is X?"

いかがですか is more formal and polite than どうですか. They are used to ask an opinion about something.

日本語のクラスは どうですか 。

How is Japanese class?

日本語のクラスはやさしくておもしろいです。

Japanese class is easy and interesting.

新しいアパートは いかがですか 。

How is (your) new apartment?

新しいアパートはべんりですが、しずかではありません。

(My) new apartment is convenient, but it isn't quiet.

7j　XはどんなYですか　　"What kind of Y is X?"

This construction is used to ask about X's characteristics with regard to category Y.

山本さんのへやは どんな へやですか。

What kind of room is Yamamoto-san's?

山本さんのへやはきれいで大きいへやです。

Yamamoto-san's room is a pretty and spacious room.

スミスさんのともだちは どんな ひとですか。

What kind of person is your friend, Smith-san?

私のともだちはげんきでしんせつなひとです。

My friend is an energetic and kind person.

7k　こちら／そちら／あちら　　"this／that direction"

こちら／そちら／あちら are another set of the こ・そ・あ words. Their original meanings are directions, but they are frequently used to refer to a person in polite speech.

このかた ＝ こちら　　　そのかた ＝ そちら　　　あのかた ＝ あちら

こちらはソンさんです。　　　　　*This is Son-san.*
あちらはどなたですか。　　　　　*Who is that person over there?*
あちらは石川先生です。　　　　　*That's Ishikawa-sensei.*

Because these are respectful expressions, you cannot use them for yourself, i.e. if your name is Son, you cannot say こちらはソンです, or worse yet, こちらはソンさんです.

<ruby>練<rt>れん</rt>習<rt>しゅう</rt>問<rt>もん</rt>題<rt>だい</rt></ruby>

I.   Using adjectives, describe each situation.

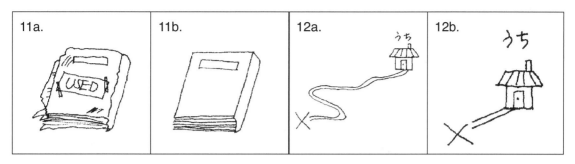

Now, say the negative form of each adjective.

II.　Using the word for each body part, describe each person below.

れい

たなかさんは、<u>かみがながくて、目が小さい</u>です。

たなかさん　　　　さとうさん　　　　スミスさん　　　　ウィルソンさん
　　ブラウンさん　　まえださん　　　　　シンさん　　　　よしださん

III. Ask your partner about his/her house or his/her friend and circle the appropriate adjectives in the boxes.

れい

A: Bさんの家はきれいですか。

B: いいえ、私の家はきれいじゃありません。
私の家はきたないです。

| きれい | （きたない） |

_____さんの家　　　　　　_____さんのともだち

きれい	きたない
しずか	うるさい
新しい	古い

まじめ	ふまじめ
やさしい	いじわる
おもしろい	つまらない

Organize your partner's responses and write sentences, using multiple adjectives, to describe his/her house and friend. Use が if you combine adjectives of positive and negative values.

1. _____さんの家は_____

　　_____。

2. _____さんのともだちは_____

　　_____。

IV. Following the example, ask your partner about each item.

れい1

A: Bさんのへやはどんなへやですか。

B: 私のへやは、広くてきれいなへやです。

れい2

A: Bさんのへやはどんなへやですか。

B: 私のへやは、きれいじゃありませんが、広いへやです。
(or) 私のへやは、広いですが、きれいじゃありません。

へや	
日本語のクラス	
コンピューター	
ともだち	
車	

V. Circle the most appropriate word. If more than one word can be used, discuss the differences.

1. 私の大学のキャンパスは 〔あまり／とても／ぜんぜん〕 広いです。
2. 日本語の先生は 〔あまり／とても／ぜんぜん〕 しんせつです。
3. せいぶつ学のクラスは 〔あまり／とても／ぜんぜん〕 おもしろいです。
4. 日本語のクラスは 〔ちょっと／とても／ぜんぜん〕 おもしろくありません。
5. ダウンタウンは 〔あまり／とても／ぜんぜん〕 にぎやかです。
6. ダウンタウンは 〔ちょっと／ぜんぜん／とても〕 しずかじゃありません。
7. りょうのごはんは 〔ぜんぜん／あまり／とても〕 おいしくありません。
8. 日本りょうりは 〔とても／あまり／ぜんぜん〕 高いです。でも、〔とても／あまり／ぜんぜん〕 おいしいです。
9. ヨセミテは 〔とても／あまり／ぜんぜん〕 きれいです。
10. けいざい学のクラスは 〔とても／あまり／ちょっと〕 つまらないです。
11. フランス語は 〔とても／ちょっと／ぜんぜん〕 むずかしいです。

VI. Look at ジョーンズさん's schedule this week and discuss the time and location of each of her activities. Use 「X で Y があります」。

れい

Q: 月曜日に何かありますか。

A: はい、<u>月曜日</u>の九時から十時まで<u>日本語のクラス</u>で<u>テスト</u>があります。

21 Monday	25 Friday
9:00-10:00 _____ テスト 日本語のクラス	12:00 デモ　大学 _____
22 Tueday	26 Saturday
7:00-9:00 となりのトトロ* _____ California Theater	6:00 ソンさんの家 _____ パーティー
23 Wednesday	27 Sunday
1:30-4:00 Workshop _____ コンピューターラボ	Macy's セール _____
24 Thursday _____ _____	*Japanese animation film

VII.　よみましょう。

ルイスさんはだいがくせいです。ルイスさんは、せが高くて、かみが長いです。そして、目が大きくてきれいです。

ルイスさんは、まじめであたまがいい*ひとです。英語とフランス語をはなすことができます。でも、日本語をはなすことはできません。

ルイスさんのルームメートはウォンさんです。ウォンさんは、せがひくくて、かみがみじかいです。そして、げんきでおもしろいひとです。

ウォンさんはドイツ語や、かんこく語などをはなすことができます。日本語もはなすことができます。

> *あたまがいい smart

○ ですか。×ですか。

1.　（　　）ルイスさんはせが高いです。
2.　（　　）ルイスさんはまじめじゃありません。
3.　（　　）ルイスさんは日本語をはなすことはできません。
4.　（　　）ウォンさんはルイスさんのルームメートです。
5.　（　　）ウォンさんはげんきですが、おもしろくありません。
6.　（　　）ウォンさんは日本語をはなすことはできません。

新しい漢字

新しい	石川	大きい	暗い	車	大学	高い
あたら	いしかわ	おお	くら	くるま	だいがく	たか
長い	入る	広い	古い	目	安い	
なが	はい	ひろ	ふる	め	やす	

新しい使い方
<small>つか　かた</small>

明るい <small>あか</small>	お金 <small>かね</small>	小さい <small>ちい</small>	山下 <small>やました</small>

Stroke Count and Stroke Order

As explained in Lesson 3, more than 1,000 漢字 <small>かんじ</small> are necessary to read Japanese, and you will learn a few more than 300 of them in this textbook. A question arises: How can we organize such a large number of 漢字? Unlike vocabulary, they cannot be listed by あいうえお, because, normally, each 漢字 has more than one reading.

One way to arrange 漢字 is to use their stroke counts. 一 is written with one stroke; 二, 七, 八, 十, and 人 have two strokes; 三, 千, 土, 小, 山, 上, and 下 have three strokes, and so forth. Although not very efficient (and you will learn better ways in subsequent lessons), this method can accomplish the task.

In order to arrange 漢字 by stroke count, you need to know their correct stroke order. For example, 山 may appear to have four strokes, rather than three, if you do not know that its second stroke contains an angle (凵).

Stroke order is important for another reason as well. If you write very carefully (mimicking the printed character), it does not matter how you write it. For example, we can write the letter *a* backwards. But if you write it quickly, this manner of writing will result in an unintelligible character. So, whenever you learn new 漢字, carefully follow the stroke order in the table.

明	丨	冂	冃	日	旷	明	明	明		
あか（るい）	*shining/clearness:* 明日（あした）*tomorrow*									
新	丶	亠	六	立	立	辛	辛	亲	亲
	新	新	新						
あたら （しい）	*new*								
石	一	丆	不	石	石				
いし	*stone:* 石川 *Ishikawa*								

川	ノ	川	川						
かわ	*river:* 石川 *Ishikawa*								
大	一	ナ	大						
ダイ・おお(きい)	*big:* 大学 *college, university*								
金	ノ	入	人	仐	仐	仐	金	金	
キン・かね	*gold:* 金曜日 *Friday,* お金 *money*								
暗	I	冂	日	日	日'	旷	旷	晬	晬
	晬	暗	暗						
くら(い)	*dark / gloomy*								
車	一	厂	冂	戸	亘	亘	車		
くるま	*car*								
高	'	亠	广	亠	古	卢	高	高	高
									高
たか(い)	*expensive / tall*								
小	亅	小	小						
こ・ちい(さい)	*small:* 小山さん *Koyama,* 小さい *small*								
長	I	厂	乍	乍	巨	長	長	長	
なが(い)	*long*								
入	ノ	入							
はい(る)	*to enter (this* 漢字 *is the mirror image of* 人 *person.)*								
広	'	亠	广	広	広				
ひろ(い)	*spacious / wide*								
古	一	十	十	古	古				
ふる(い)	*old*								

目	丨	冂	冃	月	目				
め	*eye*								
安	丶	丷	宀	安	安	安			
やす（い）	*cheap / inexpensive*								

漢字の復習
かんじ　ふくしゅう

I.　よみかた (way of reading) をかきましょう。

1.	会う		20.	小山	
2.	明るい		21.	今晩	
3.	明日		22.	下	
4.	新しい		23.	先生	
5.	行く		24.	大学	
6.	石川		25.	高い	
7.	今		26.	食べる	
8.	上		27.	小さい	
9.	家		28.	長い	
10.	大きい		29.	飲む	
11.	買う		30.	入る	
12.	学生		31.	広い	
13.	昨日		32.	古い	
14.	今日		33.	本	
15.	金曜日		34.	見る	
16.	暗い		35.	安い	
17.	来る		36.	山下	
18.	車		37.	山本	
19.	五月		38.	留学生	

II.　Categorize each word in the above table.

Personal names: _____

Occupations, statuses: _____

Locations, institutions: _____

Temporal expressions: _____

Characteristics: _____

Activities: _____

Things: _____

III.　よみましょう。

1.　石川先生は新しい車を買いました。

2.　私は今、お金がありません。

3.　今晩、山本さんといっしょにおすしを食べるつもりです。

4.　英語のじしょは三十七ドルでした。

5.　小山さんは昨日、大学に来ませんでした。

新しい語彙

(イ)：い -adjective　　(ナ)：な -adjective

明るい	(イ)	bright
あし		foot, leg
あたま		head
新しい	(イ)	new
あちら		that direction
あまり		(not) much
いい	(イ)	good
いかが		how (respectful)
いじわる	(ナ)	mean
いつも		always
うるさい	(イ)	noisy
おいしい	(イ)	delicious
大きい	(イ)	big, large
おもしろい	(イ)	interesting

かみ		hair
きたない	(イ)	dirty
きれい	(ナ)	clean, beautiful
くち		mouth
暗い	(イ)	dark
ケーキ		cake
げんき	(ナ)	energetic
コース		course
こちら		this direction
しずか	(ナ)	quiet
しつれい	(ナ)	rude
しんせつ	(ナ)	kind
せ		body height
セール		sale

せまい	㋑	narrow, small		はな		nose
ぜんぜん		(not) at all		ひくい	㋑	low, short (height)
そちら		that direction		広い	㋑	spacious, wide
高い	㋑	expensive, high		ふべん	㋥	inconvenient
小さい	㋑	small		ふまじめ	㋥	not serious
ちかい	㋑	near		古い	㋑	old
ちょっと		a little		べんり	㋥	convenient
つまらない	㋑	trivial, boring		まじめ	㋥	serious
て		hand, arm		まずい	㋑	not tasty / yucky
デモ		demonstration		みじかい	㋑	short (length)
どう		how		みみ		ear
とおい	㋑	far		むずかしい	㋑	difficult
とても		very		目		eye
どんな		what kind of		やさしい	㋑	easy, gentle
長い	㋑	long		安い	㋑	cheap, inexpensive
にぎやか	㋥	lively		ラボ		laboratory
入る	㋒	to enter				

なまえ

ウィルソン	Wilson		とうきょう（東京）	Tokyo
おおさか（大阪）	Osaka		まえだ	Maeda
シン	Singh		山下	Yamashita
スミス	Smith		ルイス	Lewis

第八課 LESSON 8

だいはっか

かぞく
Family

あに　　ひとり　　いもうと　　ふたり
兄が一人と 妹 が二人います
I have a brother and two sisters

会話

1　ミラー　：これは山本さんのごりょうしんのしゃしんですか。

　　　　　　Is this a picture of your parents, Yamamoto-san?

　　山本　：ええ。父と母は今、東京にいます。

　　　　　　Yes, my father and mother are living in Tokyo now.

2　ソン　：ご兄弟がいらっしゃいますか。

　　　　　　Do you have any siblings?

　　山本　：ええ、兄が一人と妹が二人います。

　　　　　　Yes, I have one older brother and two younger sisters.

3　山本　：兄はニューヨークの大学でべんきょうしています。上の妹は東京の大学の学生です。下の妹はまだ高校生です。

　　　　　　My brother is studying at a university in New York. The older of my younger sisters is a student at a university in Tokyo. The younger one is still a high school student.

4　ミラー　：そうですか。じゃ、山本さんは六人かぞくですね。

　　　　　　I see. So you have a six-person family, then.

　　山本　：そうです。

　　　　　　That's right.

5　山本　：きょねんのふゆやすみに妹たちがあそびに来ました。それで、いっしょにタホへスキーをしに行きました。

　　　　　　Last winter my sisters came to visit me, and we (all) went to Tahoe to go skiing.

　　ソン　：いいですねえ。私もことしのふゆ、スキーをするつもりです。

　　　　　　That's nice. I plan to go skiing this winter, too.

6　山本　：そうですか。ところで、何か飲みませんか。ジュースはいかがですか。

　　　　　　Oh, you are? By the way, would you like to drink something? How about some juice?

　　ソン　：ありがとうございます。でも、今は、けっこうです。

　　　　　　Thank you, but I'm fine right now.

7　山本　：そうですか。ミラーさんは。

　　　　　　All right. What about you, Miller-san?

　　ミラー　：それじゃ、いただきます。

　　　　　　(Lit.) Well then, I'll have some.

　　　　　　Actually, I'll have some. Thank you.

8 山本 ：じゃあ、ちょっと、まって下^ださい。

Okay. Please wait a moment.

使^{つか}い方^{かた}

1 りょうしん is used to refer to your own parents; use ごりょうしん when referring to others' parents, cf. **8h**.

2 兄 "older brother" and 弟 "younger brother" can be combined to form a compound noun 兄弟, which then means "siblings".

5 それで means "therefore/so that". It appears sentence-initially.

も "also" need not share exactly the same predicate with a preceding sentence. Here, 山本さん *went* skiing at Tahoe last year, and ソンさん *plans to go* this year.

6 ところで "by the way" is used to change the topic of the conversation.

けっこう means "fine, nice, wonderful", etc. If you are offered something but you do not wish to accept it, say けっこうです "I'm fine". Here, ソンさん is very polite, so she first says "thank you" and then adds でも、今は、けっこうです "but I'm fine right now".

7 If you wish to accept an offer, say はい、いただきます。いただく means "to accept something gratefully/with thanks", cf. 第一課, **1a**.

文法^{ぶんぽう}

8a	Verb Conjugation: てフォーム	
8b	てフォーム + 下さい	"Please do ~"
	てフォーム + 下さいませんか	"Would you please do ~?"
8c	ないフォーム + で下さい	"Please don't do ~"
	ないフォーム + で下さいませんか	"Would you please not do ~?"
8d	てフォーム + いる	"be VERB-ing"
8e	まだ	"still"
8f	X はどうですか／いかがですか	"How about X?"
8g	Counting People	
8h	かぞく	

8a　Verb Conjugation: てフォーム

The てフォーム is one of the most commonly used verb forms in Japanese, but deriving it is messy due to historical changes of the Japanese language. Historically, the てフォーム developed from the Pre-ますフォーム + the connective particle て. However, in Modern Japanese it is easier to derive it from the Dictionary フォーム.

Although small in number, the る -verbs are straightforward; drop る and add て.

食べる	→	食べ て		おしえる	→	おしえ て
いる	→	い て		見る	→	見 て

The two irregular verbs are:

来る	→	来て		する	→	して

It is the う -verbs that make things difficult. But because the てフォーム is so important, let us tackle this problem. Recall that the Dictionary フォーム of う -verbs ends with a syllable from the う line.

ら	や	ま	ば	ぱ	は	な	だ	た	ざ	さ	が	か	あ
り		み	び	ぴ	ひ	に	ぢ	ち	じ	し	ぎ	き	い
る	ゆ	む	ぶ	ぷ	ふ	ぬ	づ	つ	ず	す	ぐ	く	う
れ		め	べ	ぺ	へ	ね	で	て	ぜ	せ	げ	け	え
ろ	よ	も	ぼ	ぽ	ほ	の	ど	と	ぞ	そ	ご	こ	お

← Dictionary フォーム

There are 14 such syllables, but no Dictionary フォーム ends with ず, づ, ふ, ぷ, or ゆ. So we need to consider only 9 syllables.

九	八	七	六	五	四	三	二	一
ら	ま	ば	な	た	さ	が	か	あ
り	み	び	に	ち	し	ぎ	き	い
る	む	ぶ	ぬ	つ	す	ぐ	く	う
れ	め	べ	ね	て	せ	げ	け	え
ろ	も	ぼ	の	と	そ	ご	こ	お

う:	会う	→	会って	*meet*
	うたう	→	うたって	*sing*
	買う	→	買って	*buy*
	つかう	→	つかって	*use*

く：	あるく	→	あるいて	walk
	いただく	→	いただいて	receive
	かく	→	かいて	write
	きく	→	きいて	listen, hear
	ひく	→	ひいて	play (a stringed instrument)
ぐ：	およぐ	→	およいで	swim
す：	かえす	→	かえして	return
	かす	→	かして	lend
	はなす	→	はなして	talk, speak
つ：	まつ	→	まって	wait
	もつ	→	もって	hold, have
ぬ：	しぬ	→	しんで	die
ぶ：	あそぶ	→	あそんで	play (have fun)
	よぶ	→	よんで	call
む：	飲む	→	飲んで	drink
	よむ	→	よんで	read
る：	帰る	→	帰って	go home
	がんばる	→	がんばって	do one's best
	つくる	→	つくって	make
	とる	→	とって	take
	入る	→	入って	enter

Note that ぐ is just the voiced version of く. So it can be said that if the final syllable of the Dictionary フォーム contains a voiced consonant (ぐぬぶむ, but not る), て is realized as で.

The verb 行く is irregular in its てフォーム. Unlike かく → かいて and きく → きいて, 行く becomes 行って.

kak–u	→	kaite		kik–u	→	kiite		ik–u	→	itte

てフォーム Song: Sung to the tune of "Twinkle, Twinkle, Little Star"*

ぬ／む／ぶ　→　んで
る／う／つ　→　って
く　　　　→　いて
ぐ　　　　→　いで
す　　　　→　して

→　う -verbs

Those are all the う -verbs.

Followed by the る -verbs:

Take off the る, add a て

→　る -verbs

くる（来る）→　きて（来て）
する　　　　→　して
いく（行く）→　いって（行って）

→　Irregular verbs

ぬ む ぶんで るう つって くいて ぐいで すし て

Those are all the う verbs Fol-lowed by the る verbs Take off the

る add a て くるきて するして いくいっ て

*By Mieko Aono

8b　てフォーム + 下さい　　　　　　**"Please do ~"**
　　てフォーム + 下さいませんか　　　**"Would you please do ~?"**

て

When asking someone to do something, てフォーム + 下さい／下さい　ません か is used. In English, using the question form "Would you ~?／Wouldn't you ~?" is more polite than the request form "Please do ~". Similarly, てフォーム + 下さいませんか "Wouldn't you ~?" is more polite than てフォーム + 下さい "Please do ~". Generally, longer expressions are more polite than their shorter counterparts.

ケーキを食べて下さい。

Please eat the cake.

本をよんで下さいませんか。

(Lit.) Won't you?

Would you please read the book?

でんしゃで行って下さい。

Please go there by train.

小山さんと来て下さいませんか。

(Lit.) Won't you?

Would you please come with Koyama-san?

そとではなして下さいませんか。

(Lit.) Won't you?

Would you please talk outside?

しゃしんをとって下さい。

Please take a picture.

8c   ないフォーム + で下さい   **"Please don't do ~"**

ないフォーム + で下さいませんか   **"Would you please not do ~?"**

When you ask someone not to do something, you need ないフォーム + で下さい／下さいませんか. Like in English, ないフォーム + で下さいませんか "Would you please not do ~?" is more polite than ないフォーム + で下さい "Please don't do ~".

このへやに入らないで下さい。

Please don't enter this room.

ここでうたをうたわないで下さい。

Please don't sing songs here.

今、ピアノをひかないで下さいませんか。

Would you please not play the piano now?

タクシーで行かないで下さい。

Please don't go there by taxi.

これは、つかわないで下さいませんか。

(Lit.) This, would you mind not using it please?

Would you mind not using this please?

8d　てフォーム + いる　"be VERB-ing"

 With an action verb, this construction means that someone is currently doing something.

今、何をしていますか 。　*What are you doing now?*

| テレビを見ています。
I'm watching TV. | べんきょうしています。
I'm studying. | しんぶんをよんでいます。
I'm reading the newspaper. |

Like in English, this construction can be used to describe some event in progress.

あめがふっています。

It's raining.

Also similar to English "be VERB-ing", てフォーム + います
can be used to express habitual (repetitive) activities.

妹は高校に行っています。	*(Lit.) My younger sister goes (is going) to a high school.* *My younger sister is in high school.*
兄はニューヨークでしごとをしています。	*My brother is working in New York.* *My brother works in New York.*
私はニューヨークタイムズをよんでいます。	*I read The New York Times.*

8e　まだ　"still"

In 第五課, **5i**, we studied まだ "yet" that occurs in a negative answer.

| バスはもう来ましたか。 | *Did the bus already come (and gone)?* |
| いいえ、 まだ です。 | *No, not yet.* |

When まだ appears in an affirmative sentence, it means "still".

下の妹は まだ 高校生です。

The younger of my younger sisters is still a high school student.

まだ 早いですから、帰らないで下さい。

It's still early, so please don't go home.

8f　X はどうですか／いかがですか　"How about X?"

In 第七課, we studied 「X はどうですか／いかがですか」 to request opinions about X. The same construction can be used to offer something.

おちゃは いかがですか 。

How about some tea / Would you like some tea?

ありがとうございます。いただきます。

Thank you, I'll have some.

ありがとうございます。でも、今は、けっこうです。

Thank you, but I'm fine right now. (cf. Usage Note **6**)

8g　Counting People

一人	ひとり	六人	ろくにん
二人	ふたり	七人	しちにん／ななにん
三人	さんにん	八人	はちにん
四人	よにん	九人	くにん／きゅうにん
五人	ごにん	十人	じゅうにん
		何人	なんにん

8h　かぞく

Like many languages, Japanese provides a rich vocabulary for kinship terms. A pair of plain and respectful forms exists for each relationship. The Japanese commonly use the respectful form to address parents, grandparents, uncles, aunts, and older siblings (instead of the pronoun *you*).

おばさん、おはよう。	*Good Morning, Aunt X.*
おじさん、こんにちは。	*Hi, Uncle X.*
お母さんもいっしょに行く？	*Mom, are you going with us?*

Respectful forms are also used to refer to someone else's family member(s). Use a plain form when you talk about your family members with other persons.

お父^{とう}さんはおげんきですか。

はい、ありがとうございます。父^{ちち}はげんきです。

How's your father?

Yes, thank you. He's fine.

	Respectful	Plain		Respectful	Plain
Family	ごかぞく	かぞく	*Grandfather*	おじいさん	そふ
Parents	ごりょうしん	りょうしん	*Grandmother*	おばあさん	そぼ
Father	お父^{とう}さん	父^{ちち}	*Uncle*	おじさん	おじ
Mother	お母^{かあ}さん	母^{はは}	*Aunt*	おばさん	おば
Siblings	ご兄弟^{きょうだい}	兄弟	*Nephew*	おいごさん	おい
Older brother	お兄^{にい}さん	兄^{あに}	*Niece*	めいごさん	めい
Younger brother	弟^{おとうと}さん	弟	*Husband*	ごしゅじん	しゅじん
Older sister	お姉^{ねえ}さん*	姉^{あね}	*Wife*	おくさん	かない
Younger sister	妹^{いもうと}さん	妹	*Child*	おこさん	こども
			Grandchild	おまごさん	まご

* Note that in おねえさん the long え is written as ええ, rather than ×おね い さん.

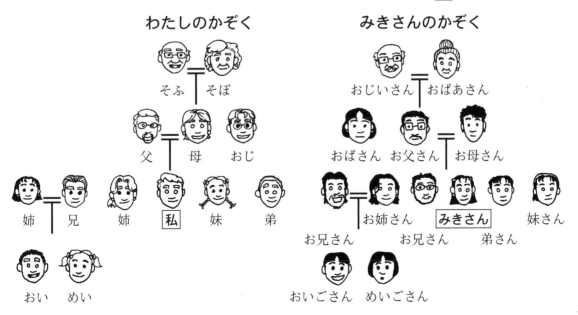

わたしのかぞく　　みきさんのかぞく

| X | は | Y | が | Z人 | | います |

(1) 私は 弟が 一人 と 姉が 二人 います。

I have one younger brother and two older sisters.

(2) お兄さんが {います / いらっしゃいます} か。

Do you have an older brother?

いいえ、兄はいません。でも、弟が 二人 います。

No, I don't have an older brother, but I do have two younger brothers.

(3) ごかぞくは何人(なんにん)ですか。

How many people are there in your family?

かぞくは、父と母と私の三人です。

In my family, there are three people: father, mother, and myself.

私は三人かぞくです。

(Lit.) As for me, it's a three-person family.

I have a three-person family.

(4) ご兄弟は何人ですか。

How many siblings do you have?

兄弟は二人です。兄が一人と妹が一人います。

I have two siblings: an older brother and a younger sister.

私は三人兄弟です。

(Lit.) I'm one of three siblings.

I have two siblings.

(5) 山本さんはご兄弟がいらっしゃいますか。

Does Yamamoto-san have siblings?

はい、山本さんはお兄さんが一人と妹さんが二人います。

Yes, Yamamoto-san has an older brother and two younger sisters.

山本さんは四人兄弟です。

(Lit.) Yamamoto-san is one of four siblings.

Yamamoto-san has three siblings.

When you describe the size of your かぞく, don't forget to count yourself.

練習問題

I.　　Look at the pictures below and find out how many people of each category are in each of them.

例

れい
例

おとこ　　ひと
A: 男の人は何人いますか。

B: （男の人は）二人います。

おんな
A: じゃあ、女の人は何人いますか。

B: （女の人は）一人います。

男の人＿二＿人　　　女の人＿一＿人

男の人　＿＿＿＿＿人　　　日本人　　＿＿＿＿＿人　　　男の先生　＿＿＿＿＿人

女の人　＿＿＿＿＿人　　　アメリカ人　＿＿＿＿＿人　　　女の先生　＿＿＿＿＿人

学生　＿＿＿＿＿人　　　男の学生　＿＿＿＿＿人

先生　＿＿＿＿＿人　　　女の学生　＿＿＿＿＿人

II.   Look at the pictures of やまださん's and やすかわさん's families, and practice asking and
answering questions about each family.

例
<ruby>例<rt>れい</rt></ruby>

A: やまださんはお姉さんがいらっしゃいますか。

B: はい、やまださんはお姉さんが一人いらっしゃいます。

A: お姉さんのおなまえは。

B: ともこさんです。

A: やまださんはお兄さんもいらっしゃいますか。

B: いいえ、やまださんはお兄さんはいらっしゃいません。

やまださんのごかぞく

父   母
しげる   みどり

やまだ   姉   弟
ともこ あきら

	何人	なまえ
お父さん		
お母さん		
お姉さん	人	
お兄さん	人	
妹さん	人	
弟さん	人	

やまださんはごりょうしんと _____ が _____ 人と _____ が _____ 人
いらっしゃいます。やまださんのごかぞくは _____ 人です。

やすかわさんのごかぞく

父   母   兄
みきお ちよこ ひろし

妹   妹   やすかわ
けいこ めぐみ

	何人	なまえ
お父さん		
お母さん		
お姉さん	人	
お兄さん	人	
妹さん	人	
弟さん	人	

やすかわさんはごりょうしんと _____ が _____ 人と _____ が _____ 人
いらっしゃいます。やすかわさんのごかぞくは _____ 人です。

III.　Talk with your partner about his/her family.

例1 (X さんは) ご兄弟がいらっしゃいますか。

　　はい、(私は) 兄が<u>一人</u>と妹が<u>一人</u>います。

　　(or) いいえ、(私は) 兄弟はいません。

例2 (X さんの) ごかぞくは何人ですか。

　　(私のかぞくは) <u>三人</u>です。

　　(私のかぞくは) <u>父</u>と<u>母</u>と<u>私</u>です。

　　(or) (私のかぞくは) <u>六人</u>です。

　　(私は) <u>りょうしん</u>と姉が<u>二人</u>と弟が<u>一人</u>います。

IV.　Practice making requests using the following verbs in the てフォーム＋下さい.

1.	いる	11.	帰る	21.	飲む
2.	会う	12.	かす	22.	入る
3.	あそぶ	13.	かりる	23.	はなす
4.	あるく	14.	きく	24.	ピアノをひく
5.	行く	15.	来る	25.	べんきょうする
6.	おきる	16.	食べる	26.	まつ
7.	おしえる	17.	つかう	27.	見る
8.	およぐ	18.	つくる	28.	もつ
9.	買う	19.	とる	29.	よぶ
10.	かえす	20.	ねる	30.	よむ

V.　Suppose that you are a teacher of this class. Look at the pictures below and practice making requests with your classmates.

例　先生: X さん、カタカナをべんきょうして下さい。

VI.　Using the list in Exercise IV, practice making the ないフォーム＋下さい.

VII.　Look at the pictures below and ask your classmate not to do the things indicated in the pictures.

例

A:　Bさん、私のビールを飲まないで下さい。

B:　すみません。

VIII.　Look at the pictures below and describe what's going on with てフォーム＋います.

例

Q:　何をしていますか。

A:　てがみをかいています。

IX. Practice conversations in which one person offers the things indicated in each picture below, and the other person accepts or declines the offer.

例

A: Bさん、何か飲みませんか。ジュースはいかがですか。

B: ありがとうございます。じゃあ、いただきます。

(or) ありがとうございます。でも、今はけっこうです。

X. The pictures below indicate what きむらさん does regularly on weekends. Practice asking and telling what きむらさん regularly does on weekends.

例

A: きむらさんはいつも土曜日のあさ、何をしていますか。

B: ジョギングをしています。

	土曜日	日曜日
あさ		
ごご		
晩		

Now interview your classmates and find out what they regularly do on weekends.

XI. よみましょう。

私のなまえはヤングです。今、大学三ねん生です。

父はアメリカ人ですが、母は日本人です。私は兄が一人と弟が一人います。

兄は今、日本で英語をおしえています。弟はまだ高校生です。

昨日は日曜日でしたが、私は一時に大学のとしょかんへ行きました。私はいつも日曜日に大学のとしょかんでべんきょうしています。

としょかんにともだちの古川さんがいました。私は古川さんのとなりで二時半まで日本語のクラスのしゅくだいをしました。

三時に古川さんといっしょにカフェテリアへコーヒーを飲みに行きました。

そして、三時四十五分までカフェテリアで古川さんとはなしました。それから、私は家へ帰りました。

〇 ですか。×ですか。

1. （　　）ヤングさんは、お姉さんはいません。妹さんもいません。
2. （　　）ヤングさんのお兄さんは今、アメリカの大学で英語をおしえています。
3. （　　）ヤングさんの弟さんは大学生です。
4. （　　）ヤングさんはいつも日曜日に大学のとしょかんでべんきょうしています。
5. （　　）ヤングさんは昨日、三時から三時四十五分までとしょかんでしゅくだいをしました。

XII. Look at the pictures below and answer the questions with まだ.

例

Q: よしださんの弟さんは大学生ですか。

A: いいえ、まだ高校生です。

1.　今、九時ですか。

いいえ、まだ ＿＿＿＿＿＿＿＿＿＿＿＿＿＿＿＿＿＿＿＿ です。

2.　よしださんはもう三ねん<ruby>生<rt>せい</rt></ruby>ですか。

いいえ、まだ ＿＿＿＿＿＿＿＿＿＿＿＿＿＿＿＿＿＿＿＿ です。

3.　今日は土曜日ですか。

いいえ、まだ ＿＿＿＿＿＿＿＿＿＿＿＿＿＿＿＿＿＿＿＿ です。

4.　もう東京ですか。

いいえ、まだ ＿＿＿＿＿＿＿＿＿＿＿＿＿＿＿＿＿＿＿＿ です。

<ruby>新<rt>あたら</rt></ruby>しい<ruby>漢字<rt>かんじ</rt></ruby>

<ruby>兄<rt>あに</rt></ruby>	<ruby>姉<rt>あね</rt></ruby>	<ruby>妹<rt>いもうと</rt></ruby>	お<ruby>母<rt>かあ</rt></ruby>さん	お<ruby>父<rt>とう</rt></ruby>さん	<ruby>弟<rt>おとうと</rt></ruby>	<ruby>男<rt>おとこ</rt></ruby>
お<ruby>兄<rt>にい</rt></ruby>さん	お<ruby>姉<rt>ねえ</rt></ruby>さん	<ruby>女<rt>おんな</rt></ruby>	<ruby>帰<rt>かえ</rt></ruby>る	<ruby>兄弟<rt>きょうだい</rt></ruby>	<ruby>高校生<rt>こうこうせい</rt></ruby>	<ruby>父<rt>ちち</rt></ruby>
<ruby>東京<rt>とうきょう</rt></ruby>	<ruby>母<rt>はは</rt></ruby>	<ruby>早<rt>はや</rt></ruby>い				

<ruby>新<rt>あたら</rt></ruby>しい<ruby>使<rt>つか</rt></ruby>い<ruby>方<rt>かた</rt></ruby>

<ruby>下<rt>くだ</rt></ruby>さい	<ruby>大学生<rt>だいがくせい</rt></ruby>	〜<ruby>人<rt>にん</rt></ruby>	<ruby>人<rt>ひと</rt></ruby>	<ruby>一人<rt>ひとり</rt></ruby>	<ruby>二人<rt>ふたり</rt></ruby>	<ruby>古川<rt>ふるかわ</rt></ruby>

Radicals: Introduction

Suppose that you had to invent an ideographic writing system. You would need many symbols to represent ideas. You could begin with a line, circle, triangle, square, simplified pictures of daily items, etc. But you would soon run out of symbols and start thinking about combining old ones in order to form new symbols. How would you go about combining symbols then?

You have already seen that the symbol for the sun 日 appears in various 漢字 (時, 曜, 昨, 明, 晩, 暗), and you recognize that those 漢字 have some semantic connections with the sun, e.g. time, brightness. In this lesson, you have learned 女 "female", which also appears (albeit skinnier in shape) in 姉 "older sister" and 妹 "younger sister".

Such frequently recurring parts are called *radicals*. They are used for classifying 漢字 into groups, and they broadly suggest the meaning or reading of the 漢字. There are seven major types of radicals; they vary according to the location in which they appear:

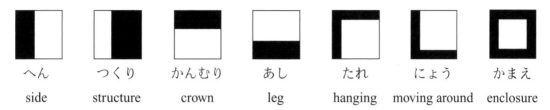

へん	つくり	かんむり	あし	たれ	にょう	かまえ
side	structure	crown	leg	hanging	moving around	enclosure

日 and 女 belong to the へん group and are called 日へん and 女へん, respectively.

兄 あに・キョウ	ノ 口 口 尸 兄
	older brother: お兄さん（おにいさん）*older brother,* 兄弟 *siblings*
▉姉 あね	く 乡 女 女' 女' 女' 妒 姉
	older sister: お姉さん（おねえさん）*older sister,* 姉妹（しまい）*female siblings exists, but* 兄弟 *is more commonly used for siblings regardless of their genders*
▉妹 いもうと	く 乡 女 女' 女二 妊 妹 妹
	young sister
母 はは	ノ 口 口 母 母
	mother: お母さん（おかあさん）*mother*
父 ちち	ノ ハ 少 父
	father: お父さん（おとうさん）*father*
弟 おとうと・ダイ	、 ゛ 当 当 弟 弟 弟
	younger brother: 兄弟 *siblings*
男 おとこ	ノ 口 冊 冊 田 男 男
	male

女	く	夕	女						
おんな	*female: this* かんじ *appears in* 姉 *and* 妹								
帰	`	リ	刂	刂	刂	刂	帚	帚	帰	帰
かえ（る）	*to go home / return*								
下	一	丁	下						
した・くだ（さい）	*below / under / down:* 下さい *(Lit.) please give downward*								
高	`	亠	亠	亣	古	戸	高	高	高	高
コウ・たか（い）	*high / expensive / tall:* 高校 *high school,* 高校生 *high school student*								
校	一	十	才	木	朾	朾	杧	栌	校	校
コウ	*school:* 高校 *high school,* 高校生 *high school student*								
東	一	厂	币	币	百	車	車	東		
トウ	*east:* 東京 *Tokyo (east capital)*								
京	`	亠	亠	亣	古	亨	京	京		
キョウ	*capital:* 東京 *Tokyo (east capital)*								
人	ノ	人							
ジン・ニン・ひと	*person:* 日本人 *Japanese people,* 男の人 *man,* 女の人 *woman,* 一人（ひとり）*one person,* 二人（ふたり）*two persons,* 三人 *three persons*								
早	`	口	日	日	旦	早			
はや（い）	*early: this* かんじ *contains the sun* 日								

漢字の復習
<ruby>漢<rt>かん</rt></ruby><ruby>字<rt>じ</rt></ruby>の<ruby>復<rt>ふく</rt></ruby><ruby>習<rt>しゅう</rt></ruby>

I.　よみましょう。

1.　弟は金曜日に中間しけんがあります。
2.　シュミットさんはドイツ人の留学生です。
3.　シュミットさんのアパートは広いですが、暗いです。
4.　ご兄弟は何人いますか。
5.　まだ早いですから、帰らないで下さい。

II.　あたまのうんどうです。

1.　私は兄弟がたくさんいます。私は姉が一人と妹が三人と弟が一人います。私は何人兄弟ですか。
　　＿＿＿＿＿＿＿＿＿＿＿＿＿＿＿＿＿＿＿＿ 兄弟です。

2.　私は兄が二人と妹が一人います。父と母はげんきです。私は何人かぞくですか。
　　＿＿＿＿＿＿＿＿＿＿＿＿＿＿＿＿＿ です。

3.　私は大学一ねん生です。男の兄弟が一人います。高校生です。私の兄弟は兄ですか。姉ですか。弟ですか。妹ですか。
　　＿＿＿＿＿＿＿＿＿＿＿＿＿＿＿＿＿ です。

4.　私は高校生です。高校三ねん生です。兄弟が二人います。一人は大学生です。男です。一人は高校一ねん生です。女です。私は兄がいますか。姉がいますか。弟がいますか。妹がいますか。
　　＿＿＿＿＿＿＿＿＿＿＿＿＿＿＿ と ＿＿＿＿＿＿＿＿＿＿＿＿ がいます。

新しい語彙
<ruby>新<rt>あたら</rt></ruby>しい<ruby>語彙<rt>ごい</rt></ruby>

X<ruby>人<rt>にん</rt></ruby>	*(counter for people)*		<ruby>妹<rt>いもうと</rt></ruby>	*younger sister (plain)*
<ruby>兄<rt>あに</rt></ruby>	*older brother (plain)*		<ruby>妹<rt>いもうと</rt></ruby>さん	*younger sister (resp)*
<ruby>姉<rt>あね</rt></ruby>	*older sister (plain)*		うた	*song*
あめ	*rain*		うたう	ウ	*to sing*
あるく	ウ	*to walk*	おい	*nephew (plain)*
いただく	ウ	*to receive (respectful)*	おいごさん	*nephew (respectful)*

お母さん	mother (respectful)		ことし	this year		
おくさん	wife (respectful)		こども	child (plain)		
おこさん	child (respectful)		ごりょうしん	parents (respectful)		
おじ	uncle (plain)		しごと（する）	job		
おじいさん	grandfather (respect)		しぬ	ウ	to die
おじさん	uncle (respectful)		ジュース	juice		
お父さん	father (respectful)		しゅじん	husband (plain)		
弟	younger brother (plain)		そふ	grandfather (plain)		
弟さん	younger brother (resp)		そぼ	grandmother (plain)		
お兄さん	older brother (respect)		タクシー	taxi		
お姉さん	older sister (respect)		父	father (plain)		
おば	aunt (plain)		ところで	by the way		
おばあさん	grandmother (respect)		（しゃしんを）とる	ウ	to take (a picture)
おばさん	aunt (respectful)		何人	how many people		
おまごさん	grandchild (respect)		母	mother (plain)		
かす	ウ	to lend	早い	イ	early
かぞく	family (plain)		一人	one person		
かない	wife (plain)		二人	two persons		
兄弟	siblings (plain)		ふゆ	winter		
きょねん	last year		ふる	ウ	to fall (weather)
けっこう	fine, nice, wonderful		まご	grandchild (plain)		
高校	high school		まだ	still		
高校生	high school student		まつ	ウ	to wait
ごかぞく	family (respectful)		めい	niece (plain)		
ご兄弟	siblings (respectful)		めいごさん	niece (respectful)		
ごしゅじん	husband (respectful)		もつ	ウ	to have, hold

よぶ	ウ	to call, summon

りょうしん		parents (plain)

なまえ

シュミット	Schmidt
古川	Furukawa

やすかわ	Yasukawa
よこはま（横浜）	Yokohama

第九課 LESSON 9

レストランで
At a Restaurant

何が一番好きですか
What do you like the most?

おしながき

とんかつ
Breaded and deep
fried pork cutlet
9 ドル

かきフライ
Breaded and deep
fried oysters
１１ドル

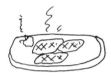
ぎゅうてりやき
Grilled beef with
teriyaki sauce
9 ドル

すし
１３ドル

てんぷら
Deep fried prawns
and vegetables
１２ドル

うなじゅう
Broiled eel
over rice
１２ドル

ちゃわんむし
Egg custard with
chicken and shrimp
5 ドル

カレーライス
Curry sauce
over rice
8 ドル

カツどん
とんかつ over rice
8 ドル

てんどん
てんぷら over rice
8 ドル

おやこどん
Chicken and egg over rice
6 ドル

ざるそば
Cold buckwheat noodles
5 ドル

きつねうどん
きつねそば
Noodles in a hot soy sauce broth
with deep fried seasoned tofu
6 ドル

たぬきうどん
たぬきそば
Noodles in a hot soy sauce broth
with tempura batter pieces
6 ドル

すきやき
Thinly sliced beef,
vegetables, and tofu
cooked in sukiyaki sauce
１２ドル

しゃぶしゃぶ
Paper-thin slices of beef and
various vegetables dipped by the
diners in a pot of boiling broth
１２ドル

おこのみやき
Pancake with cabbage
and various ingredients
7 ドル

お飲みもの
   さけ　　　　　3ドル
   ビール　　　　3ドル
   コーヒー　　　2ドル
   コーラ　　　　2ドル
   ジュース　　　2ドル

デザート
   アイスクリーム　　2ドル

おしながき:	menu
うどん:	wheat noodles
そば:	buckwheat noodles

会話

1　ソン　　：あっ、もう十二時ですね。おなかがすきましたね。

Oh, it's already 12 o'clock. I'm hungry. (Aren't you?)

　　　ミラー　：ええ。何か食べに行きましょうか。

Yes. Shall we go eat something?

2　ソン　　：いいですね。ミラーさんは何が好きですか。

Sure. What do you like?

　　　ミラー　：私は何でも好きですが、ソンさんはどうですか。

I like anything. What about you, Son-san?

3　ソン　　：私は日本りょうりが一番好きです。でも、ちゅうかりょうりもとても好きです。

I like Japanese food the most, but I also really like Chinese food.

　　　ミラー　：そうですか。今日は、日本りょうりとちゅうかりょうりとではどちらの方がいいですか。

Well, which do you prefer today, Japanese or Chinese food?

4　ソン　　：そうですねえ、今日は、日本りょうりの方がちゅうかりょうりよりいいです。

Well, today I guess I'd prefer Japanese over Chinese.

　　　ミラー　：じゃあ、日本りょうりを食べに行きましょう。

Let's go eat Japanese food, then.

（レストランで）

5　ウェイター　　：いらっしゃいませ。どうぞこちらへ。
　　　　　　　　　　　Welcome. Right this way, please.

6　ウェイター　　：<ruby>何<rt>なん</rt></ruby>になさいますか。
　　　　　　　　　　　What would you like?

　　　ソン　　　　　：私はとんかつにします。
　　　　　　　　　　　I'll have the pork cutlet.

7　ウェイター　　：お飲みものは。
　　　　　　　　　　　And to drink?

　　　ソン　　　　　：お<ruby>茶<rt>ちゃ</rt></ruby>を下さい。
　　　　　　　　　　　Tea, please.

　　　ミラー　　　　：私はカレーライスとコーラをおねがいします。
　　　　　　　　　　　I'll have curry rice and cola, please.

8　ウェイター　　：はい。とんかつが<ruby>一<rt>ひと</rt></ruby>つとカレーライスが一つとコーラが一つ、そしてお茶ですね。しょうしょうお<ruby>待<rt>ま</rt></ruby>ち下さい。
　　　　　　　　　　　Sure. That's one pork cutlet, curry rice, cola, and tea, right?
　　　　　　　　　　　Please wait just a moment.

<ruby>使<rt>つか</rt></ruby>い<ruby>方<rt>かた</rt></ruby>

2　We have learned 何 "what", 何か "something", and 何も "nothing (with a negative predicate)". 何でも means "anything" with an affirmative predicate.

In 第七課, we studied 「Xはどうですか」 "How is X?". This construction can also be used to ask the addressee's opinion regarding some activity, e.g. ソンさんはどうですか "How about you, Son-san?". ソンさんはどうですか could mean "How is Son-san" in some contexts.

5　いらっしゃいませ is a standard expression for greeting customers when they enter a small shop or a restaurant. どうぞこちらへ literally means "please this way".

6　なさいますか is an honorific form of しますか. Honorific forms will be studied systematically in 第十九課.

7　「Xをおねがいします」 and 「Xを下さい」 are used when ordering at a restaurant. おねがいします is politer than 下さい.

お茶をもう一ぱい下さい。   *One more cup of tea please* (cf. **9f**).

おかんじょう（を）おねがいします。   *Check please.*

8   「Xが COUNTER」(e.g. とんかつが一つ) is a common way to repeat an order.

しょうしょう means "every little", and お待ち下さい is a politer equivalent to 待って下さい.

ぶんぽう
文法

> **9a**   XはYが 好きです／きらいです／上手（じょうず）です／下手（へた）です／とくいです
> "X likes／hates／is good at／is bad at／is good at Y"
> **9b**   Nominalization
> **9c**   Comparative
> **9d**   Superlative
> **9e**   Xを下さい／下さいませんか   "Please give me X"
> **9f**   Counters
> **9g**   Xにする   "decide on X／make something X"

9a   XはYが 好きです／きらいです／上手です／下手です／とくいです
"X likes／hates／is good at／is bad at／is good at Y"

In 第七課, we studied the は－が construction:

| TOPIC は **SUBJECT** が ADJECTIVE |

山下さん|は|、目|が|大きいです。

(Lit.) As for Yamashita-san, her eyes are big. / Yamashita-san has big eyes.

日本語のクラス|は|、先生|が|しんせつです。

(Lit.) Regarding the Japanese class, the teachers are sympathetic.

The Japanese class has sympathetic teachers.

This pattern can also be used to express:

| TOPIC は **OBJECT** が ADJECTIVE |

ソンさん|は|日本りょうり|が|好きです。   *Son-san likes Japanese food.*

私|は|さかな|が|きらいです。   *I hate fish.*

私|は|え|が|下手です。   *I'm bad at (painting／drawing) pictures.*

（X さんは）どんな食べものが好きですか。　　*What kind of food do you like, X-san?*

安川さん は ピアノ が 上手です。　　*Yasukawa-san is good at (playing) the piano.*

私 は イタリアりょうり が とくいです。　　*I'm good at (cooking) Italian food.*

上手 vs. とくい

Both 上手 and とくい mean that someone (marked with は) is good at some activity, but they are not necessarily interchangeable. 上手 is an *objective* adjective; とくい is a *subjective* adjective. 上手 indicates that the person is skillful at the activity based on someone else's (objective) judgment or standard. For example, in the case of 安川さんはピアノが上手です, we understand that it is the speaker who

私はあたまがいいです。

私はハンサムです。

私は日本語が上手です。

considers that 安川さん is skillful (安川さん might or might not think so). とくい, on the other hand, indicates that the topic person considers that the activity is his/her own forte (other people might or might not agree with it).

It is generally regarded as a boastful act to assert your skillfulness (and other positive qualities) as an objective fact. So do not use 上手 for yourself; use とくい instead.

9b　Nominalization

In order to say you like to *do something*, rather than you like something, you need to change the activity clause into a noun phrase. This process is called *nominalization*. Nominalized clauses can be used as nouns. To nominalize a clause, add の after the Dictionary フォーム of the verb.

日本語を書く の はむずかしいです。　　*Writing Japanese is difficult.*

ギターをひく の が好きです。　　*I like playing the guitar.*

すきやきを作る の はかんたんです。

Making sukiyaki is easy.

てんぷらを作る の はどうですか。

How (difficult) is it to make tempura ?

What does making tempura involve?

てんぷらを作る の はやさしく{ありません／ないです}。

Making tempura isn't easy.

そうじする の は好き{じゃありません／じゃないです}。

I don't like to clean (the room).

9c　Comparative

When you compare two things or two activities, you need to use a special construction. The complete patterns are:

ＡとＢとでは、どちらの方がＸですか。	Between A and B, which one is X-er?
ＡとＢとでは、Ａの方がＢよりＸです。	Between A and B, A is X-er than B.

Unlike English, Japanese has no special form of adjectives for comparison (e.g. *small-er*). で here is the location marker that appears in 家でパーティーがあります; 方 means "direction/side". So the literal translations are:

ＡとＢとでは、どちらの方がＸですか。	In A and B, which side is X?
ＡとＢとでは、Ａの方がＢよりＸです。	In A and B, the A side, rather than B, is X.

アメリカと中国とでは、どちらの方が大きいですか。

Of the U.S. and China, which one is larger?

アメリカと中国とでは、アメリカの方が中国より大きいです。

Of the U.S. and China, the U.S. is larger than China.

(United Nations Demorgraphic Yearbook 2000)

When it is obvious from the context, some element(s) may be omitted.

ＡとＢとでは、どちらの方がＸですか。	Which one is X-er, A or B?
どちらがＸですか。	Which is X-er?

アメリカと中国とでは、どちらの方が大きいですか。

Which one is larger, the U.S. or China?

どちらが大きいですか。

Which is larger?

ＡとＢとでは、Ａの方がＢよりＸです。	Between A and B, A is X-er than B.
Ａの方がＢよりＸです。	A is X-er than B.
Ａの方がＸです。	A is X-er.

中国とアメリカとでは、アメリカの方が中国より大きいです。

Between China and the U.S., the U.S. is larger than China.

アメリカの方が中国より大きいです。

The U.S. is larger than China.

アメリカの方が大きいです。

The U.S. is larger.

You can also change the word order.

BよりAの方がXです。　　　　　　　　A is X-er than B.

中国よりアメリカの方が大きいです。

The U.S. is larger than China.

いぬよりねこの方がかわいいです。

Cats are cuter than dogs.

てがみよりEメールの方がべんりです。

Email is more convenient than letters.

コンピューターは、アメリカより日本の方が高いです。

When it comes to computers, Japan is more expensive than the U.S.

When a nominalized clause appears before の方が, both instances of の are deleted, e.g.:

読む の ＋ の 方が → 読む方が.

Before より, the use of の is optional; omission of の is more common, however.

(1)　日本語を話すのと読むのとでは、どちらの方がむずかしいですか。

Which is more difficult, speaking or reading Japanese?

日本語を 読む方が 話す (の) よりむずかしいです。

日本語を話す (の) より 読む方が むずかしいです。

Reading Japanese is more difficult than speaking it.

(2)　スポーツをするのとえいがを見るのとでは、どちらの方が好きですか。

Which do you like more, playing sports or watching movies?

えいがを 見る方が スポーツをする (の) より好きです。

スポーツをする (の) よりえいがを 見る方が 好きです。

I prefer watching movies to playing sports.

(3)　日本りょうりは、作るのと食べるのとでは、どちらの方がたのしいですか。

When it comes to Japanese food, which do you enjoy more, cooking or eating?

もちろん、 食べる方が 作る (の) よりたのしいです。

もちろん、作る (の) より 食べる方が たのしいです。

I enjoy eating more than cooking, of course.

(4) 私はダウンタウンに行きます。でんしゃで行くのとバスで行くのとでは、どちらの方が
はやいですか。

I'm going downtown. Which is faster, going by train or by bus?

でんしゃで行く方が バスで行く（の）よりはやいです。

バスで行く（の）より でんしゃで行く方が はやいです。

Going by train is faster than going by bus.

9d Superlative

To compare more than two entities, 一番 "number one / first" is used. The literal translation is "Among A and B and C, A is number one X".

AとBとCとでは、Aが一番Xです。　　Among A, B, and C, A is the X-est.

In comparative questions, we use どちらの方, regardless of what is compared. In superlative questions,
by contrast, an appropriate WH-word（どれ, だれ／どなた, どこ）must be selected according to the
compared items.

Among A, B, and C, which is the X-est?	
AとBとCとでは、 どれ が一番Xですか。	Things
Among A, B, and C, who is the X-est?	
AとBとCとでは、 だれ が一番Xですか。	People (Plain)
AとBとCとでは、 どなた が一番Xですか。	People (Polite)
Among A, B, and C, which place is the X-est?	
AとBとCとでは、 どこ が一番Xですか。	Places

(1) イタリアりょうりとちゅうかりょうりと日本りょうりとでは、どれが一番おいしい
ですか。

Which do you like most, Italian, Chinese, or Japanese cuisine?

イタリアりょうりとちゅうかりょうりと日本りょうりとでは、イタリアりょうりが一
番おいしいです。

Of Italian, Chinese, and Japanese cuisine, I like Italian the most.

(2) おんがくをきくのはたのしいですね。クラシックとジャズとロックとでは、どれが一番
好きですか。

*Listening to music is enjoyable, isn't it? Which (do you think) is most enjoyable, classical
music, jazz, or rock?*

ジャズが一番好きです。

Jazz is the most enjoyable.

(3) 英語と日本語とロシア語とでは、どれが一番むずかしいですか。

Which is the most difficult, English, Japanese, or Russian?

ロシア語が一番むずかしいです。

Russian is the most difficult.

(4) テニスとゴルフとバスケットボールとでは、どれが一番とくいですか。

Which are you best at, tennis, golf, or basketball?

テニスが一番とくいです。

I'm best at tennis.

(5) ミラーさんとソンさんとキムさんとでは、だれが一番せが高いですか。

Who is the tallest, Miller-san, Son-san, or Kim-san?

キムさんが一番せが高いです。

Kim-san is the tallest.

(6) ニューヨークとロサンゼルスとサンフランシスコとでは、どこが一番大きいですか。

Which is the largest, New York, Los Angeles, or San Francisco?

ニューヨークが一番大きいです。

New York is the largest.

Like comparisons, the clauses must be nominalized in the superlative construction.

(7) スキーをする の とテニスをする の とお
よぐ の とでは、どれが一番好きですか。

Which do you like most, skiing,

playing tennis, or swimming?

およぐ の が一番好きです。

I like swimming the most.

(8) 日本語は、読む の と書く の と話す の とでは、どれが一番やさしいですか。

In Japanese, which is the easiest, reading, writing, or speaking?

話す の が一番やさしいです。

Speaking is the easiest.

(9) 私は、かんじをれんしゅうする の ときょうかしょを読む の としゅくだいをする の とでは、しゅくだいをする の が一番きらいです。

(Lit.) Of practicing kanji, reading the textbook, and doing assignments, I dislike doing assignments most.

Of practicing kanji, reading the textbook, and doing assignments, doing assignments is what I dislike most.

If you want to mention a specific category X, rather than individual items in that category, 「Xの中(なか)で」 can be used. If you use this pattern in a question, use 何 "what", instead of どれ "which", because どれ requires a list of choices. As you can see, English has a similar restriction on "which".

(10) スポーツ の中で 、 何 が一番おもしろいですか。

In sports, what is the most interesting?

(11) スポーツ の中で 、 何 を見るのが一番好きですか。

In sports, what do you like to watch most?

(12) 日本りょうり の中で 、 何 が一番好きですか。

Of Japanese cuisine, what do you like most?

9e   Xを下さい／下さいませんか   "Please give me X"

In 第八課, てフォーム + 下さい "please do ~" was studied. When you request a thing, 「Xを下さい／下さいませんか」 is used. 下さい is appropriate in such situations as shopping and ordering at a restaurant; 下さいませんか is used when you want to be more polite. If you feel like saying simply *Give it to me*, use 下さい; if you want to say *Would / Could you give it to me?*, use 下さいませんか.

コーヒーを下さい。
Give me coffee.

石川先生、ハンドアウトを下さいませんか。
Ishikawa-sensei, could you give me (a copy of) the handout?

このまちのちずを下さいませんか。
Could you give me a map of this town?

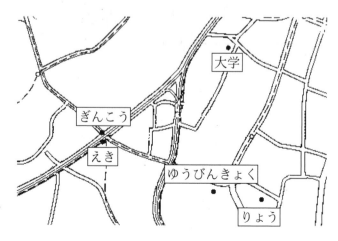

9f   Counters

In English, we can just add a number to a noun to specify the quantity of the entity: e.g. one book, two persons, three cars, etc. Japanese requires the use of *counters*. Selection of a particular counter depends on the nature and the general shape of the object.

Entity	Examples	Counter	1
人	people	～人 （り・にん）	一人 ひとり
Things (general)	fruits, hamburger, furniture	～つ	一つ ひとつ
Things (general)	fruits, hamburger, furniture	～こ	一こ いっこ
Thin, flat things	paper, records, shirts, skirts, floppies, CDs	～まい	一まい いちまい
Long, cylindrical objects	pens, pencils, umbrellas, bottles, audiotapes, video-tapes, movies, flowers	～本（ほん ・ぽん・ぼん）	一本 いっぽん
Liquid, grains, noodles, etc.	cups of tea, coffee, juice, soup noodles, rice, domburi	～はい・ ～ばい・ ～ぱい	一ぱい いっぱい
Machines	cars, bicycles, computers, TVs, cameras, washing machines	～だい	一だい いちだい
Bound things	books, magazines	～さつ	一さつ いっさつ
Years		～年	一年 いちねん
Months		～か月	一か月 いっかげつ
Hours		～時間	一時間 いちじかん
Minutes		～分 （ふん・ぷん）	一分 いっぷん
円		～円	一円 いちえん
Dollars		～ドル	一ドル いちドル
Cents		～セント	一セント いっセント

2	3	4	5	6
二人 ふたり	三人 さんにん	四人 よにん	五人 ごにん	六人 ろくにん
二つ ふたつ	三つ みっつ	四つ よっつ	五つ いつつ	六つ むっつ
二こ にこ	三こ さんこ	四こ よんこ	五こ ごこ	六こ ろっこ
二まい にまい	三まい さんまい	四まい よんまい よまい	五まい ごまい	六まい ろくまい
二本 にほん	三本 さんぼん	四本 よんほん	五本 ごほん	六本 ろっぽん
二はい にはい	三ばい さんばい	四はい よんはい	五はい ごはい	六ぱい ろっぱい
二だい にだい	三だい さんだい	四だい よんだい よだい	五だい ごだい	六だい ろくだい
二さつ にさつ	三さつ さんさつ	四さつ よんさつ	五さつ ごさつ	六さつ ろくさつ
二年 にねん	三年 さんねん	四年 よねん	五年 ごねん	六年 ろくねん
二か月 にかげつ	三か月 さんかげつ	四か月 よんかげつ	五か月 ごかげつ	六か月 ろっかげつ
二時間 にじかん	三時間 さんじかん	四時間 よじかん	五時間 ごじかん	六時間 ろくじかん
二分 にふん	三分 さんぷん	四分 よんぷん	五分 ごふん	六分 ろっぷん
二円 にえん	三円 さんえん	四円 よえん	五円 ごえん	六円 ろくえん
二ドル にドル	三ドル さんドル	四ドル よんドル	五ドル ごドル	六ドル ろくドル
二セント にセント	三セント さんセント	四セント よんセント	五セント ごセント	六セント ろくセント

7	8	9	10	?
七人 しちにん ななにん	八人 はちにん	九人 きゅうにん くにん	十人 じゅうにん	何人 なんにん
七つ ななつ	八つ やっつ	九つ ここのつ	十 とお	いくつ
七こ ななこ	八こ はっこ はちこ	九こ きゅうこ	十こ じっこ じゅっこ	何こ なんこ
七まい ななまい	八まい はちまい	九まい きゅうまい	十まい じゅうまい	何まい なんまい
七本 ななほん	八本 はっぽん はちほん	九本 きゅうほん	十本 じっぽん じゅっぽん	何本 なんぼん
七はい ななはい	八ぱい はっぱい はちはい	九はい きゅうはい	十ぱい じっぱい じゅっぱい	何ば(は)い なんばい なんはい
七だい ななだい しちだい	八だい はちだい	九だい きゅうだい くだい	十だい じゅうだい	何だい なんだい
七さつ ななさつ	八さつ はっさつ	九さつ きゅうさつ	十さつ じっさつ じゅっさつ	何さつ なんさつ
七年 しちねん ななねん	八年 はちねん	九年 くねん きゅうねん	十年 じゅうねん	何年 なんねん
七か月 ななかげつ しちかげつ	八か月 はっかげつ はちかげつ	九か月 きゅうかげつ	十か月 じっかげつ じゅっかげつ	何か月 なんかげつ
七時間 しちじかん ななじかん	八時間 はちじかん	九時間 くじかん	十時間 じゅうじかん	何時間 なんじかん
七分 ななふん	八分 はっぷん はちふん	九分 きゅうふん	十分 じっぷん じゅっぷん	何分 なんぷん
七円 ななえん	八円 はちえん	九円 きゅうえん	十円 じゅうえん	何円 なんえん
七ドル ななドル	八ドル はちドル	九ドル きゅうドル	十ドル じゅうドル	何ドル なんドル
七セント ななセント	八セント はっセント はちセント	九セント きゅうセント	十セント じっセント じゅっセント	何セント なんセント

When a counter quantifies the subject or direct object, it normally appears after the subject or direct object. Note that は, が, and を do not appear after the counter.

SUBJECT	は／が	COUNTER	VERB
DIRECT OBJECT	を	COUNTER	VERB

あそこに クラスメートが 六人 います。　　　　*Six of my classmates are over there.*

石川先生は 車が 二だい あります。　　　　*Ishikawa-sensei has two cars.*

ボストンで Tシャツを 一まい 買いました。　　　*I bought a T-shirt in Boston.*

ウィスキーを 二本 下さい。　　　　*Give me two bottles of whiskey.*

マグカップが いっこ／一つ あります。　　　*There is a mug.* (or)

　　　　　　　　　　　　　　　　　　I /We / etc. have one mug.

お茶を もう一ぱい 下さい。　　　　*Please give me one more cup of tea.*

9g　Xにする　　　"decide on X / make something X"

As mentioned in Usage **6**, なさいます is an honorific form (to be discussed in 第十九課) of します。

ウェイター　：何になさいますか。

　　　　　　(Lit.) What will you decide on? / What would you like to order?

ソン　　　　：私はとんかつにします。

　　　　　　(Lit.) I decide on the pork cutlet. / I'll have the pork cutlet.

ミラー　　　：私はカレーライスにします。

　　　　　　(Lit.) I decide on the curry rice. / I'll have the curry rice.

パーティーは七時にしましょう。

(Lit.) As for the party, let's decide on 7 o'clock. / Let's make the party start at 7.

その話は明日にしましょう。

(Lit.) As for that matter, let's decide on it tomorrow. / Let's talk about it tomorrow.

<ruby>練習問題<rt>れんしゅうもんだい</rt></ruby>

I.　クラスメートにききましょう。

<ruby>例<rt>れい</rt></ruby>

Q: X さんは<u>えをかくの</u>が好きですか。

A:　はい、<u>えをかくの</u>が好きです。

　　(or) いいえ、<u>えをかくの</u>は好きじゃありません。きらいです。

例

1.　　　　　2.　　　　　3.

4.　　　　　5.　　　　　6.　　　　　7.

II.　クラスメートにききましょう。

1.	どんなおんがくが好きですか。	
2.	どんなスポーツがとくいですか。	
3.	どんな食べものがきらいですか。	
4.	何が { 上手 とくい } ですか。	
5.	何が下手ですか。	
6.	何をするのが好きですか。	
7.	何をするのがきらいですか。	

III.　<ruby>第九課会話<rt>だいきゅうかかいわ</rt></ruby>のメニューを見て、オーダーしましょう。

例　ウェーター　：　いらっしゃいませ。何になさいますか。

　　A　　　　　：　＿＿＿＿＿＿＿＿＿＿＿＿＿を下さい／おねがいします。

　　ウェーター　：　はい。＿＿＿＿＿＿＿＿＿＿＿ですね。お飲みものは。

　　A　　　　　：　＿＿＿＿＿＿＿＿＿＿＿＿＿を下さい／おねがいします。

　　ウェーター　：　はい。しょうしょうお待ち下さい。

IV.　クラスメートにききましょう。

例

A:　かんじとひらがなとでは、どちらの方がむずかしいですか。

B:　かんじの方がひらがなよりむずかしいです。

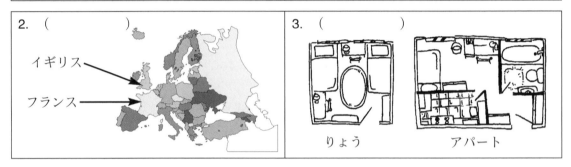

例　（むずかしい）

漢字　ひらがな

1.　（　　　　　）

マクドナルド　バーガーキング

2.　（　　　　　）

イギリス

フランス

3.　（　　　　　）

りょう　アパート

V.　クラスメートにききましょう。

例

A:　日本語を話すのと書くのとではどちらの方がおもしろいですか。

B:　話す方が書くよりおもしろいです。

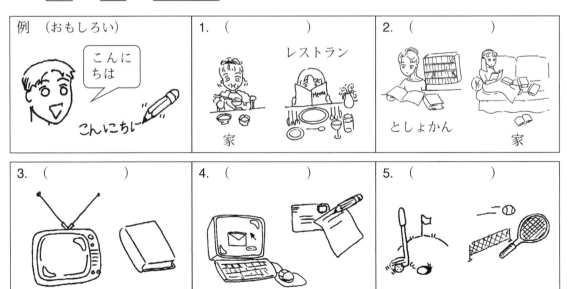

例　（おもしろい）

こんにちは

こんにちは

1.　（　　　　　）

レストラン

家

2.　（　　　　　）

としょかん　家

3.　（　　　　　）

4.　（　　　　　）

5.　（　　　　　）

VI.　クラスメートにききましょう。

例

A:　日本語と中国語と英語とではどれが一番むずかしいですか。

B:　中国語が一番むずかしいです。

VII.　クラスメートにききましょう。

例

A:　おんがくの中で何が一番好きですか。

B:　クラシックが一番好きです。

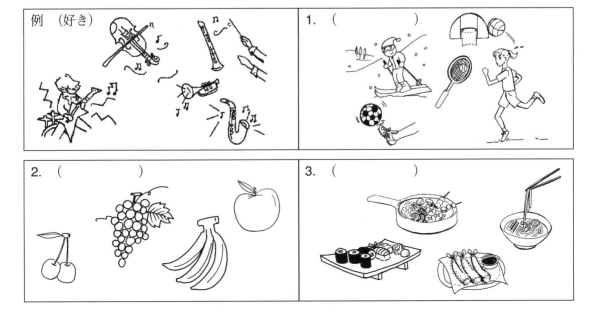

VIII.　クラスメートにききましょう。

例

A:　日本語を話すのと書くのと読むのとではどれが一番むずかしいですか。

B:　そうですね。書くのが一番むずかしいです。

IX.　クラスメートにききましょう。

例

A:　Bさんは、Tシャツがありますか。

B:　はい、Tシャツがあります。

　　(or) いいえ、Tシャツはありません。

A:　何まいありますか。

B:　六まいあります。

4.			6.		
5.			7.		

いいましょう。

例　　_____ さんはTシャツが_____ あります。

(or) _____ さんはTシャツはありません。

1. _____さんはマグカップが _____。
2. _____さんはペンが_____。
3. _____さんはじしょが_____。
4. _____さんはかばんが_____。
5. _____さんはかさが_____。
6. _____さんはCDが_____。
7. _____さんはコンピューターが_____。

X.　　クラスメートと話しましょう。

例

A:　レストランへ行きませんか。

B:　いいですねえ。行きましょう。

A:　どのレストランにしましょうか。

B:　日本りょうりのレストランにしましょうか。

A:　そうですね。そうしましょう。

　　(or) あのう、ちょっと……。イタリアりょうりのレストランにしませんか。

例	レストランへ行きましょう。	日本りょうり／イタリアりょうり／ちゅうかりょうり
1.	おんがくをききましょう。	ジャズ／クラシック／ロック
2.	えいがを見ましょう。	アクション(action)／ホラー(horror) ／コメディー(comedy)
3.	デザートを食べましょう。	ケーキ／アイスクリーム／くだもの
4.	としょかんでべんきょうしましょう。	ごぜん十一時／ごご三時／ごご七時

XI.   買いものしましょう。

例

A: いらっしゃいませ。

B: あのう、<u>りんご</u>*、ありますか。

A: はい、ありますよ。

B: じゃ、<u>りんご</u>を<u>三つ</u>下さい。

A: はい、<u>りんご</u>を<u>三つ</u>ですね。

B: ええ、それから、<u>オレンジ</u>を<u>八つ</u>下さい。

A: はい。<u>1,250円</u>です。ありがとうございました。

> * You can as well say りんごがありますか, but the sentence without が is more natural in this context.

プライスリスト	
りんご	150円
オレンジ	100円
ビール	350円
ワイン	1,500円
ノート	180円
ペン	120円

ショッピングリスト1	
りんご	3
オレンジ	8

ショッピングリスト2	
ビール	6
ワイン	1

ショッピングリスト3	
ノート	1
ペン	3

XII.   読みましょう。

せんしゅう東京からともだちのさとうさんが来ました。

さとうさんはおんがくをきくのが好きですから、土曜日の晩、いっしょに「よし」へ行きました。「よし」はジャズクラブ (club) です。ダウンタウンにあります。

私たちは日本のビールを二本飲みました。日本のビールは高いですが、おいしいです。それから、カリフォルニアワインも一本飲みました。

「よし」に安川さんもいました。それで、いっしょにジャズをききました。

安川さんはジャズとクラシックが好きです。でも、私はクラシックは好きじゃありません。

らいしゅうのしゅうまつもさとうさんといっしょにダウンタウンへジャズをききに行くつもりです。

〇 ですか。×ですか。

1. （　　）さとうさんの家はダウンタウンにあります。
2. （　　）さとうさんは土曜日の晩、ひとりで「よし」へ行きました。
3. （　　）日本のビールは安くておいしいです。
4. （　　）この人はクラシックが好きです。
5. （　　）この人とさとうさんは、明日、いっしょにダウンタウンへジャズをききに行きます。

新しい漢字

一番 (いちばん)	～円 (えん)	お茶 (ちゃ)	書く (か)	上手 (じょうず)	好き (す)	中国 (ちゅうごく)
作る (つく)	～年 (ねん)	話 (はなし)	話す (はな)	下手 (へた)	方 (ほう)	待つ (ま)
読む (よ)						

新しい使い方

～か月 (げつ)	時間 (じ かん)	～時間 (じ かん)	中 (なか)	～本 (ほん)	安川 (やすかわ)	一つ (ひと)
二つ (ふた)	三つ (みっ)	四つ (よっ)	五つ (いつ)	六つ (むっ)	七つ (なな)	八つ (やっ)
九つ (ここの)	十* (とお)					

* Note that 十 is written as とお, **not** とう.

Radicals: 言べん・なべぶた

In 第八課, two へん radicals (日へん and 女へん) were introduced. In this lesson, we learned 好, another 女へん漢字.

Another へん radical to study here is 言 (ごんべん), which appears in 語, 話, and 読. Most 言べん漢字 are related to language.

Radicals that appear in the upper position are called かんむり "crown". 亠 in 高, 京, and 方 belongs to the かんむり group and is called なべぶた (なべ "pot" + ふた "lid"; ふた becomes ぶた by sequential voicing, cf. 第十一課, **11f**). Unlike 言べん, なべぶた does not designate any particular meaning to each 漢字.

Polysemy (Multiple Meanings)

The Japanese language does not have excess/superfluous vocabulary. What does that mean? Well, there are not many distinctive Japanese verbs or adjectives—nondistinctive in the sense that they can be used to convey different meanings depending on what they predicate. For example, in 第七課, we learned that やさしい can mean "easy" when it is used to modify an activity, but that it means "kind/gentle" when it describes a person. That is, the meaning of an adjective can be dependent on how it is used. (To some extent, this is also true in English: the meaning of *late* in *the late fee* is different from that in *the late professor*.) However, Chinese differentiates the two meanings of やさしい, so that these words are written with different 漢字 (易しい "easy" and 優しい "kind/gentle"). はやい is another such example. When it means "early", it is written as 早い (第八課), but when it means "fast", it is written as 速い (速 is not introduced in this textbook).

Similarly, かく in Japanese has a more abstract, implicit, or vague meaning than, say, "to write": i.e. "to make some marks by hand". So it can mean "to write" in てがみをかく, and it can mean "to draw" in えをかく. But these two senses of かく are differentiated by 漢字. For "to write", 書 is used, but for "to draw", a different 漢字「描」(not included in our 漢字 list) is used. This is why we do not use 書 in えをかく.

番	一	㇒	㇀	立	平	平	采	釆	番	番
バン	番	番								
	order / guard									
円	丨	冂	門	円						
エン	circle									
茶	一	十	卄	艹	芆	苓	苯	茶	茶	
チャ	tea									
書	㇇	7	㇤	彐	彐	聿	聿	書	書	書
か（く）	to write / a text									
月	㇒	刀	月	月						
ゲツ・ガツ	moon: 月曜日 *Monday,* 〜月 *month of the year,* 〜か月 *month(s)*									
上	丨	上	上							
ジョウ・うえ	top / up: 上手（じょうず）*good at*									
手	㇒	二	三	手						
	hand: 上手（じょうず）*good at,* 下手（へた）*bad at*									
■好	く	女	女	奵	好	好				
す（き）	to like									
中	丶	口	口	中						
チュウ・なか	middle / inside: 中間 *midterm,* 中国 *China*									
国	丨	冂	冂	冂	用	囯	国	国		
ゴク	country: 中国 *China*									
作	ノ	イ	亻	仁	作	作	作			
つく（る）	to make									

年	ノ	┍	乍	午	竏	年			
ネン	*year: 〜年 year(s)*								

■話	丶	二	亖	亖	言	言	言	訁	訂	託
はなし・ はな (す)	訐	話	話							
	to talk / speak									

下	一	丁	下						
した・ くだ (さい)	*below / under / down: 下さい please give downward, 下手 (へた) bad at*								

□方	丶	亠	方	方					
ホウ	*direction / side / way*								

本	一	十	才	木	本				
ホン・ポン	*origin: 本 book (origin of knowledge), 日本 Japan (sun origin), 一本 one (cylindrical thing)*								

待	ノ	ク	彳	彳	彳	往	待	待	
ま (つ)	*to wait*								

■読	丶	二	亖	亖	言	言	言	訁	訐	訪
よ (む)	訪	誌	誌	読						
	to read									

<ruby>漢<rt>かん</rt>字<rt>じ</rt></ruby>の<ruby>復<rt>ふく</rt>習<rt>しゅう</rt></ruby>

I.　　読みましょう。

1.　このお茶は千円でした。

2.　東京からサンフランシスコまで九時間です。

3.　山本さんの妹さんは高校生です。

4.　父は目が大きいです。

5.　私のおいはきょねん大学に入りました。

II. We have learned 漢字 for some counters and measuring units. Write the reading of each word in the blank square and connect it with its meaning.

例 れい	百	ひゃく
1.	十円	
2.	六時	
3.	四時間	
4.	八年	
5.	二か月	
6.	五分	
7.	十本	
8.	三つ	
9.	九人	

- hour (point in time)
- hours (duration)
- minutes
- months
- number
- people
- long, cylindrical things
- things (general)
- years
- yen

新しい語彙
あたら　ごい

X円 えん	X yen
Xか月 げつ	X month(s)
Xこ	X unit(s) (general)
Xさつ	X volume(s) of books
X時間 じかん	X hour(s)
Xセント	X cent(s)
Xだい	X machine(s)
Xドル	X dollar(s)
X年 ねん	X year(s)
Xはい	X cup(s), bowl(s), glass(es)
X本 ほん	X long, cylindrical thing(s)

Xまい	X flat thing(s)
Eメール	email
Tシャツ	T-shirt
イタリアりょうり	Italian cuisine
一番 いちばん	first, best, number one
五つ いつ	5 things
ウィスキー	whiskey
ウェイター	waiter
え	picture, drawing
オーダー (する)	order
おかんじょう	check (at a restaurant)
おなか	stomach
おねがい (する)	request

オレンジ		orange	デザート		dessert
おんがく		music	どうぞ		please
かく	⑦	to draw	十 (とお)		10 things
カレーライス		curry rice	とくい	⑪	good at
かわいい	⑥	cute	なさる	⑦	to do (respectful)
かんたん	⑪	easy	七つ (なな)		7 things
ギター		guitar	飲みもの (の)		drinks
きょうかしょ		textbook	バスケットボール		basketball
きらい	⑪	dislike	話 (はなし)		talk, story
くだもの		fruit	はやい	⑥	fast
クラシック		classical music	ハンサム	⑪	handsome
クラスメート		classmate	ハンドアウト		handout
九つ (ここの)		9 things	一つ (ひと)		1 thing
ジャズ		jazz	二つ (ふた)		2 things
上手 (じょうず)	⑪	good at	下手 (へた)	⑪	bad at
好き (す)	⑪	like	方 (ほう)		direction, side, way
すきやき		sukiyaki	マグカップ		mug
すく	⑦	to become empty	三つ (みっ)		3 things
スポーツ		sport	六つ (むっ)		6 things
そうじ (する)		cleaning	八つ (やっ)		8 things
たのしい	⑥	enjoyable, pleasant	四つ (よっ)		4 things
食べもの (た)		food	りんご		apple
ちず		map	れんしゅう (する)		practice
ちゅうかりょうり		Chinese cuisine	ロック		rock

なまえ

イギリス	England
中国 ちゅうごく	China

ボストン	Boston
ロサンゼルス（ロス）	Los Angeles

図書館
The Library

東アジア図書館へ行ったことがありますか
Have you been to the East Asian Library?

会話

1　ミラー　：もしもし、山本さんですか。ミラーです。
　　　　　　　Hello, Yamamoto-san? This is Miller.

　　　山本　　：あ、ミラーさん。おはようございます。
　　　　　　　Oh, Miller-san. Good morning.

2　ミラー　：おはようございます。おいそがしいですか。
　　　　　　　Good morning. Are you busy?

3　山本　　：今、へやをそうじしています。明日、東京から母が来るんです。
　　　　　　　I'm cleaning my room now. My mother's coming from Tokyo tomorrow.

4　ミラー　：そうですか。たいへんですね。
　　　　　　　Really. I bet it's a lot of work.

　　　山本　　：ええ。ミラーさんは。
　　　　　　　Yes. How about you?

5　ミラー　：私は日本語のしゅくだいをしているんですが、漢字がとても多いんです。
　　　　　　　それで、あまりよく分からないんです。
　　　　　　　I'm doing my Japanese homework, but there are a lot of kanji, so I don't understand
　　　　　　　it very well.

6　山本　　：そうですか。じゃあ、いっしょに東アジア図書館でべんきょうしましょうか。
　　　　　　　Is that so? Well, shall we study together at the East Asian Library?

7　ミラー　：いいですか。ありがとうございます。でも、今日は日曜日ですね。図書館は
　　　　　　　開いていますか。
　　　　　　　Would that be okay? Thank you. But today is Sunday ... Is the library open?

8　山本　：今は閉まっていますが、一時に開きますよ。ミラーさんは東アジア図書館へ
行ったことがありますか。

It's closed right now, but it opens at 1 o'clock. Have you been to the East Asian Library?

9　ミラー　：行ったことはありますが、東アジア図書館でべんきょうしたことはありま
せん。いつもほかの図書館でべんきょうしていますから。

*Yes, I've been there, but I've never studied there because I've always studied in some
other library.*

10　山本　：私は今日、東アジア図書館へ本をかえしに行くつもりです。

I plan to go to the East Asian Library to return books today.

11　ミラー　：そうですか。ところで、そうじはどのぐらいかかりますか。

You are? By the way, how long will it take to clean your room?

　　　山本　：そうですねえ、あと二時間ぐらいかかります。

Let's see ... It'll take about two more hours.

12　山本　：今何時ですか。とけいをしていませんから、分からないんです。

What time is it now? I'm not wearing a watch, so I don't know.

　　　ミラー　：今、十時半です。

It's 10:30 now.

13　山本　：そうですか。それじゃ、一時に図書館の前で会いましょうか。

I see. Well then, shall we meet in front of the library at one o'clock?

　　　ミラー　：分かりました。すみませんが、それでは、一時におねがいします。

Alright. Sorry for the trouble. I'll see you at one, then.

使い方

1　もしもし "Hello" is used exclusively for telephone calls.

2　おいそがしいですか is a polite expression to ask if the addressee is busy. The Plain フォーム
of "busy" is いそがしい.

11　そうですねえ "Let's see" is used to fill in the gap while you are thinking about what to say.

あと ＋ X (quantity expression) means "X more quantity", e.g. あと十分 "ten more minutes", あ
と五百円 "500 yen more".

13　それでは means "well then" / "if that's the case" / "given that".

文法

10a Verb Conjugation: たフォーム

The verb たフォーム is used to express that the referred event / action has been completed. Naturally, therefore, it frequently (but not always) functions as a past-tense marker. The たフォーム can be derived straightforwardly from the てフォーム; change て／で to た／だ.

会って	→	会った		食べて	→	食べた
書いて	→	書いた		見て	→	見た
話して	→	話した		来て	→	来た
待って	→	待った		して	→	した
読んで	→	読んだ				

In casual conversation, you can use the Dictionary フォーム by itself for the non-past tense, and the たフォーム by itself for the past tense.

(1) 明日、学校 (へ) 行く？

Are you going to school tomorrow?

うん、行く。

Yeah, I am.

(2) あのえいが、もう見た？

Have you already seen that movie?

うん、もう見た。

Yeah, I've already seen it.

ううん、まだ。

Nope, not yet.

Politeness encoded in polite forms is toward the addressee, not toward the person you are talking about. For example, 妹は英語を話します is a polite sentence, showing respect to the addressee, not to 妹. Usage of polite forms differs somewhat between spoken and written language. In personal letters (written to a particular addressee), you may want to use polite forms like spoken language. If you do not use polite forms in such a letter, the tone of the letter becomes casual, and possibly impolite. In formal writings (e.g. academic theses, official documents, literature), plain forms are normally used, without rendering casualness or impoliteness. This is because formal writings do not assume a particular addressee, i.e. they are supposed to be impersonal.

The negative of the Dictionary フォーム is the Negative フォーム ＋ ない (ないフォーム), whereas the negative of the たフォーム is the Negative フォーム ＋ なかった (なかったフォーム).

(3) 明日、学校 (へ) 行く？　　　　　　　　　*Are you going to school tomorrow?*
　　 ううん、行かない。　　　　　　　　　*No, I'm not.*

(4) 昨日、えいが見た？　　　　　　　　　*Did you see a movie yesterday?*
　　 ううん、見なかった。　　　　　　　　*No, I didn't (see).*

The Dictionary フォーム, たフォーム, ないフォーム, and なかったフォーム are sometimes grouped together as *plain forms*, as opposed to the *polite forms* that contain ～ます, ～ました, ～ません, or ～ませんでした.

Polite フォーム				Plain フォーム			
Non-past		Past		Non-past		Past	
Affirm-ative	Negative	Affirmative	Negative	Affirm-ative	Negative	Affirm-ative	Negative
会います	会いません	会いました	会いませんでした	会う	会わない	会った	会わなかった
あります	ありません	ありました	ありませんでした	ある	ない	あった	なかった
行きます	行きません	行きました	行きませんでした	行く	行かない	行った	行かなかった
帰ります	帰りません	帰りました	帰りませんでした	帰る	帰らない	帰った	帰らなかった
聞きます	聞きません	聞きました	聞きませんでした	聞く	聞かない	聞いた	聞かなかった
読みます	読みません	読みました	読みませんでした	読む	読まない	読んだ	読まなかった
待ちます	待ちません	待ちました	待ちませんでした	待つ	待たない	待った	待たなかった
食べます	食べません	食べました	食べませんでした	食べる	食べない	食べた	食べなかった
ねます	ねません	ねました	ねませんでした	ねる	ねない	ねた	ねなかった
います	いません	いました	いませんでした	いる	いない	いた	いなかった
見ます	見ません	見ました	見ませんでした	見る	見ない	見た	見なかった
します	しません	しました	しませんでした	する	しない	した	しなかった
来ます	来ません	来ました	来ませんでした	来る	来ない	来た	来なかった

10b たフォーム + ことがある　　"X has had the experience of VERB-ing"

た

This construction presents a past event as one's experience. Pastness is expressed by the use of the たフォーム itself. Therefore, you **do not** say たフォーム + ことがあり ました . Like the difference between the English "did ~" vs. "have done ~" constructions, ～ました emphasizes a particular past activity, whereas たフォーム + ことがあります indicates that the subject has done that activity previously. Consider the following sentences. (Pay attention to the negative scope marker は , cf. 第六課 , **6h**, in the negative answer in (1)).

(1)　日本へ行ったことがありますか。　　　　*Have you been to Japan?*

　　　はい、日本へ行ったことがあります。　　*Yes, I've been to Japan.*

　　　(cf. 日本へ行きました。)　　　　　　　*(I went to Japan.)*

　　　はい、今年、はじめて行きました。　　　*Yes, I went there this year for the first time.*

　　　いいえ、まだ日本へ行ったこと は ありません。 *No, I haven't been to Japan yet.*

(2)　日本のえいがを見たことがありますか。　　*Have you ever seen a Japanese movie?*

(3)　日本語で手紙を書いたことがありますか。　*Have you ever written a letter in Japanese?*

　　　　　　　　　　　　　　　　　　　　　　(Literally "by means of Japanese")

10c てフォーム + いる　　"X has VERB-ed"

In 第八課 , we studied てフォーム + います to express "be VERB-ing". In this lesson, we will learn another function of this construction.

Normally, when something occurs, the state of affairs changes as a result. If we want to express such a resultant state, we need to use てフォーム + います .

(1)　たちます。　 たっています 。　　　　(2)　すわります。　 すわっています 。

　　　(I'll) stand up.　*(I) am standing.*　　　　*(I'll) sit down.*　*(I) am sitting.*

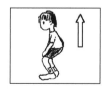  

(3)　銀行は九時に開きました。　　　　　　　*The bank opened at 9 o'clock.*

　　　今、十一時です。　　　　　　　　　　　*It's 11 o'clock now.*

　　　銀行は今、 開いています 。　　　　　　*The bank **is open** now.*

(4)　図書館は五時に閉まりました。　　　　　*The library closed at 5 o'clock.*

　　　図書館は今、 閉まっています 。　　　　*The library **is closed** now.*

Typically, adjectives refer to states of affairs, and verbs to actions. However, English has many verbs that represent states, e.g. *live, love, know, resemble.*[*] Japanese does not have many *stative verbs*; almost all Japanese verbs refer to an action or event, e.g.:

開く	become open
知る	get to know
住む	start living somewhere

> [*] We can test whether a verb is stative or not by checking if its non-past form can refer to a present situation. If it can, it is stative; if it cannot, it is non-stative. For example, whereas *I live in Tokyo* can refer to a present state, *I write a letter in Japanese* cannot be interpreted so that the speaker is in the process of writing a letter.

Thus てフォーム＋います is frequently used to express resultant states.

(5)　りょうしんは東京に住んでいます。

(Lit.) My parents are living in Tokyo.
My parents live in Tokyo.

(6)　兄がカナダから来ています。

My older brother has come from Canada.
(i.e. He's visiting me.)

(7)　母は今、大阪へ行っています。

My mother has now gone to Osaka.

(8)　早川さんはもう家に帰っています。

Hayakawa-san has gone home.
(i.e. She's at home.)

(9)　中山さんを知っていますか。

Do you know Nakayama-san?

　　はい、中山さんを知っています。

Yes, I know Nakayama-san.

　　いいえ、中山さんは 知りません 。

No, I don't know Nakayama-san.

Note that the negation of 知っています is 知りません, **not** 知っていません.

10d　Transitive vs. Intransitive Verbs

In English, many verbs can be used in two different ways. *Open*, for example, can mean an action (you *open* the door) or a process or characteristic of something (the door *opens*). Another example is *walk*. Normally, it means that some person or animal walks, e.g. *you WALK, the dog WALKS*, etc. But it can also be used transitively as in *I walk my dog every day*. When a verb is about only a single entity (the subject), it is called *intransitive*; when a verb is about (the relationship of) two entities (the subject and the direct object), it is called *transitive*. Although many English verbs are used either transitively or intransitively, as exemplified by *open* and *walk*, not all verbs can be used this way. *Vanish*, for example, can be used only as an intransitive, although it was used in both ways in classical English. You can say *When I moved the cursor, the screen vanished*, but you cannot say *I vanished the screen away*.

Japanese is very strict about the transitive-intransitive distinction. With only a handful of exceptions, Japanese verbs are either transitive or intransitive, but cannot be both. You will learn transitive-intransitive pairs later in this course. For the time being, you need to remember:

1. 　開く　　intransitive　　東アジア図書館は九時に開きます。

　　　　　　　　　　　　　　The East Asian Library opens at 9 o'clock.

　　　　　　　　Not:　　*Someone opens the East Asian Library at 9 o'clock.*

2. 　閉まる　intransitive　　そのみせは五時に閉まります。

　　　　　　　　　　　　　　That store closes at 5 o'clock.

　　　　　　　　Not:　　*Someone closes the store at 5 o'clock.*

3. 　はじめる　transitive　　私たちは七時にパーティーをはじめました。

　　　　　　　　　　　　　　We began the party at 7 o'clock.

　　　　　　　　Not:　　*The party began at 7 o'clock.*

10e Indirect Object Marker に

に	SUBJECT は／が	INDIRECT OBJECT に	DIRECT OBJECT を	VERB

　　Some verbs require both direct and indirect objects. For example, we may feel that *I sent a present* is not a complete sentence, and that we need to add a receiver, e.g. *I sent a present to my parents*. *A present* in this sentence is called the *direct object*, and *my parents* the *indirect object*. Verbs like *send*, *return*, *give* require both direct and indirect objects, unless they have already been mentioned in the conversation. Normally, the direct object is a thing, and the indirect object is a person or an organization. The direct object is marked with を ; the indirect object is marked with に .

私は Subject	りょうしんに Indirect Object	プレゼントを Direct Object	おくりました。 Predicate

I sent a present to my parents.

私はともだちにお金をかしました。
I lent some money to my friend.

私は今晩、りょうしんに手紙を書きます。
I'm going to write a letter to my parents this evening.

Like English *write*, 書く can be used as a transitive verb, e.g. 私は手紙を書きます, or it can take an indirect object, e.g. 私はりょうしんに手紙を書きます. When the sentence includes an indirect object, it strongly implies that the letter will be sent to the person(s).

かえす "return" takes an indirect object, e.g. 図書館 .

図書館に本をかえします。　　　　　　*I'm going to return the book to the library.*

When かえす appears in 「Pre-ますフォーム ＋ に ＋ 行く／来る／かえる」 "go／come／return in order to do ~", cf. 第六課, **6e**, the place plays a double role: one is the indirect object of かえす, and the other is the goal of 行く／来る／かえる.

図書館に本をかえしに行きます。　　　*I'm going to the library to return the book (to the library).*

The indirect object is often, but not always, the goal of some transfer. In the following, the indirect object ともだち designates the origin of the transfer. The interpretation of the indirect object depends on the nature of the verb.

私は ともだちに お金をかりました。　　*I borrowed some money* from my friend .

10f   Verbs of Wearing Clothing

The English verb *wear* is extremely general. People can wear makeup, glasses, clothes, jeans, shoes, a hat, wig, ring, or even a beard. In Japanese you need to select a verb appropriate to how you wear it.

A　きる is the most general *wearing* verb in Japanese. You can use it with clothes you put on and wear in the same manner as a kimono. It is also used for garments you put on by pulling downward, like a T-shirt.

スーツ　　セーター　　Tシャツ　　トレーナー　　ブラウス　　ワイシャツ　　ワンピース

ヌエンさんはいつもTシャツをきています。
Nguyen-san always wears a T-shirt.

B　はく is used with something you put on by pulling it upward, like pants. If you wear clothes consisting of two pieces, e.g. a suit or bikini, the top piece represents the manner it is worn, and you use きる.

くつ　　ジーンズ　　ショート　　スカート　　スニーカー　　ソックス　　ハイヒール
　　　　ズボン　　　パンツ

C **かける** means "hang", so it is used for glasses, which in some sense "hang from the nose."

サングラス

めがね

山本さんはめがねをかけています。
Yamamoto-san wears glasses.

D **かぶる** means "cover a body". You use it for anything you put on your head. If you put your jacket on your head to avoid the rain, you would need to use かぶる, not きる.

ぼうし

E **する** "do" is a catch-all *wearing* verb; if きる, はく, かける, and かぶる are not appropriate, する is the verb to employ. You can use it for a belt, tattoo, bandage, makeup, and accessories, to name just a few possibilities.

イヤリング

とけい

ネックレス

ネクタイ

ゆびわ

10g　かかる　　"It takes time/expense"

No particles appear after the quantity expression with かかります.

大阪<ruby>大阪<rt>おおさか</rt></ruby>から東京まで何時間かかりますか。　　*How long does it take (to get) from Osaka to Tokyo?*
三時間かかります。　　*It takes 3 hours.*

ひようは｛どの／いくら｝ぐらいかかりますか。　　*Approximately how much does it cost?*

百二十ドルぐらいかかります。　　*It costs about $120.*

X 時間　"X hour(s)"						
一時間	二時間	三時間	四時間	五時間	六時間	七時間
八時間	九時間	十時間	十一時間	十二時間		

10h　NOUN ぐらい; NOUN ごろ (に)　　　"about/approximately ~"

ぐらい is used for an approximate quantity or duration.

ホノルルまで何時間 ⌇ぐらい⌇かかりますか。　　*Approximately how many hours*
　　　　　　　　　　　　　　　　　　　　　　　does it take (to get) to Honolulu?

ホノルルまで四時間半 ⌇ぐらい⌇です。　　　*It's about 4 and a half hours to Honolulu.*

あのコンピューターはいくら ⌇ぐらい⌇ですか。　*Approximately how much is that computer?*

あのコンピューターは二千ドル ⌇ぐらい⌇です。　*That computer is about $2,000.*

三か月 ⌇ぐらい⌇日本にいました。　　　　　　*I was in Japan for about 3 months.*

X か月 "X month(s)"					
一か月	二か月	三か月	四か月	五か月	六か月
七か月	八か月	九か月	十か月	十一か月	十二か月

ごろ is used for an approximate point in time; the temporal particle に is optional with ごろ.

今日の朝、八時ごろ (に) 大学に来ました。

I came to the university around 8 o'clock this morning.

いつも、十二時ごろ (に) ねます。

I always go to bed around 12 o'clock

ごろ cannot be used to indicate an approximate cost or temporal duration.

○　五百ドルぐらいかかりました。　　　*It cost about $500.*

×　五百ドル ⌇ごろ⌇かかりました。

○　十時間ぐらいねました。　　　　　　*I slept about 10 hours.*

×　十時間 ⌇ごろ⌇ねました。

Some Japanese people use ぐらいに for an approximate point in time, e.g.

パーティーは七時 ⌇ぐらいに⌇はじめましょう。　*Let's start the party around 7 o'clock.*

However, until you become comfortable with the appropriate usage of ぐらい (duration/amount) and ごろ (に) (point in time), avoid using ぐらいに to indicate a point in time.

練習問題

I.　たフォームを作りましょう。

1.	会う	14.	買う	27.	閉まる	40.	飲む
2.	開く	15.	かえす	28.	知る	41.	入る
3.	あそぶ	16.	帰る	29.	住む	42.	はく
4.	ある	17.	かかる	30.	する	43.	はじめる
5.	あるく	18.	書く	31.	すわる	44.	話す
6.	行く	19.	かす	32.	たつ	45.	ひく
7.	いただく	20.	かぶる	33.	食べる	46.	ふる
8.	いる	21.	かりる	34.	つかう	47.	待つ
9.	うたう	22.	がんばる	35.	つかれる	48.	見る
10.	おきる	23.	きえる	36.	つく	49.	もつ
11.	おくる	24.	きく	37.	作る	50.	よぶ
12.	おしえる	25.	来る	38.	とる	51.	読む
13.	およぐ	26.	しぬ	39.	ねる	52.	分かる

II.　インタビューしましょう。

例1

Q:　昨日、でんわしましたか。

A:　はい、しました。

　　(or) いいえ、しませんでした。

Q:　だれにでんわしましたか。

A:　きむらさんにでんわしました。

例2

Q:　昨日、テレビを見ましたか。

A:　はい、見ました。

　　(or) いいえ、見ませんでした。

Q:　だれかといっしょに見ましたか。

A:　いいえ、一人で見ました。

　　(or) はい、Ｘさんと見ました。

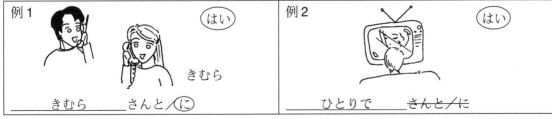

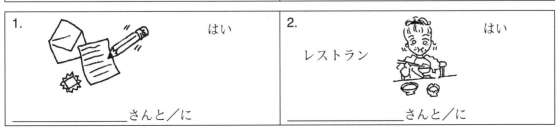

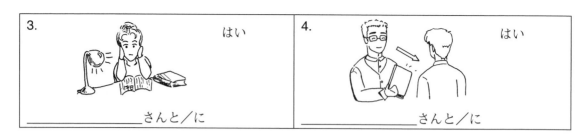

3. ＿＿＿＿＿＿＿さんと／に　　はい

4. ＿＿＿＿＿＿＿さんと／に　　はい

III.　ビンゴの時間です。「たフォーム＋ことがあります」をつかって、しつもんしてみましょう。

例

A:　Bさん、日本へ行ったことがありますか。

B:　はい、日本へ行ったことがあります。

　　(or) いいえ、日本へ行ったことはありません。

1. ＿＿＿＿＿＿＿さん

2. ＿＿＿＿＿＿＿さん

3. クラス　＿＿＿＿＿＿＿さん

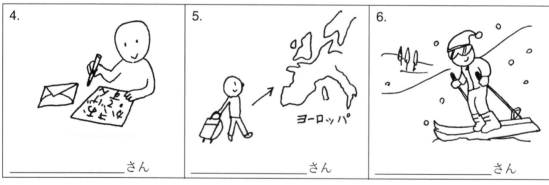

4. ＿＿＿＿＿＿＿さん

5. ＿＿＿＿＿＿＿さん

6. ＿＿＿＿＿＿＿さん

7. ＿＿＿＿＿＿＿さん

8. ＿＿＿＿＿＿＿さん

9. ＿＿＿＿＿＿＿さん

IV.　Looking at the pictures, answer the questions and fill in the blanks.

1.

お母さん、

私は月曜日から金曜日まで日本語のクラスがあります。日本語はおもしろいです。でも、ちょっとむずかしいです。

ジャック

だれが書きましたか。

_____

何を書きましたか。

_____

だれに書きましたか。

_____

　[　　　　　　]　は　[　　　　　　]　に　[　　　　　　]　を書きました。

2.

もしもし、きむらさんですか。

あ、ワトソンさん。こんにちは。

ワトソン　　きむら

何をしていますか。

_____

だれがしていますか。

_____

だれにしていますか。

_____

　[　　　　　　]　は　[　　　　　　]　に　[　　　　　　]　をしています。

3.

ホームズさん、本をかして下さい。

いいですよ。どうぞ。

ワトソン　　ホームズ

何をかしますか。

_____

だれがかしますか。

_____

だれにかしますか。

_____

　[　　　　　　]　は　[　　　　　　]　に　[　　　　　　]　をかします。

4.

ノート、ありがとうございました。

どういたしまして。

シン　　ワトソン

だれがかえしますか。

_____

だれにかえしますか。

_____

何をかえしますか。

_____

　[　　　　　　]　は　[　　　　　　]　に　[　　　　　　]　をかえします。

V.　パートナーと話しましょう。

例　Q:　きむらさんは何をきていますか。

　　A:　きむらさんはブラウスをきています。そして、スカートをはいています。

いのうえ　　　ドイル　　　きむら　　　すずき　　　シン　　　リン

VI.　ソンさんのへやはどうですか。ミラーさんのへやはどうですか。

例　A:　ソンさんのへやのテレビはついていますか。きえていますか。

　　B:　（ソンさんのへやのテレビは）ついています。

Student A

1.　You want to know the state of ソンさん's room now. Ask your partner about it and find out the current condition of the following items:
テレビ、まど、コンピューター、ドア、でんき

2.　Look at ミラーさん's room. Answer your partner's questions using 〜ています。

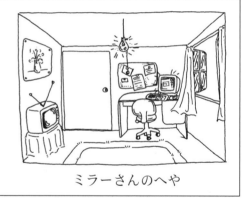

ミラーさんのへや

例　B:　ミラーさんのへやのテレビはついていますか。

　　A:　いいえ、（ミラーさんのへやのテレビは）ついていません。きえています。

Student B

1.　Look at ソンさん's room. Answer your partners questions using 〜ています。

2.　Now you want to know the state of ミラーさん's room now. Ask your partner about it and find out the current condition of the following items:
テレビ、まど、コンピューター、ドア、でんき

ソンさんのへや

VII. Look at the information below and find out if the places are open during the hours in the chart.

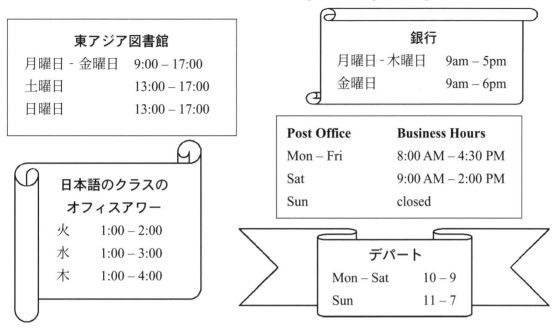

例1

Q: 月曜日のごご三時ごろ東アジア図書館は開いていますか。

A: はい、開いています。

例2

Q: 月曜日のごご三時ごろ日本語のオフィスは開いていますか。

A: いいえ、開いていません。(or) いいえ、閉まっています。

	東アジア図書館	銀行	ゆうびんきょく	日本語のオフィス	デパート
月曜日ごご三時	例1 開いています			例2 閉まっています	
火曜日ごぜん七時					
水曜日ごぜん十一時					
木曜日ごご二時					
金曜日ごご七時					
土曜日ごぜん八時					
日曜日ごご六時					

VIII.　The following chart provides the time and fare between two stations on a しんかんせん.
パートナーに聞きましょう。

例^{れい}1

Q:　東京から名古屋^{な ご や}までどのぐらいかかりますか。

A:　一時間四十分かかります。

例2

Q:　東京から名古屋^{な ご や}までいくらぐらいかかりますか。

A:　一まん千円ぐらいかかります。

	東京	名古屋^{な ご や}	京都^{きょうと}	新大阪^{しんおおさか}	広島^{ひろしま}	博多^{はか た}
東京		100 分	138 分	145 分	236 分	298 分
		11,340 円	14,190 円	14,720 円	18,050 円	21,720 円
名古屋^{な ご や}	100 分		36 分	52 分	134 分	196 分
	11,340 円		5,900 円	6,640 円	14,550 円	18,860 円
京都^{きょう と}	138 分	36 分		14 分	96 分	158 分
	14,190 円	5,900 円		3,040 円	11,760 円	16,390 円
新大阪^{しんおおさか}	145 分	52 分	14 分		80 分	142 分
	14,720 円	6,640 円	3,040 円		10,710 円	15,560 円
広島^{ひろしま}	236 分	134 分	96 分	80 分		61 分
	18,050 円	14,550 円	11,760 円	10,710 円		9,310 円
博多^{はか た}	298 分	196 分	158 分	142 分	61 分	
	21,720 円	18,860 円	16,390 円	15,560 円	9,310 円	

しんかんせんのえき

IX.　読みましょう。

私は２０００年から２００２年まで二年日本に住んでいました。

日本の銀行は九時から三時まで開いていました。ゆうびんきょくは九時から五時まででした。土曜日には、大きいゆうびんきょくは開いていましたが、小さいゆうびんきょくは閉まっていました。

私は今、アメリカに住んでいます。アメリカの銀行は五時まで開いています。そして、私の家のちかくのゆうびんきょくはごぜん八時半から開いています。土曜日も九時から十二時まで開いています。

私は高校ですうがくをおしえています。九時から四時まで高校でしごとをしていますが、ゆうびんきょくや銀行などへ行くことができます。ですから、アメリカの銀行やゆうびんきょくはとてもべんりです。

〇 ですか。×ですか。

1.　（　　）この人は日本に住んだことはありません。
2.　（　　）日本の銀行は九時から五時まででした。
3.　（　　）日本の小さいゆうびんきょくは土曜日には開いていませんでした。
4.　（　　）今日は木曜日です。今ごぜん八時四十分です。この人の家のちかくのゆうびんきょくは今、開いています。
5.　（　　）この人は今、高校生です。

新しい漢字

開く	朝	多い	漢字	銀行	閉まる	知る
住む	手紙	図書館	前			

新しい使い方
　　<ruby>使<rt>つか</rt></ruby>い<ruby>方<rt>かた</rt></ruby>

<ruby>学校<rt>がっこう</rt></ruby>	<ruby>今年<rt>ことし</rt></ruby>	<ruby>中山<rt>なかやま</rt></ruby>	<ruby>早川<rt>はやかわ</rt></ruby>	<ruby>東<rt>ひがし</rt></ruby> アジア　<ruby>分<rt>わ</rt></ruby>かる

Radicals: 国がまえ・門がまえ
　　　　　　　<ruby>国<rt>くに</rt></ruby>がまえ・<ruby>門<rt>もん</rt></ruby>がまえ

囗 This type of radical is called かまえ "enclosure". 囗 (in 国, 図) belongs to this group and is called 国がまえ (国 "country" + かまえ; like なべふた ＞ なべぶた, かまえ becomes がまえ by sequential voicing, cf. 第十一課, **11f**). The meaning of a 漢字 with this radical is generally associated with some institution.

Another かまえ to learn in this lesson is 門 (in 開・閉), which is called 門がまえ. 門 by itself is a 漢字 and means "gate". Obviously, it is reasonable for a gate to appear in 開く and 閉まる.

囗開 あ (く)	丨	ｱ	尸	尸	尸	門	門	門	門	閂
	閈	開								
	to open									
朝 あさ	一	十	十	古	吉	直	卓	朝	朝	
	朝	朝								
	morning: (this 漢字 contains both the sun 日 and the moon 月.)									
多 おお (い)	ノ	ク	タ	タ	多	多				
	abundant									
学 ガク・ガッ	丶	ﾞ	ッ	ﾂﾞ	兴	学	学	学		
	study: 学生 student (studying person), 留学生 foreign student, 大学 college, 学校 school									
漢 カン	丶	氵	氵	氵	汁	汁	汁	汁	漢	
	漢	漢	漢							
	Han dynasty: 漢字 kanji									

字	丶	丷	宀	宇	宁	字			
ジ	*letter:* 漢字 *kanji*								

銀	ノ	八	个	牟	牟	牟	金	金	釒	釒
ギン	釒	鈤	銀	銀						
	silver: 銀行 *bank (the place where silver goes),* 金 *gold is included in this* 漢字.									

行	ノ	ク	彳	彳	行	行			
コウ・い (く)	*to go:* 銀行 *bank (the place where silver goes)*								

■閉	丨	冂	冂	門	門	門	門	門	閂	閉
し(まる)	閉									
	to close									

知	ノ	𠂉	匕	矢	矢	知	知	知	
し(る)	*to know*								

住	ノ	亻	亻	住	住	住	住		
す(む)	*to live*								

手	一	二	三	手					
て	*hand:* 上手 (じょうず) *good at,* 下手 (へた) *bad at,* 手紙 *letter*								

紙	乙	幺	幺	糸	糸	糸	紵	紅	紙	紙
かみ・がみ	*paper:* 手紙 *letter*									

■図	丨	冂	冂	冈	図	図			
ト	*to plan / a diagram:* 図書館 *library (a mansion to keep texts)*								

書	フ	ラ	ヲ	圭	圭	聿	書	書	書
ショ・か (く)	*to write / a text:* 図書館 *library (a mansion to keep texts)*								

館	ノ	人	⺀	今	今	今	負	食	食ˋ	食ˋ
カン	飣	飣	館	館	館	館				
	mansion: 図書館 library (a mansion to keep texts)									
東	一	厂	戸	戸	車	車	東	東		
トウ・ひがし	east: 東京 Tokyo (east capital), 東アジア East Asia									
前	丶	丷	丷	产	广	前	前	前	前	
まえ	in front of									
分	ノ	八	分	分						
フン・プン・わ（かる）	to divide: 一分（いっぷん）one minute, 二分（にふん）two minutes, 分かる to under-stand									

漢字の復習

I. 　　読みましょう。

1. この大学の図書館はとても古いです。
2. 母は中国に住んでいます。
3. 弟の学校は小さいです。
4. 銀行へ行きましたが、閉まっていました。
5. 小山さんのお父さんは英語が上手です。

II. Insert the specified 漢字 in the center box and identify two or three words, reading either top-down or left to right.

1. Write 行.

ま	銀	作
古		く
小	ち	東

2. Write 書.

時	母	け
図		館
京	く	手

3. Write 手.

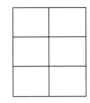

見	上	帰
下		紙
中	広	間

4. Write 学.

小	大	日
英		校
中	生	字

5. Write 中.

上	前	男
多		国
好	間	下

新しい語彙
あたら ごい

ⓘ : Intransive   ⓣ : Transitive   Ⓘ : Irregular verb

開く あ	ⓦ ⓘ	to open
いくら		how much
いそがしい	ⓘ	busy
イヤリング		earrings
インタビュー (する)		interview
多い おお	ⓘ	many, plenty
おくる	ⓦ ⓣ	to send
オフィスアワー		office hours
かかる	ⓦ ⓘ	to take (time, expense)
かける	ⓡ ⓣ	to wear (glasses)
学校 がっこう		school
かぶる	ⓦ ⓣ	to wear (hat, cap)
漢字 かんじ		Chinese characters
きえる	ⓡ ⓘ	to turn off

きる	ⓡ ⓣ	to wear (dress, shirt, suit)
サングラス		sunglasses
ジーンズ		jeans
時間 じかん		time
閉まる し	ⓦ ⓘ	to close
ショートパンツ		shorts
知る し	ⓦ ⓣ	to get to know
スーツ		suit
スカート		skirt
スニーカー		sneakers
ズボン		trousers, pants
住む す	ⓦ ⓘ	to start living somewhere

する　　　Ⅰ t		to wear (accessory)
すもう		Sumo wrestling
すわる　　ウ i		to sit down
セーター		sweater
ソックス		socks
たつ　　　ウ i		to stand up
つく　　　ウ i		to turn on
でんき		electricity, electric light
でんわ（する）		telephone
ドア		door
トレーナー		sweatshirt
ネクタイ		necktie
ネックレス		necklace
パートナー		partner
ハイヒール		high heeled shoes
はく　　　ウ t		to wear (shoes, socks, trousers)

はじめて		for the first time
はじめる　ル t		to start
ひよう		expense
ブラウス		blouse
プレゼント（する）		present
ぼうし		hat, cap
ほか		other
まど		window
めがね		glasses
ゆびわ		ring
よく		well
ワイシャツ		dress shirt
分かる　　ウ t		to understand
ワンピース		dress

なまえ

ジャック	Jack
しんおおさか（新大阪）	Shin-Osaka
東アジア	East Asia
ホノルル	Honolulu
中山	Nakayama

なごや（名古屋）	Nagoya
ヌエン	Nguyen
はかた（博多）	Hakata
ひろしま（広島）	Hiroshima
ヨーロッパ	Europe

ジャパンクラブで
At the Japan Club

コールさんの前にすわっている人はだれですか
Who's the person sitting in front of Cole-san?

会話

かいわ

1　ミラー　：ソンさん、あの、めがねをかけている女の人はだれですか。

Son-san, who's that woman wearing glasses?

　　ソン　：あの人はコールさんです。コールさんは英文学部の大学院生です。

えいぶんがくぶ　だいがくいんせい

That's Cole-san. She's a graduate student in the English Literature Department.

2　ミラー　：そうですか。静かな人ですね。

しず

Oh. She's a (pretty) quiet person, isn't she?

　　ソン　：ええ。コールさんはエッセーを書くのが上手です。時々、大学の新聞に
エッセーを書いています。

ときどき　しんぶん

*Yes. Cole-san is good at writing essays. From time to time, she writes (is writing)
essays for the University newspaper.*

3　ミラー　：へえ、すごいですね。コールさんの前にすわっている人はだれですか。

Really? That's great. Who's the person sitting in front of Cole-san?

4　ソン　：早川さんです。早川さんはにっけいアメリカ人です。せいぶつ学部の二年生
です。

にねんせい

*That's Hayakawa-san. Hayakawa-san is Japanese-American and a sophomore (2nd
year) in the Biology Department.*

5　ミラー　：そうですか。あの、音楽を聞いている人はだれですか。

おんがく　き

Oh. And who's that person listening to the music?

6　ソン　：あの人はラウールさんです。ラウールさんとキムさんはバスケットボールが
上手です。大学のチームのせんしゅです。

*That's Raoul-san. He and Kim-san are good at basketball. They're players on our
college team.*

7　ミラー　：へえ。キムさんはどの人ですか。

Really? Which one is Kim-san?

8　ソン　：キムさんは、ラウールさんの後ろにすわっている人です。

うし

He's the person who is sitting behind Raoul-san.

9　ミラー　：ああ、目が大きくて、背が高い男の人ですか。

せ

Oh, that tall guy with large eyes?

ソン　　：ええ、そうです。
Yes, that's right.

10　ミラー：ソンさんもバスケットボールができますか。
Son-san, can you play basketball too?

ソン　　：ええ、できますが、あまり上手じゃありません。ミラーさんは。
Yes, I can, but I'm not very good at it. What about you, Miller-san?

ミラー：私もだめです。
I'm no good either.

使い方

1　文学 means "literature". The 漢字「英」 is frequently used to refer to England in Sino-Japanese compound words, e.g. 英語, 英国 "Great Britain".

学 "study" + 部 "section" means an "academic department". When the preceding word ends with 学, the second 学 is normally omitted (cf. Appendix B for a list of college majors).

音楽	＋	学部　→	音楽学部
文学	＋	学部　→	文学部
せいぶつ学	＋	学部　→	せいぶつ学部

2　X に Y を書く means either "write Y to X" or "write Y for X", depending on the context. Here, the natural interpretation is that コールさん writes essays **for** the university newspaper.

4　にっけい is written in 漢字 as 日系, which consists of 日 "Japan" and 系 "lineage".

かん国系アメリカ人	Korean-American
中国系アメリカ人	Chinese-American
ドイツ系アメリカ人	German-American
メキシコ系アメリカ人	Mexican-American
ユダヤ系アメリカ人	Jewish-American

10　だめ is a な -adjective and used to express a broad range of negative judgments, e.g. *no good, useless, hopeless,* etc. In this conversation, ミラーさん uses it to mean that he is not skillful at playing basketball.

文法
<ruby>文法<rt>ぶんぽう</rt></ruby>

11a　Noun Modification by Verbs
11b　Past Tense of い-Adjectives
11c　Past Tense of です
11d　Noun Modification by Adjectives
11e　Object Marker が
11f　Sequential Voicing

11a　Noun Modification by Verbs

So far, we have learned that there are three ways to modify nouns:

(i)　NOUN + の + NOUN (第二課)

先生のお<ruby>名前<rt>な まえ</rt></ruby>	*Sensei's name*
アメリカの車	*American car*
日本人の留学生	*foreign student from Japan*
学生の早川さん	*Hayakawa-san, who is a student*

(ii)　い-ADJECTIVE (Plain Form) + NOUN (第七課)

おもしろい手紙	*interesting letter*
おいしいお茶	*delicious tea*
広いへや	*spacious room*

(iii)　な-ADJECTIVE + な + NOUN (第七課)

<ruby>元気<rt>げん き</rt></ruby>な女の人	*energetic woman*
きれいなこうえん	*beautiful park*
静かな高校生	*quiet high-school student*

Like in English, e.g. *the park (that) I like*, nouns in Japanese can also be modified by a clause. Unlike English, however, the modifying clause in Japanese **always precedes** the noun being modified.

Modifier

NOUN + の
い-ADJECTIVE (Plain フォーム)
な-ADJECTIVE + な
CLAUSE (Plain フォーム)

+　　NOUN

Note that the predicate of the modifying clause (or *relative clause*) must be in a Plain フォーム, e.g. the Dictionary, た, ない, or なかったフォーム, cf. 第十課, **10a**, rather than in a Polite フォーム, e.g. 〜ます, 〜ました, 〜ません, 〜ませんでした, cf. 第六課, **6b**. The use of a Polite フォーム makes the speech polite to the addressee. When a sentence contains a noun-modification clause, it includes more than one predicate. In order to show politeness, you use the Polite フォーム of only the sentence-final predicate (i.e. the main-clause predicate). If you use the Polite フォーム of the relative-clause predicate, your speech will usually become extremely awkward. (This rule also applies to relative clauses with an adjective or a nominal predicate, cf. **11d**.)

Let us now practice noun modification with verbs.

A When the modified (head) noun is identical to the *subject* of the relative clause.

You say:

(1a) That's a bus.

If the bus is visible, (1a) is not very informative. What you want to convey is:

(1b) The bus goes to Yosemite.

So, you combine (1a) and (1b) to make (1c).

Head Noun   Relative Clause
(1c) That's a bus which goes to Yosemite.

The Japanese counterparts of (1a)-(1b) are:

(1d)　　あれはバスです。　　　　　　　　*That over there is a bus.*
(1e)　　（あの）バスはヨセミテへ行きます。　*The bus goes to Yosemite.*

Like English examples (1a)-(1b), the main clause is (1d); (1e) is to modify the バス. Now we combine them: because these two sentences have the same noun (バス), the second バス is deleted. If you did not delete it, the sentence would sound like the ungrammatical English sentence, *That's the bus that the bus goes to Yosemite.*

あれは バス です。　　　　　　　　Main Clause

↑

バスは ヨセミテへ行きます　　　　　Modifying Clause

In order to maintain the politeness level of your speech, you keep the main-clause predicate in its Polite フォーム (です). Then, in order to make your utterance natural, you need to convert the modifying-clause predicate (行きます) to its Plain フォーム. Because 行きます is non-past affirmative, its Plain フォーム is the Dictionary フォーム, 行く.

あれは バス です。 　　　　　　　　　Main Clause

Ø ヨセミテへ 行きます 行く 　　　Modifying Clause

Not: 　　　× あれはヨセミテへ行きますバスです。

The Japanese relative clause always precedes the head noun:

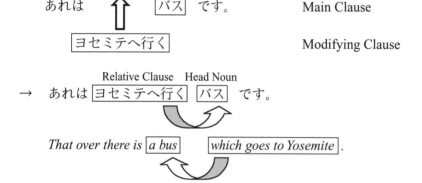

あれは 　　　 バス です。 　　　Main Clause

ヨセミテへ行く 　　　　　　　　　Modifying Clause

　　　　　　　　　Relative Clause　　Head Noun
→ 　あれは ヨセミテへ行く バス です。

That over there is a bus 　who goes to Yosemite.

(2) 　あの人は留学生です。 　　　　　　*That person over there is a foreign student.*
　　（あの）留学生はタイから来ました。 　*The foreign student came from Thailand.*

(a) 　Delete the noun that is identical to the head noun.

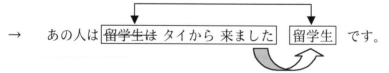

→ 　あの人は 留学生は タイから 来ました 留学生 です。

(b) 　Change the predicate of the modifying clause to its Plain フォーム.

→ 　あの人は タイから 来ました 来た 留学生 です。

→ 　あの人は タイから来た 留学生 です。

That person over there is a foreign student 　who came from Thailand.

(3) コールさんは大学院生です。　　　　　　*Cole-san is a graduate student.*

　　 (その) 大学院生はテレビを見ません。　　*The graduate student doesn't watch TV.*

　　→　　コールさんは テレビを見ない 　大学院生 　です。

Cole-san is a graduate student 　 who doesn't watch TV .

(4) 中山さんは大学生です。

Nakayama-san is an undergraduate student.

　　(その) 学生は昨日クラスに来ませんでした。

The student didn't come to class yesterday.

　　→　　中山さんは昨日クラスに来なかった学生です。

Nakayama-san is the student who didn't come to class yesterday.

(5) キムさんは男の人です。

　　(その) 男の人はラウールさんの後ろにすわっています。

　　→　　キムさんはラウールさんの後ろにすわっている男の人です。

(6) ヤングさんは学生です。

　　(その) 学生は日本語ができます。

　　→　　ヤングさんは日本語ができる学生です。

(7) ミラーさんは学生です。

　　(その) 学生はふゆやすみに日本へ行きます。

　　→　　ミラーさんはふゆやすみに日本へ行く学生です。

(8) 早川さんは学生です。

　　(その) 学生はコールさんの前にいます。

　　→　　早川さんはコールさんの前にいる学生です。

(9) 図書館はビルです。

　　(その) ビルはゆうびんきょくのとなりにあります。

　　→　　図書館はゆうびんきょくのとなりにあるビルです。

(10) 安川さんは学生です。

　　(その) 学生は昨日オフィスへ来ました。

　　→　　安川さんは昨日オフィスへ来た学生です。

B | When the modified (head) noun is identical to the *object* of the relative clause.

(11a)　これはビデオです。

This is a video.

(11b)　私はらいしゅう（この）ビデオをかります。

I'm going to rent the video next week.

Like the previous case, you need to delete the noun that is identical with the head; otherwise, it would sound like *This is the video that I'm going to rent the video next week.*

(11c)　→　これは 私がらいしゅう　ビデオを かります ビデオ です。

Note that in (11b) 私 appears with the topic marker は, whereas in (11c) it appears with the subject marker が. This is because being a modifier of a noun of the main clause, the relative clause is "embedded" in that noun phrase. In principle, the topic, about which the rest of the sentence is concerned, can appear only in the main clause, not in an embedded clause or subordinate clause (cf. 第十四課, **14b**). Thus, you need to convert は to が when the clause modifies a noun.

(11d)　→　これは 私がらいしゅう かります かりる ビデオ です。

This is the video that I'm going to rent next week.

(12) これはじしょです。

This is a dictionary.

私はいつも（この）じしょをつかっています。

I always use the dictionary.

(a)　Delete the noun that is identical with the head noun.

→　これは 私がいつも じしょを つかっています じしょ です。

(b)　Change the predicate of the modifying clause to its Plain フォーム.

→　これは 私がいつも つかっています つかっている じしょ です。

This is the dictionary that I use regularly.

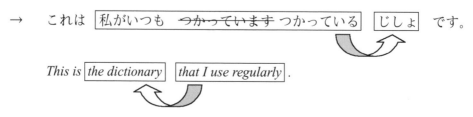

(13) これはりょうりです。

This is a dish (cooking).

私は（この）りょうりをかんがえました。

(Lit.) I thought of the dish. /I invented the dish.

→　これは私がかんがえたりょうりです。

　　This is the dish that I invented.

(14) これはえいがです。

私は（この）えいがを見ませんでした。

→　これは私が見なかったえいがです。

11b　Past Tense of い -Adjectives

In English, adjectives do not conjugate because they occur with the verb *be*, which conjugates: e.g. *It is interesting /It <u>was</u> interesting*. In Japanese, the い -adjectives can occur without です, and they do conjugate to show the affirmative-negative opposition and different tenses. The Dictionary フォーム (the plain non-past form) of い -adjectives ends with い, e.g. 明るい, 暗い, 新しい, 多い —which we have studied already.

To make the plain past form (i.e. たフォーム) of an い -adjective, you drop い and add 〜かった. Note that いい exhibits irregularity, cf. (6).

(1)　むずかしい　→　むずかしかった
　　昨日のテストはむずかしかったです。
　　Yesterday's test was difficult.

(2)　あつい　　→　あつかった
　　ハワイはあつかったです。
　　It was hot in Hawaii.

(3)　かたい　　→　かたかった
　　あのスーパーで買ったにくはかたかったです。
　　The meat I bought at that supermarket was tough.

(4)　つまらない　→　つまらなかった
　　昨日読んだしょうせつはつまらなかったです。
　　The novel I read yesterday was boring.

(5) すずしい → すずしかった

アラスカはすずしかったです。

It was cool in Alaska.

(6) いい → よかった

あのレストランのサービスは よかった です。

That restaurant's service was good.

The past negative form of an い -adjective is 〜くなかった (です) or 〜くありませんでした. 〜くありませんでした is more formal than 〜くなかった (です).

(7) カナダはあまりさむくなかったです。

It wasn't too cold in Canada.

(8) しけんはむずかしくありませんでした。

The test / exam was not difficult.

When two or more adjectives are conjoined, only the final one conjugates to show the tense of the sentence; the preceding one takes the てフォーム.

(9) 昨日食べたピザはやわらかくて、おいしくありませんでした。

(Lit.) The pizza I ate yesterday was soft and not delicious.

The pizza I ate yesterday was soft and didn't taste good.

Stem			さむ -	い -
Before Noun			さむ - い	い - い
Plain	Affirmative	Non-past	さむ - い	い - い
		Past	さむ - かった	よ - かった
	Negative	Non-past	さむ - く - ない	よ - く - ない
		Past	さむ - く - なかった	よ - く - なかった
Polite	Affirmative	Non-past	さむ - い - です	い - い - です
		Past	さむ - かった - です	よ - かった - です
	Negative	Non-past	さむ - く - ない - です さむ - く - ありません	よ - く - ない-です よ - く - ありません
		Past	さむ - く - なかった - です さむ - く - ありませんでした	よ - く - なかった - です よ - く - ありませんでした

もっと知りたい人へ
FOR THOSE WITH BURNING CURIOSITY

When multiple adjectives are used, the non-final negative adjective becomes 〜くなくて (い -adjectives) or 〜じゃなくて (な -adjectives).

ソンさんが作ったケーキはあまり あまくなくて 、おいしかったです。

The cake that Son-san made was not very sweet and was delicious.

タホは さむくなくて 、たのしかったです。

Tahoe was not cold and was fun / enjoyable.

しけんは かんたんじゃなくて 、たいへんでした。

(Lit.) The exam was not easy and was tough.

The exam was not easy, so it was tough / painful / etc.

古川さんのアパートは 静かじゃなくて 、よくありませんでした。

Furukawa-san's apartment was not quiet, and was not good.

11c　Past Tense of です

The following table shows various forms of です.

Plain	Affirmative	Non-past	だ	六ドルだ	*It's $6.*
		Past	だった	六ドルだった	*It was $6.*
	Negative	Non-past	じゃ - ない	六ドルじゃない	*It's not $6.*
		Past	じゃ - なかった	六ドルじゃなかった	*It was not $6.*
Polite	Affirmative	Non-past	です	六ドルです	*It's $6.*
		Past	でした	六ドルでした	*It was $6.*
	Negative	Non-past	じゃ - ない - です じゃ - ありません	六ドルじゃないです 六ドルじゃありません	*It's not $6.*
		Past	じゃ - なかった - です じゃ - ありません - でした	六ドルじゃなかったです 六ドルじゃありませんでした	*It was not $6.*

早川さんのせんもんは英文学じゃないです。

Hayakawa-san's major isn't English literature.

プレゼントはクッキーでした。

The gift was cookies.

Like English adjectives, な -adjectives occur with です:

Stem			きれい　　　べんり	
Before Noun			きれい - な	べんり - な
Plain	Affirmative	Non-past	きれい - だ	べんり - だ
		Past	きれい - だった	べんり - だった
	Negative	Non-past	きれい - じゃ - ない	べんり - じゃ - ない
		Past	きれい - じゃ - なかった	べんり - じゃ - なかった
Polite	Affirmative	Non-past	きれい - です	べんり - です
		Past	きれい - でした	べんり - でした
	Negative	Non-past	きれい - じゃ - ない - です きれい - じゃ - ありません	べんり - じゃ - ない - です べんり - じゃ - ありません
		Past	きれい - じゃ - なかった - です きれい - じゃ - ありません - でした	べんり - じゃ - なかった - です べんり - じゃ - ありません - でした

中山さんはとても元気でした。

Nakayama-san was very cheerful.

図書館は、今日は静かじゃありませんでした。

The library wasn't quiet today.

昨日行ったレストランはあまりきれいじゃなかったです。

The restaurant I went to yesterday wasn't very clean.

When you conjoin two or more い - and/or な -adjectives, only the final one conjugates to show the tense of the sentence.

バスはおそくてとてもふべん です 。　　　*The bus* is *slow and very inconvenient.*

バスはおそくてとてもふべん でした 。　　*The bus* was *slow and very inconvenient.*

図書館はきれいで 明るいです 。　　　*The library* is *clean and bright.*

図書館はきれいで 明るかったです 。　　*The library* was *clean and bright.*

11d   Noun Modification by Adjectives

In both English and Japanese, most adjectives can serve in two ways: (i) as a modifier, occurring before the noun and (ii) as a predicate:

(i)   大きい まど　　　　　　*a* large *window*　　　　Modifier

(ii)   そのまどは 大きい です。　　*The window is* large .　　Predicate

Generally, adjectives maintain the same meaning regardless of their positions. (There are, however, some exceptions, e.g. *the late professor* vs. *The professor was late*.) The predicative use of an adjective can also modify a noun when it appears in a relative clause, e.g. *That is the professor who was late.*

Like in noun modification with verbs, the noun in the relative clause that is identical to the head noun must be deleted. Also, when an い-adjective appears as a relative-clause predicate, its Plain フォーム must be used.

(1)　ルイスさんは学生です。　　　　　　　*Lewis-san is a student.*
　　（その）学生は背が高いです。　　　　*The student is tall.*

　　(a)　Delete the noun that is identical to the head noun.

　　→　　ルイスさんは ┃学生は 背が高いです┃ ┃学生┃ です。

　　(b)　Change the predicate of the modifying clause to its Plain フォーム.

　　→　　ルイスさんは ┃背が 高いです 高い┃ ┃学生┃ です。

　　　　Lewis-san is a student who is tall.

(2)　これはおかしです。　　　　　　　　*This is a snack.*
　　（この）おかしはあまくないです。　　*The snack is not sweet.*

　　→　　これは┃あまくない┃ ┃おかし┃ です。　*This is a snack that is not sweet.*

(3)　私はせんしゅう、ビデオをたくさん見ました。
　　I watched a lot of videos last week.
　　これはおもしろかったビデオです。
　　These are videos that were amusing.
　　これはおもしろくなかったビデオです。
　　These are videos that were not amusing.

You can use multiple adjectives in a relative clause:

山下さんは目が大きくてやさしい人です。

(Lit.) Yamashita-san is a person who has big eyes and is kind.

Yamashita-san is a kind person with big eyes.

コールさんは静かでまじめな大学院生です。

(Lit.) Cole-san is a graduate student who is quiet and serious.

Cole-san is a quiet and serious graduate student.

もっともっと知りたい人へ
FOR THOSE WITH EVEN MORE CURIOSITY

Note that sentences like あれはおいしいおかしです can be structurally ambiguous between the modifier and predicate constructions.

Modifier:　　あれは　[おいしい　おかし]　です
　　　　　　　　　　　　ADJECTIVE　　NOUN

Predicate:　　あれはおかしです。

　　　　　　（あの）おかしはおいしいです。

→　　あれは　~~おかしは~~ おいしいです　　おかし　　です。

→　　あれは　~~おいしいです~~ おいしい　　おかし　　です。

→　　あれは　おいしい　　　　　おかし　　です。
　　　　　　　REL. CLAUSE　　　HEAD NOUN

11e Object Marker が

が　The great majority of verbs take を as the direct object marker, whereas a small number of verbs requires に, e.g. ともだち に 会います. Recall that in 第九課 we studied な-adjectives that require が-marked objects, e.g. 私は音楽が好きです. Some verbs behave like な-adjectives and take が-marked objects. You have already learned two such verbs, namely 分かる and できる.

(1)　先生、この漢字 が 分かりません。
Sensei, I don't understand this kanji.

(2)　ラウールさんはうんてん が できます。
Raoul-san can drive (do driving).

(3)　ヌエンさんはダンス が できます。
Nguyen-san can dance.

Sentences (2) and (3) are equivalent to ラウールさんはうんてんをすることができます and ヌエンさんはダンスをすることができます, respectively. Normally, the object of できる is a verbal noun or a noun that connotes some action/activity. However, when a noun is clearly associated with some verb(s), regular nouns can appear as the object of できる.

私はスペイン語を話すことができます。
I can speak Spanish.
私はスペイン語ができます。
I can speak/read/understand Spanish.

11f Sequential Voicing

The character 々 in 時々 indicates that the preceding 漢字 is repeated, i.e. 時時. However, with 時々, the first 漢字 is pronounced as とき, but the second one as どき. That is, the first consonant of the second 時 acquires voicing ([t] → [d]). This phenomenon is called *sequential voicing*. Sequential voicing tightens the bond between the two parts of a word. Another example of sequential voicing is 手紙, which consists of two parts: 手 "hand" and 紙 "paper". When 紙 is used by itself, it is pronounced as かみ, but when it is part of the complex word 手紙, かみ becomes がみ ([k] → [g]). Although sequential voicing is very common, it does not occur in all compound words, so you have to remember when it occurs and when it does not. Here are some more examples of sequential voicing:

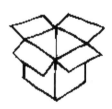

本 *book*	+	はこ *box*	→	本ばこ *book case*
大 (きい) *big*	+	とおり *street*	→	大どおり *boulevard*
人 *person*	+	人 *person*	→	人々 *people*
すし *sushi*	+	す *vinegar*	→	すしず *sushi vinegar*

The sound [ji] is usually represented by the letter じ, but when ち becomes [ji] because of sequential voicing, ぢ is used.

そこ *bottom*	+	ちから *power*	→	そこ ぢ から *latent power*
はな *nose*	+	ち *blood*	→	はな ぢ *nose blood*
わる (い) *bad*	+	ちえ *intelligence*	→	わる ぢ え *cunning*

Similarly, [zu] is usually written as ず, but when つ becomes [zu], づ is used.

こ (小) *small* ＋ つつみ *package* → こ|づ|つみ *parcel*

まつば *pine leaf* ＋ つえ *cane* → まつば|づ|え *crutch*

みか (く三日) *3rd day* ＋ つき (月) *moon*

→ みか|づ|き (三日月) *crescent moon (3rd-day moon)*

れんしゅうもんだい
練習問題

I. どの人ですか。いいましょう。

例 山下さんはコーヒーを飲んでいる人です。

1. 小山さんは＿＿＿＿＿＿＿＿＿＿＿＿＿＿＿＿＿＿＿＿＿＿＿＿人です。

2. 早川さんは＿＿＿＿＿＿＿＿＿＿＿＿＿＿＿＿＿＿＿＿＿＿＿＿人です。

3. 古川さんは＿＿＿＿＿＿＿＿＿＿＿＿＿＿＿＿＿＿＿＿＿＿＿＿人です。

4. 安川さんは＿＿＿＿＿＿＿＿＿＿＿＿＿＿＿＿＿＿＿＿＿＿＿＿人です。

5. 中山さんは＿＿＿＿＿＿＿＿＿＿＿＿＿＿＿＿＿＿＿＿＿＿＿＿人です。

6. 山本さんは＿＿＿＿＿＿＿＿＿＿＿＿＿＿＿＿＿＿＿＿＿＿＿＿人です。

7. ささきさんは＿＿＿＿＿＿＿＿＿＿＿＿＿＿＿＿＿＿＿＿＿＿＿＿人です。

II.　シュミットさんとルイスさんとリンさんはAさんのともだちです。ジョーンズ さんと
　　　ブラウンさんとドイルさんはBさんのともだちです。どんな人ですか。パートナーに聞
　　　きましょう。

例

Q：　パクさんはどんな人ですか。

A：　パクさんはまいにちテニスをしている人です。

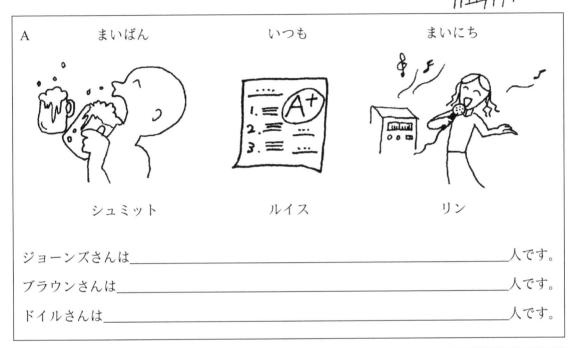

ジョーンズさんは＿＿＿＿＿＿＿＿＿＿＿＿＿＿＿＿＿＿＿＿＿人です。

ブラウンさんは＿＿＿＿＿＿＿＿＿＿＿＿＿＿＿＿＿＿＿＿＿人です。

ドイルさんは＿＿＿＿＿＿＿＿＿＿＿＿＿＿＿＿＿＿＿＿＿人です。

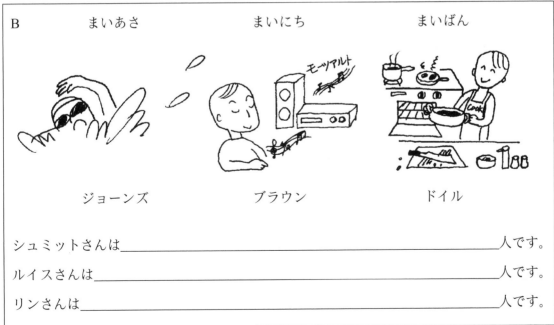

シュミットさんは＿＿＿＿＿＿＿＿＿＿＿＿＿＿＿＿＿＿＿＿＿人です。

ルイスさんは＿＿＿＿＿＿＿＿＿＿＿＿＿＿＿＿＿＿＿＿＿人です。

リンさんは＿＿＿＿＿＿＿＿＿＿＿＿＿＿＿＿＿＿＿＿＿人です。

III.　Paraphrase each sentence by using the noun modification construction.

例　早川さんは土曜日にこのえいがを見ました。

　　→　　これは<u>早川さんが土曜日に見たえいが</u>です。

1.　コールさんは昨日、このクッキーを作りました。

　　→　これは＿＿＿＿＿＿＿＿＿＿＿＿＿＿＿＿＿

　＿＿＿＿＿＿＿＿＿＿＿＿＿＿＿＿＿＿＿＿＿＿＿＿。

2.　私は今晩このピザを食べます。

　　→　これは＿＿＿＿＿＿＿＿＿＿＿＿＿＿＿＿＿

＿＿＿＿＿＿＿＿＿＿＿＿＿＿＿＿＿＿＿＿＿＿＿＿。

3.　キムさんはまいにちこのじしょをつかっています。

　　→　これは＿＿＿＿＿＿＿＿＿＿＿＿＿＿＿＿＿

　＿＿＿＿＿＿＿＿＿＿＿＿＿＿＿＿＿＿＿＿＿＿＿＿。

4.　ラウールさんは明日このビデオを見ます。

　　→　これは＿＿＿＿＿＿＿＿＿＿＿＿＿＿＿＿＿

＿＿＿＿＿＿＿＿＿＿＿＿＿＿＿＿＿＿＿＿＿＿＿＿。

5.　コールさんはこのエッセーを書きました。

　　→　これは＿＿＿＿＿＿＿＿＿＿＿＿＿＿＿＿＿

　＿＿＿＿＿＿＿＿＿＿＿＿＿＿＿＿＿＿＿＿＿＿＿＿。

IV.　日本語のクラスでパーティーをします。えを見ていいましょう。

例　ヤングさんは何をする人ですか。

ヤング　　　　きむら　　　　安川　　　　中山　　　　ブラウン

ヤング	ヤングさんは手紙を書く人です。
きむら	
安川	
中山	
ブラウン	

V.　何をした人ですか。パートナーに聞きましょう。

• 「ハムレット」を書きました。	• ロックをうたいました。
• 月へ行きました。	• ミッキーマウスのえいがを作りました。
• ふねでアメリカへ来ました。	• ゲティスバーグ (Gettysburg) で話しました。
• 「イマジン」を書きました。	• ひこうきを作りました。

例

Q:　シェークスピアは何をした人ですか。

A:　シェークスピアは「ハムレット」を書いた人です。

1.　リンカーンは_____人です。

2.　コロンブスは１４９２年に _____人です。

3.　ニール・アームストロングは _____人です。

4.　ジョン・レノンは _____人です。

5.　ディズニーは _____人です。

6.　ライト兄弟は_____兄弟です。

7.　エルビス・プレスリーは _____人です。

VI.　Plain past negative form をいいましょう。

例　会う　　　　　会わなかった

1.　開く
2.　ある
3.　あるく
4.　あそぶ
5.　行く
6.　いただく
7.　いらっしゃる
8.　いる
9.　うたう
10.　おきる
11.　おくる
12.　おしえる
13.　およぐ
14.　買う
15.　かえす

16.　帰る
17.　かかる
18.　書く
19.　かける
20.　かす
21.　かぶる
22.　かりる
23.　がんばる
24.　きえる
25.　聞く
26.　きる
27.　来る
28.　しぬ
29.　閉まる
30.　知る

31.　(おなかが)すく
32.　住む
33.　する
34.　すわる
35.　たつ
36.　食べる
37.　つかう
38.　つかれる
39.　つく
40.　作る
41.　できる
42.　とる
43.　なさる
44.　ねる
45.　飲む

46.　はじめる
47.　入る
48.　はく
49.　話す
50.　ひく
51.　ふる
52.　待つ
53.　見る
54.　もつ
55.　よぶ
56.　読む
57.　分かる

VII. どんな人ですか。かんがえましょう。
　　 ないフォームをつかいましょう。

例 コールさんはテレビを見ない人です。

コール

1. 早川さん

2. キムさん

3. ラウールさん

クラシック
ジャズ
ロック
ブルース

4. ペレスさん

5. 早川さん

VIII. Adjective の polite past affirmative form をいいましょう.

例　明るいです　　　　　　明るかったです

1. 新しいです
2. あついです
3. あまいです
4. いいです
5. いじわるです

6. うるさいです
7. おいしいです
8. 多いです
9. おそいです
10. おもしろいです

11. かたいです
12. かわいいです
13. かんたんです
14. きたないです
15. きらいです

16. きれいです	29. たいへんです	42. ふまじめです
17. 暗いです	30. 高いです	43. 古いです
18. けっこうです	31. たのしいです	44. 下手です
19. 元気です	32. だめです	45. べんりです
20. ざんねんです	33. 小さいです	46. まじめです
21. 静かです	34. つまらないです	47. まずいです
22. しつれいです	35. とおいです	48. みじかいです
23. 上手です	36. ちかいです	49. むずかしいです
24. しんせつです	37. にぎやかです	50. やさしいです
25. 好きです	38. 早いです	51. 安いです
26. すごいです	39. ひくいです	52. やわらかいです
27. すずしいです	40. 広いです	53. わるいです
28. せまいです	41. ふべんです	

IX.　VIII の adjective の polite past negative form をいいましょう。

X.　Talk with your partner about your high-school days.

例　《高校、家にちかい》

A：　高校は家にちかかったですか。*

B：　はい、ちかかったです。

　　　(or) いいえ、ちかくなかったです／ちかくありませんでした。

> * X は Y にちかい
> 　X is close to Y

1.　《カフェテリアの食べもの、おいしい》 5.　《しゅくだい、多い》

2.　《クラス、たのしい》 6.　《先生、どう》

3.　《しけん、むずかしい》 7.　《make your own question》

4.　《きょうしつ、きれい》

XI.　読みましょう　　　　　　　　　　　* X は Y からとおい　　X is far from Y

 私はライです。今、アメリカに住んでいますが、日本に住んだことがあります。二年、東京に住んでいました。

そして、東京の高校へ行きました。私が行った高校は家からとおかったです。* まいにち、でんしゃで高校へ行きました。

べんきょうはちょっとむずかしかったですが、先生はとてもしんせつでした。

いいともだちを作りましたから、クラスはとてもたのしかったです。一番いいともだちは東山（ひがしやま）さんです。私は東山さんといっしょに京都（きょうと）や奈良（なら）へ行きました。

そして、おいしい日本りょうりを食べました。

らいしゅう、東山さんが日本からあそびに来ます。いっしょにサンフランシスコへ行くつもりです。

○ ですか。×ですか。

1. （　　）ライさんは今、日本に住んでいます。
2. （　　）ライさんは日本の高校でべんきょうしました。
3. （　　）高校はライさんの家からとおくありませんでした。
4. （　　）ライさんはじてんしゃで高校へ行きました。
5. （　　）ライさんといっしょに京都（きょうと）へ行った人は東山さんです。
6. （　　）ライさんと東山さんは、きのう、サンフランシスコで日本りょうりを食べました。

XII. パートナーにインタビューしましょう。Multiple adjectives をつかって下さい。

1. 日本りょうりを食べたことがありますか。どうでしたか。
2. がいこくへ行ったことがありますか。どうでしたか。
3. どこの高校へ行きましたか。どうでしたか。
4. ともだちの家／アパート／りょうへ行ったことがありますか。どうでしたか。

XIII.　山下さんはどんな人ですか。いいましょう。

例　山下さんは目が ___大きい___ 人です。

1.　山下さんはかみが _____ 人です。
2.　山下さんはくだものが _____ 人です。
3.　山下さんは _____ 人です。
4.　山下さんは _____ 人です。
5.　山下さんは _____ 人です。

XIV.　あなたのともだちはどんな人ですか。いいましょう。

新しい漢字

後ろ うしろ	英文学 えいぶんがく	音楽 おんがく	学部 がくぶ	聞く き	元気 げんき	静か しず
新聞 しんぶん	背 せ	大学院生 だいがくいんせい	名前 なまえ			

新しい使い方

大どおり おお	方 かた	紙 かみ	小づつみ こ	月 つき	手 て	時々 ときどき
～年生 ねんせい	東山 ひがしやま	人々 ひとびと	本ばこ ほん			

Radicals: 人べん・行人べん
にん　ぎょうにん

亻 in 作 and 住 is called 人べん. This radical is derived
from 人 by rotating and stylizing it. 人べん signals that
the meaning of the 漢字 is related to some human activity, e.g. 作
る "make" and 住む "live".

イ in 行・待・後 is called 行人べん（ぎょう＋にんべん）. This name is derived from 行, which can be read as ぎょう. Like 人べん, the meaning of 行人べん漢字 is related to some human activity, but such relationships are less transparent than those with 人べん.

■後	ノ	ク	イ	彳	彳	彳	彳	後	後	
うし（ろ）	*back (location / spatial orientation)*									
英	一	十	艹	艹	艹	芯	苎	英		
エイ	*gifted / England:* 英語 *English,* 英文学 *English literature*									
■文	丶	亠	ナ	文						
ブン	*sentence / text:* 英文学 *English literature,* 日本文学 *Japanese literature*									
音	丶	亠	立	立	立	产	音	音	音	
オン	*sound:* 音楽 *music (comfort by sound)*									
楽	丶	亻	竹	白	白	白	泊	泊	泊	楽
	楽	楽	楽							
	comfort / ease: 音楽 *music (comfort by sound)*									
部	丶	亠	立	立	立	产	音	音	咅	部
	部									
	section / department: 学部 *academic department*									
■方	丶	亠	方	方						
ホウ・かた	*direction / side / way:* あの方 *person over there (polite)*									
紙	乙	幺	幺	幺	糸	糸	糸	紅	紅	紙
かみ・がみ	*paper:* 手紙 *letter*									
元	一	二	元	元						
ゲン	*origin:* 元気 *energetic*									

気	ノ	ノ	ヒ	气	気	気		
キ	spirit: 元気 energetic							

□聞									
ブン・き（く）									

□聞	丨	冂	冋	冋	門	門	門	門	門
ブン・き（く）	門	閂	聞	聞					
	to listen: 新聞 newspaper (news hearing)								

静	一	十	圭	主	丰	青	青	青	青	靑
しず（か）	靜	静	静	静						
	quiet									

新	丶	亠	立	亠	立	立	辛	辛	亲	亲
シン・あたら（しい）	新	新	新							
	new: 新聞 newspaper (new hearing)									

背	一	十	北	北	北	北	背	背	背	
せ	stature / back (anatomical)									

院	゛	了	阝	阝	阝	阝	阼	陀	陀	院
イン	institution: 大学院 graduate school, 大学院生 graduate student									

月	ノ	刀	月	月					
ゲツ・ガツ・つき	moon: 月曜日 Monday, 〜月 month of the year, 〜か月 month(s)								

時	丨	冂	日	日	日一	日十	昨	昨	時	時
ジ・とき	time: 時間 time / hours									

名	ノ	ク	夕	夕	名	名			
な	name: 名前 name								

漢字の復習

I.　　読みましょう。

1.　母は音楽を聞くのが好きです。
2.　今晩は月がきれいですね。
3.　音楽の先生は英文学部の大学院生の後ろにいます。
4.　ここにお名前を書いて下さい。
5.　あのアパートは安くて静かです。

II.　　Write the reading of each word and connect it with the opposite meaning.

例	明るい	あかるい ●		● 上手	
1.	開く	●		● 後ろ	
2.	新しい	●		● きらい	
3.	大きい	●		● 暗い	くらい
4.	背がひくい	●		● 安い	
5.	下手	●		● 閉まる	
6.	好き	●		● たくさん／多い	
7.	すこし	●		● 小さい	
8.	高い	●		● 古い	
9.	前	●		● 背が高い	

新しい語彙

あつい	イ	*hot*	おかし		*snack*
あまい	イ	*sweet*	おそい	イ	*slow, late*
いう	ウ i	*to say, speak, talk*	がいこく		*foreign country*
うんてん（する）		*driving*	学部		*academic department*
英文学		*English literature*	かたい	イ	*tough, hard*
エッセー		*essay*	紙		*paper*
大どおり		*boulevard*	かんがえる ル t		*to think*

クッキー		cookie
クラブ		club
小づつみ		parcel
サービス (する)		service
さむい	イ	cold
しょうせつ		novel
(お) す		vinegar
すごい	イ	terrific
すずしい	イ	cool
ステレオ		stereo (set)
せいぶつ学		biology
せんしゅ		sports player
そこ		bottom
だめ	ナ	no good
ダンス (する)		dance
ち		blood
チーム		team
ちえ		intelligence, wisdom
ちから		power
つえ		cane

月		moon
できる	ル　i	to be able to do ~
とおり		street
時々		sometimes
にく		meat
にっけい		of Japanese ancestry
はこ		box
ピザ		pizza
ビデオ		video
人々		people
ふね		boat, ship
ブルース		blues
本ばこ		bookshelf
まいあさ		every morning
まいにち		everyday
まいばん		every evening
もらう	ウ　t	to receive
やわらかい	イ	soft
らいしゅう		next week
わるい	イ	bad

なまえ

アームストロング	Armstrong
アラスカ	Alaska
エルビス	Elvis
コロンブス	Columbus

シェークスピア	Shakespeare
ジャパン	Japan
ジョン	John
タイ	Thailand

ディズニー	*Disney*	プレスリー	*Presley*
デトロイト	*Detroit*	ペレス	*Perez*
なら（奈良）	*Nara*	ミッキーマウス	*Mickey Mouse*
ニール	*Neil*	ライト<ruby>兄弟<rt>きょうだい</rt></ruby>	*Wright Brothers*
ハムレット	*Hamlet*	リンカーン	*Lincoln*
ハワイ	*Hawaii*	レノン	*Lennon*
<ruby>東山<rt>ひがしやま</rt></ruby>	*Higashiyama*		

第十二課 LESSON 12
だいじゅうに か

買い物
もの
Shopping

あまい物が少しほしいですね
すこ
We want something sweet, right?

<ruby>会<rt>かい</rt></ruby><ruby>話<rt>わ</rt></ruby>

1　ソン　　：今晩、何を食べましょうか。

What shall we eat for dinner tonight?

　　　小山　：そうですねえ、私はのりまきが食べたいです。

Hmmm ... well, I'd like to have some norimaki.

2　ソン　　：いいですね。私も日本<ruby>料理<rt>りょうり</rt></ruby>が<ruby>大好<rt>だいす</rt></ruby>きです。でも、私はのりまきを作ったこと
はありません。

Great. I really love Japanese food, too. But I've never made norimaki.

　　　小山　：だいじょうぶですよ。私は作ったことがありますから。

That's alright. I've made them before.

3　ソン　　：ああ、よかった。このあいだ、ミラーさんものりまきを食べたがっていまし
たよ。

Wonderful. Recently Miller-san has also been wanting to eat norimaki.

　　　小山　：じゃあ、ミラーさんをよびましょう。

Well then, let's invite Miller-san.

4　ソン　：ええ、そうしましょう。ところで、のりまきは何で作りますか。

Yes, let's do so. By the way, what is norimaki made of?

　　　小山　：ごはんや、のりや、たまごなどで作ります。おすもつかいます。

It's made of rice, seaweed, eggs, and such. And vinegar, too.

　　　ソン　：そうですか。じゃ、すぐに買いに行きましょう。

I see. Well then, let's go shopping right away.

（店^{みせ}で）

5　店員^{てんいん}　：いらっしゃいませ。

Welcome.

6　ソン　：日本の食べ物がいろいろありますね。

They have all kinds of Japanese food here.

　　　小山　：ええ、この店は安くて便利^{べんり}で、とてもいいですよ。

Yes, this shop is inexpensive and convenient, so it's very good.

7　小山　：このお米^{こめ}はいくらですか。

How much is this rice?

　　　店員　：７ドルです。

7 dollars.

8　ソン　：デザートはどうしますか。あまい物が少しほしいですね。

What about dessert? We want something sweet, right?

　　　小山　：そうですね。ようかんを一本買いましょうか。

Certainly. Shall we buy a stick of yokan?

（レジで）

9　小山　：じゃ、おねがいします。

This is it.

　　　店員　：のりが二ドル五十セント、おすが三ドル、お米が七ドル、ようかんが三ドル五十セント。全部^{ぜんぶ}で十六ドルです。

The seaweed is $2.50, vinegar $3.00, rice $7.00, and yokan $3.50. All together, it's $16.00.

10　小山　：はい。じゃあ、二十ドル。

Okay, here's $20.00.

11　店員　　：はい、ありがとうございます。四ドルのおつりです。
　　　　　　　　Thank you, and here's $4 in change.

12　小山　　：どうも。
　　　　　　　　Thanks.

　　店員　　：ありがとうございました。また、どうぞ。
　　　　　　　　Thank you very much. Please (come) again.

使い方
（つか　かた）

1　のりまき is a kind of すし, vinegared rice rolled in のり (toasted dried laver) with various fillings in the center. まき is the Pre- ますフォーム of まく "to roll / wrap".

2　だいじょうぶ originally meant "big strong man". Today, it means "safe / all right".

3　ああ、よかった is a casual phrase to express your feeling of relief.

　　先生：　こんしゅうおぼえる漢字は八つです。
　　学生：　ああ、よかった。

　If what you have just heard is very significant, use わあ、よかった, instead of ああ、よか
　った.

　　先生：　こんしゅうは、しゅくだいがありません。
　　学生：　わあ、よかった。

　このあいだ consists of この "this" and あいだ "interval". This phrase means "a little while ago".

6　いろいろ (な -adjective) consists of a repetition of いろ "color" and indicates "various" or "a lot / many". It can be used as a quantifier and thus appears frequently after noun phrases (cf. **12g**). 日本の食べ物がいろいろありますね is equivalent to いろいろな日本の食べ物がありますね or 日本のいろいろな食べ物がありますね.

8　ようかん is a thick jellied confection made of adzuki beans. It is commonly molded into sticks, so the counter for a long object, 本, is used here.

9　In 第九課, we studied the expression Xをおねがいします to make an order at a restaurant. おねがいします can also be used whenever you make a request. Here, 小山さん asks the 店員 to calculate the total price.

12　どうも is an abbreviation of どうもありがとうございます or どうもありがとうございました.

Politest	どうもありがとうございます／ございました。
↑ Casual	どうもありがとう
↓ Most casual	どうも

<ruby>文法<rt>ぶんぽう</rt></ruby>

12a	**X**がほしいです	"I / We want X"
	Xはほしくありません	"I / We don't want X" (formal)
	Xはほしくないです	"I / We don't want X" (less formal)
12b	**X**は**Y**をほしがっている	"X wants Y"
12c	Pre-ますフォーム+たいです	"I / We want to do ~"
	たくありません	"I / We don't want to do ~"
	たくないです	"I / We don't want to do ~"
12d	**X**は Pre-ますフォーム+たがっている	"X wants to do ~"
12e	どうして／なぜ	"Why ~?"
	Plain フォーム+からだ	"It is because ~"
12f	Material Marker で	
12g	Quantifiers	

12a	**X**がほしいです	"I / We want X"
	Xはほしくありません	"I / We don't want X" (formal)
	Xはほしくないです	"I / We don't want X" (less formal)

ほしい is an い-adjective although it is semantically similar to a verb. The negative scope marker は appears in the place of が in negative sentences.

（私は）<ruby>水<rt>みず</rt></ruby>がほしいです。	*I want some water.*
おさけ は ほしくありません。	*I don't want any sake.*
ビールもほしくないです。	*I don't want any beer either.*

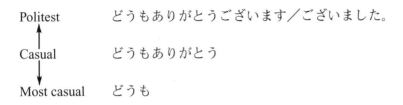

In declarative sentences, the subject is understood to be the speaker; in questions, the subject is the addressee.

【たんじょう日】

何がほしいですか。	*What do you want?*
花がほしいです。	*I'd like some flowers.*
何もほしくないです。	*I don't want anything.*

NON-PAST	PAST
ほしいです	ほしかったです
ほしくありません	ほしくありませんでした
ほしくないです	ほしくなかったです

【去年のたんじょう日】

何がほしかったですか。
What did you want?
車がほしかったです。
I wanted a car.

じしょはほしくありませんでした。
I didn't want a dictionary.
かばんもほしくなかったです。
I didn't want a briefcase either.

It is acceptable to express your own desire, but it is not polite to ask the addressee's desire directly in Japanese society. This is also true in English to a certain extent, so the euphemistic question *Would you like some coffee?*, instead of *Do you want some coffee?*, is frequently used. It is safer to avoid Xがほしいですか when you are supposed to show respect to the addressee.

12b　XはYをほしがっている　　　"X wants Y"

In English, you can use the same word to describe the mental (psychological, emotional, sensation, etc.) states of both yourself and other persons, e.g. "I *want* some coffee" and "Son-san *wants* some coffee". In Japanese, expressions like ほしい／〜たい (cf. **12c**) can be used only when you have direct access to the source (your brain). Therefore, you cannot use such expressions with a third-person subject, because you do not have direct access to others' mental states in ordinary situations. You can *guess / infer* others' mental states, but you never *know* them with the same degree of certainty as you know about yourself. In this respect, the Japanese language is very rigid and forces its users to draw a strict line between themselves and others. For a third-person subject, ほしがっている (the Dictionary フォーム is ほしがる) is used, instead of ほしい. ほしがっている literally means "showing a sign of one's feelings / desires". Unlike ほしい, which behaves like an adjective, ほしがる is a genuine verb. Note that the particle to mark the direct object with ほしがる is を, whereas that with ほしい is が.

(私は) ワイン が ほしいです。
I want some wine.
古川さんはワイン を ほしがっています。
Furukawa-san wants some wine.

(私は) ラップトップ が ほしかったです。
I wanted a laptop.
弟はラップトップ を ほしがっていました。
My brother wanted a laptop.

(私は) CD プレーヤー が ほしいです。
I want a CD player.
ルームメートは CD プレーヤー を ほしがっています。
My roommate wants a CD player.

Here, again, guessing another person's desires may be interpreted as presumptuous. So avoid ほしがっている with a subject that refers to a person to whom you need to show respect.

12c　PRE-ますフォーム＋　たいです　　　　"I / We want to do ~"
　　　　　　　　　　　　たくありません　　"I / We don't want to do ~"(formal)
　　　　　　　　　　　　たくないです　　　"I / We don't want to do ~"(less formal)

If you want something, X がほしい is used; if you want to *do* something, Pre- ますフォーム ＋ たいです is used instead. Like ほしい, this construction makes the phrase like an い-adjective. This irregularity is understandable because wanting something and wanting to do something are both psychological states, rather than actions or events, and states are normally expressed by adjectives, rather than verbs. Literally, Pre- ますフォーム＋たいです means that "I'm in the state of wanting to do something".

(私は) 日本へ留学したいです。　　　　　*(Lit.) I want to go studying abroad to Japan.*
　　　　　　　　　　　　　　　　　　I want to study abroad in Japan.
(私は) べんきょうしたくありません。　*I don't want to study.*

The direct object of the verb can be marked either with が or を. In negative sentences, は -marking is most natural.

（私は）パン　が　食べたいです。

I want to eat bread.

（私は）きれいな日本のにわが見たいです。

I want to see a beautiful Japanese garden.

（私は）漢字　は　おぼえたくないです。

I don't want to memorize kanji.

（私は）ポップコーン　を　作りたいですから、
でんしレンジがほしいです。

I want to make popcorn, so I want a microwave oven.

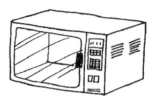

NON-PAST	PAST
～たいです	～たかったです
～たく｛ありません / ないです｝	～たく｛ありませんでした / なかったです｝

昨日は、ラボへ行きたくありませんでした。頭（あたま）がいたかったんです。

I didn't want to go to the lab yesterday. I had a headache.

つかれましたから、せんたくはしたくなかったです。

Because I got tired, I didn't want to do my laundry.

12d　X は PRE- ますフォーム + たがっている　　　"X wants to do ~"

ます

If you need to say *someone wants to do something*, this construction is used. However, like ほしがっている , describing another's mental state is a risky business (you may sound presumptuous), so use this construction with great care. (You will learn safer expressions later in this course.) If X is a family member or close friend, the use of this construction is acceptable. Unlike ～たいです , the direct object of ～たがっています is always marked with を .

姉は来年（らいねん）アフリカへ行きたがっています。

My (older) sister wants to go to Africa next year.

弟はタイ料理　を　ならいたがっています。

My (younger) brother wants to learn Thai cooking.

母は大きいれいぞうこ　を　買いたがっています。

My mother wants to buy a large refrigerator.

ルームメートはスピーチコンテストにでたがっていました。

My roommate wanted to enter a speech contest.

SUBJECT	WANT A THING	WANT TO DO
You	花がほしいです	花 { が / を } 買いたいです
Other	花をほしがっています	花を買いたがっています

12e　どうして／なぜ　　　　"Why ~?"
　　PLAIN フォーム + からだ　　"It is because ~"

In 第五課, we studied a limited use of どうして, e.g.:

私は今晩十二時までべんきょうします。

I'm going to study until midnight tonight.

どうして ですか。　　　　　　　　　　*Why?*

明日、しけんが ありますから 。　　　　*Because I have a test tomorrow.*

In this lesson, you learn to use どうして and なぜ with other predicates in the form of どうして／な
ぜ〜のですか or どうして／なぜ〜んですか. To answer such a question, you can use Plain フォー
ム + からです "It is because ~".

A　　Verbs

どうして 十二時までべんきょうするんですか。*Why are you going to study until midnight?*

明日、しけんが あるからです 。　　　　*Because I have a test tomorrow.*

なぜ チョコレートを食べないのですか。　*Why don't you eat chocolate?*

ダイエット しているからです 。　　　　*Because I'm on a diet.*

なぜ しゅくだいをしないんですか。　　　*Why don't you do your homework?*

しつもんが 分からないからです 。　　　*Because I don't understand the question(s).*

どうして 今朝、じゅぎょうにでなかったん　*Why didn't you attend class this morning?*
ですか。

ねぼう したからです 。　　　　　　　　*Because I overslept.*

どうして デモに来なかったんですか。　　*Why didn't you come to the demonstration?*

ばしょが 分からなかったからです 。　　*Because I didn't know the place.*

　　　　　　　　　　　　　　　　　　　(or) Because I couldn't find the place.

B　　い-Adjectives

| どうして | パーティーに行かないんですか。 | *Why aren't you going to the party?* |
| いそがしいからです | 。 | *Because I'm busy.* |

| どうして | 日本語をとらないんですか。 | *Why aren't you taking Japanese?* |
| おもしろくないからです | 。 | *Because it's not interesting.* |

なぜ じゅぎょうをやすんだんですか。　　*Why did you skip class?*
頭が いたかったからです 。　　*Because I had a headache.*

なぜ セーターをきなかったんですか。　　*Why didn't you wear a sweater?*
さむくなかったからです 。　　*Because it wasn't cold.*

C　　な-Adjectives

どうして あきに日本へ行きたいんですか。　　*Why do you want to go to Japan in fall?*
日本のあきは きれいだからです 。　　*Because the fall is beautiful in Japan.*

なぜ うたわないんですか。　　*Why don't you sing?*
私はうたが 上手じゃないからです 。　　*Because I'm no good at singing.*

どうして その家を買わなかったのですか。　　*Why didn't you buy that house?*
ばしょが ふべんだったからです 。　　*Because the location was inconvenient.*

なぜ シンさんと話さなかったんですか。　　*Why didn't you talk with Singh-san?*
しんせつじゃなかったからです 。　　*Because she was unkind.*

D　　Norminal Predicates

なぜ 家にいるんですか。　　*Why are you at home?*
今日は 土曜日だからです 。　　*Because it's Saturday today.*

どうして その本を読まないのですか。　　*Why don't you read that book?*
かんこく語じゃないからです 。　　*Because it's not in Korean.*

なぜ ひるごはんを食べなかったんですか　　*Why didn't you eat lunch?*
ハンバーガーだったからです 。　　*Because it was hamburgers.*
私はにくは食べません。　　*I don't eat meat.*

どうして その車を買わなかったのですか。　　*Why didn't you buy that car?*
セールじゃなかったからです 。　　*Because it wasn't on sale.*

Like English *Why?*, どうしてですか／なぜですか can be interpreted as criticism or a challenge, so use it carefully.

12f　Material Marker　で

X は Y で作る　"X is made of / from Y"
Y で X を作る　"SUBJECT makes X with Y"

In 第四課, we studied the location marker で and the instrumental marker で. で is also used to mark materials of / from which something is made.

クッキーは、こむぎこや、バターや、さとうなどで作ります。
Cookies are made of flour, butter, sugar, and other things.
すきやきは、ぎゅうにくとやさいで作ります。
Sukiyaki is made of beef and vegetables.
私はとりにくですきやきを作りますよ。
I make sukiyaki with chicken.

12g　Quantifiers

In 第九課, we studied counters. When a counter quantifies the subject or direct object, it normally appears **after** the subject or direct object.

SUBJECT	が	COUNTER	VERB
DIRECT OBJECT	を	COUNTER	VERB

ともだちが　二人　あそびに来ました。　　*Two of my friends visited me.*

ワインを　三本　買いました。　　*I bought three bottles of wine.*

If the preceding noun is **not** the subject or direct object, the counter cannot quantify it.

	SUBJECT	INDIRECT OBJECT		DIRECT OBJECT	VERB
×	私は	ともだちに	三人	手紙を	書きました。
○	私は	三人のともだちに		手紙を	書きました。

Counters are a subset of the larger category of *quantifiers*. Quantifiers specify the quantity of the noun (entity) they modify. Some quantifiers are:

いろいろ	*various*	たくさん	*a lot, many*
少し	*a little, some*	ちょっと	*a little, some (colloquial)*
全部	*all*		

In English, quantifiers can appear after the noun only when the noun is the subject, e.g. *All the students were happy = The students were all happy*. In Japanese, quantifiers can appear after the subject or direct object.

| おもしろい読み物が | いろいろ ありますね。 | *There's all kinds of interesting readings, isn't there?* |

ともだちが	たくさん あそびに来ました。	*Lots of my friends came to visit me.*
お茶が	少し ほしいですね。	*We want some tea, don't we?*
本を	全部 読みました。	*I read all of the books.*
		(or) I read the entire book.

れんしゅうもんだい
練 習 問題

I.　Following the example below, create and practice dialogues, using phrases from box A and appropriate reasons from box B.

れい
例

A:　今日、あそびに行きません。

B:　どうして行かないんですか。

　　(or) どうしてですか。

A:　お金がないからです。

A	B
例　今日、あそびに行きません。	a.　さむいです。
1.　プレゼントを買いました。	b.　くつが買いたかったです。
2.　図書館でしゅくだいをします。	c.　来年、日本へ行きます。
3.　今日、およぎません。	d.　おもしろくないです。
4.　日本語をべんきょうしています。	e.　きれいでした。
5.　明日、大学へ来ません。	f.　お金がありません。
6.　晩ごはんを食べませんでした。	g.　ひまじゃありませんでした。
7.　このビデオは買いません。	h.　静かです。
8.　デパートへ行きました。	i.　土曜日です。
9.　えいがは見ませんでした。	j.　おいしくありませんでした。
10.　富士山のしゃしんをたくさんとりました。	k.　明日はともだちのたんじょう日です。

II.　Following the example, make your own dialogs.

例

A：　どうして、<u>昨日、クラスへ来なかった</u>んですか。

X：　<u>ねぼうした</u>からです。

III.　クラスメートに聞きましょう。そして、名前を書きましょう。

例

A:　Xさん、ピアノがほしいですか。

X:　はい、(ピアノが)ほしいです。

　　(or)いいえ、(ピアノは)ほしくありません。

　　If the answer is yes, put his / her name in ⬚ III.

IV.　パートナーと話しましょう。そして、名前を書きましょう。

例

A:　だれかピアノをほしがっていますか。

B:　はい、Xさんが(ピアノを)ほしがっています。

　　(or)いいえ、だれも(ピアノは)ほしがっていません。

　　Put the person's name in ⬚ IV.

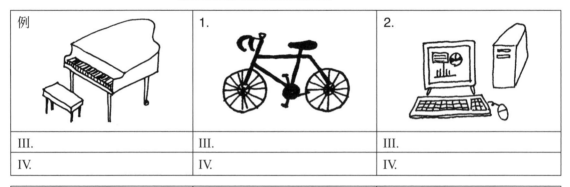

例	1.	2.
III.	III.	III.
IV.	IV.	IV.

3.	4.	5.
III.	III.	III.
IV.	IV.	IV.

6.	7.	8.
III.	III.	III.
IV.	IV.	IV.

V.　クラスメートに聞きましょう。そして、名前を書きましょう。

例

A:　X さん、デパートで買い物がしたいですか。

X:　はい、(買い物が) したいです。

　　(or) いいえ、(買い物は) したくありません。

　　If the answer is yes, put his/her name in | V. _____ |.

VI.　パートナーと話しましょう。そして、名前を書きましょう。

例

A:　だれかデパートで買い物をしたがっていますか。

B:　はい、X さんが (買い物を) したがっています。

　　(or) いいえ、だれも (買い物は) したがっていません。

　　Put the person's name in | VI. _____ |.

うなぎ

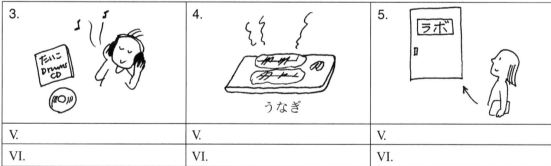

高校のともだち

VII.　パートナーと話しましょう。

<ruby>例<rt>れい</rt></ruby>

A:　おすしのごはんは何で作りますか。

B:　米やすやさとうなどで作ります。

A:　ああ、そうですか。

みそしる　(Miso Soup)

みず	2 カップ
みそ (miso)	30g
とうふ	100g
ねぎ (green onion)	2本
インスタントだしのもと	少し
(instant Japanese stock)	

チキンカレー　(Chicken Curry)

とりにく	500g
たまねぎ	3つ
にんじん	1本
じゃがいも	2つ
にんにく (garlic)	少し
しょうが (ginger)	少し
カレールー	1はこ
(instant curry sauce mix)	

おすしのごはん

米	3 カップ (cup)
さけ	少し
だしこぶ (kelp)	15 cm
す	大さじ (tablespoon) 4 ¼
さとう	大さじ 1½
しお	小さじ (teaspoon) 2

さけのてりやき　(Salmon Teriyaki)

さけ	2 きれ (piece)
しょうゆ	大さじ 1
みりん	大さじ 1
(sweet cooking sake)	

もっと話しましょう。

チョコレートケーキは？

ハンバーガーは？

ピザは？

VIII.　読みましょう。

私はカラオケが好きです。日本のうたがうたいたいです。でも、日本のうたは知りません。

それで、せんしゅうの土曜日に日本まちへCDを買いに行きました。小さい店に日本のうたのCDがありました。CDは一まい２５ドルでした。

高かったですが、CDを三ま
い買いました。

それから、本やへ行きまし
た。日本語の本がたくさん
ありました。

私はべんきょうがきらいです。で
も、日本のうたのいみが知りたい
です。それで、日本語のじしょを
買いました。

日本のスーパーへも行
きました。そして、よう
かんを買いました。
ルームメートがほし
がっていたからです。

私は日本のうたをれん
しゅうするつもりです。
そして、カラオケでう
たいたいです。

○ ですか。×ですか。

1. （　　）この人は日本のうたをうたいたがっています。
2. （　　）日本のうたのCDはあまり高くありませんでした。
3. （　　）この人はCDを五まい買いました。
4. （　　）この人は日本語のべんきょうが好きですから、日本語のじしょを買いました。
5. （　　）この人のルームメートはようかんを買いました。

IX.　このショッピングリストはみなさんが買った物です。パートナーと話しましょう。

例　ショッピングリスト1

A:　何を買いましたか。
B:　りんごとオレンジを買いました。
A:　そうですか。りんごをたくさん買いましたか。
B:　いいえ、（りんごは）三つ買いました。
A:　オレンジも三つ買いましたか。
B:　いいえ、オレンジは二十こ買いました。
A:　そうですか。

ショッピングリスト1	
りんご	3
オレンジ	20

ショッピングリスト2	
コーラ	6
ビール	24

X.　たなかさんと安川さんと山本さんとシンさんがリストを作りました。リストを見て下さい。そして、パートナーと話しましょう。

^{れい}
例

A:　たなかさんは何をしますか。

B:　ダンスパーティーをします。

A:　そうですか。たなかさんはともだちを何人よびますか。

B:　（たなかさんはともだちを）六人よびたがっています。

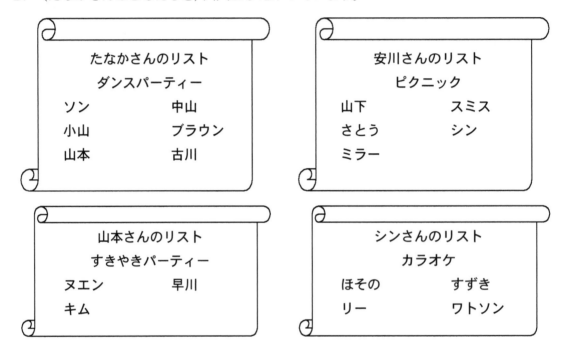

たなかさんのリスト
ダンスパーティー

ソン	中山
小山	ブラウン
山本	古川

安川さんのリスト
ピクニック

山下	スミス
さとう	シン
ミラー	

山本さんのリスト
すきやきパーティー

ヌエン	早川
キム	

シンさんのリスト
カラオケ

ほその	すずき
リー	ワトソン

^{あたら}新 しい^{かんじ}漢字

^{あたま}頭	^{か もの}買い物	^{きょねん}去年	^{こめ}米	^{すこ}少し	^{ぜんぶ}全部	^{た もの}食べ物
^{てんいん}店員	^{はな}花	^{べんり}便利	^{みせ}店	^{よ もの}読み物	^{りょうり}料理	

新しい^{つか かた}使い方

^{けさ}今朝	^{だいす}大好き	^{みず}水	^{らいねん}来年	たんじょう^び日

Radicals: 草かんむり・麻だれ

In 第九課, we learned the かんむり "crown" type radical of なべぶた (冖 in 高, 京, 方, 文). 艹 in 英, 茶, and 花 is another かんむり radical called 草かんむり* (草 "grass" + かんむり). As the name suggests, the meaning of most 草かんむり漢字 is related to plants. Although not common in modern Japanese, 英 can be read as はなぶさ and means a "cluster of flowers".

The radicals that appear in this position are called たれ "hanging". The radical 广 in 広 (第七課) and 店 (this lesson) is called 麻だれ. 麻 means "hemp" and is read as あさ (訓読み) or マ (音読み). The meaning of most 麻だれ漢字 is related to the notion of a house (i.e. a space under a roof). It might be the case that hemp was a common roofing material in ancient Japan.

*The 漢字 from which 草かんむり was derived is 艸. It looks like grass, doesn't it?

頭	一	厂	戸	口	戸	豆	豆	豇	豇	豇
あたま	頭	頭	頭	頭	頭	頭				
	head									
物	ノ	丿	牛	牛	牜	牞	物	物		
もの	*thing: this word is frequently combined with the Pre- ます form of a verb, e.g. 買い物 shopping, 食べ物 food, 読み物 something to read*									
去	一	十	土	去	去					
キョ	*to leave / be gone: 去年 last year*									
米	丶	丷	丷	半	米	米				
こめ	*rice*									
少	丿	丿	小	少						
すこ（し）	*a little (少 contains, 小 small)*									
全	ノ	人	个	仐	仝	全				
ゼン	*all: 全部 all*									

店	丶	亠	广	庁	庁	庄	店	店		
テン・みせ	*shop:* 店員 *store clerk*									
員	丶	冖	口	尸	吊	肙	冒	冒	員	員
イン	*member:* 店員 *store clerk*									
花	一	十	艹	艹	芯	芯	花			
はな	*flower*									
便	丿	亻	仁	仃	佀	佀	�	伊	便	
ベン	*convenience:* 便利 *convenient*									
利	丿	二	千	禾	禾	利	利			
リ	*benefit:* 便利 *convenient*									
水	亅	기	水	水						
スイ・みず	*water:* 水曜日 *Wednesday (day of water)*									
来	一	丆	冖	平	平	来	来			
き(ます)・く(る)・こ(ない)	*to come:* 来年 *next year*									
料	丶	丷	丷	半	半	米	米	米	米	料
リョウ	*materials;* 料理 *cooking*									
理	一	丁	干	王	玌	玑	珂	珂	理	理
リ	理									
	reason: 料理 *cooking*									

<ruby>漢<rt>かん</rt></ruby><ruby>字<rt>じ</rt></ruby>の<ruby>復<rt>ふく</rt></ruby><ruby>習<rt>しゅう</rt></ruby>

I.　　読みましょう。

1.　姉は去年、東京の大学院に入りました。
2.　せんもんは英文学ですが、英語がよく分かりません。
3.　安かったですから、お米をたくさん買いました。
4.　キムさんは背がとても高いです。
5.　お金がありませんから、買い物をすることはできません。

II.　　Write the reading of each word and identify the word category it best fits.

<ruby>例<rt>れい</rt></ruby>	兄	あに	school • (family) • other
1.	妹		school • family • other
2.	家		school • family • other
3.	英文学		school • family • other
4.	お父さん		school • family • other
5.	弟さん		school • family • other
6.	お姉さん		school • family • other
7.	音楽		school • family • other
8.	買い物		school • family • other
9.	学生		school • family • other
10.	学校		school • family • other
11.	兄弟		school • family • other
12.	高校生		school • family • other
13.	米		school • family • other
14.	先生		school • family • other
15.	大学院生		school • family • other
16.	中間しけん		school • family • other
17.	図書館		school • family • other
18.	母		school • family • other
19.	店		school • family • other
20.	留学生		school • family • other

新しい語彙

CD プレーヤー	CD player
あき	autumn
いたい　　　　イ	painful
いみ	meaning
いろいろ　　　ナ	various, many kinds of
うなぎ	eel
おつり	change
おぼえる　　ル t	to memorize
カラオケ	karaoke
ぎゅうにく	beef
今朝	this morning
このあいだ	some time ago, the other day
こむぎこ	wheat flour
（お）米	(uncooked) rice
こんしゅう	this week
さけ	salmon
（お）さとう	sugar
しお	salt
じゃがいも	potato
じゅぎょう	class
しょうゆ	soy sauce
スピーチコンテスト	speech contest
せんたく（する）	laundry

全部	all
ダイエット（する）	diet
だいじょうぶ　　ナ	alright, okay
大好き　　　　ナ	to like very much
たまご	egg
たまねぎ	onion
たんじょう日	birthday
チョコレート	chocolate
でる　　　　ル i	to attend, enter (a contest)
店員	store clerk
でんしレンジ	microwave oven
とうふ	tofu
とりにく	chicken
なぜ	why
ならう　　　　t	to learn
にわ	garden
にんじん	carrot
ねぎ	green onion
ねぼうする I i	to oversleep
のり	laver (type of seaweed)
のりまき	seaweed wrapped sushi
ばしょ	location, place
バター	butter

パン		bread
ひま	㋤	leisure, not busy
ほしい	㋑	want, desire
ほしがる	㋒ t	to show signs of desire
ポップコーン		popcorn
水 <ruby>みず</ruby>		water
みなさん		everyone (respectful)
ようかん		sweet jellied adzuki bean paste

やさい		vegetable
よぶ	㋒ t	to invite
読み物		readings
来年		next year
ラップトップ		laptop
留学 (する)		studying abroad
れいぞうこ		refrigerator
レジ		cash register

なまえ

アフリカ	Africa

ふじさん (富士山)	Mt. Fuji

手紙
A Letter

たの
会えるのを楽しみにしています
We're looking forward to seeing you

かいわ
会話

1　ミラー　：山本さん、今、いそがしいですか。

　　　　　　　Yamamoto-san, are you busy now?

　　山本　　：いいえ。どうしてですか。

　　　　　　　No, why?

2 ミラー　：あのう、じつは、ちょっとおねがいがあるんですけれど……。

Well, I have a little favor to ask of you ...

　　　山本　：はい、何ですか。

Sure, what is it?

3 ミラー　：私は冬休みに、日本へホームステイに行くんです。

I'm going to Japan for a homestay during winter break.

　　　山本　：へえ、日本へ行くんですか。それはいいですね。

Oh, you're going to Japan? That's great.

4 ミラー　：ええ。それで、昨日、ホストファミリーから手紙が来たんですが、むずかしい文があるんです。

Yes, and I got a letter from my host family yesterday, but there are some sentences that I don't understand well.

5 ミラー　：それから、返事を書きたいんですが、上手に書けないんです。ちょっとたすけて下さいませんか。

And I'd like to write a reply, but I won't be able to write it very well. Do you think you could help me out a little?

　　　山本　：いいですよ。

Sure.

6 ミラー　：おねがいします。

Thank you.

7 ミラーさん、お元気ですか。私達もみんな元気です。

8 そちらは寒いですか。こちらはとても寒いです。でも、まゆみとたろうはとてもよろこんでいます。先週、ゆきがふったからです。それで、こども達は、にわでゆきだるまを作りました。

9 みんなミラーさんに早く会いたがっています。ミラーさんが来た時に、みんなでいっしょに奈良や京都へ行きましょう。

10 では、冬休みに会えるのを楽しみにしています。

11 さようなら

12 平成十七年十一月六日　　秋山いさお

13

14 ジミー・ミラーさま

7　*Dear Miller-san, how are you? We're all doing fine too.*

8　*Is it cold over there? It's very cold here. But Mayumi and Taro are happy because we had snow last week. The kids made a snowman in the garden.*

9　*Everyone here is eager to meet you soon. When you come here, let's all go to Nara, Kyoto, and so on.*

10　*We look forward to seeing you during your winter break.*

11　*See you then (goodbye).*

12　*November 6, 2005*

13　*Isao Akiyama*

14　*Mr. Jimmy Miller*

使い方

2　じつは literally means "the fact is ～" (じつ "reality" + は). This expression is frequently used to introduce some serious matter. ちょっと is used here as a hedging expression, cf. 第七課, **7g**.

　　～んですけ(れ)ど…… is equivalent to ～んですが…… (cf. 第七課, **7h** for this use of が "but"). Ending a sentence with ～んですけ(れ)ど／～んですが softens the speech. That is, if ミラーさん said おねがいがあります, his speech might sound very demanding: "I have a favor to ask of you!" おねがいがあるんですけ(れ)ど conveys the nuance "I have a favor to ask of you, (but) may I?" In spoken Japanese, the shorter form ～んですけど is more frequently used.

7　も in 私達もみんな元気です "we're all doing fine too" implies that 秋山さん assumes that ミラーさん is in good health.

8　よろこぶ "be happy／pleased" (う verb) is used with only a third-person subject. For a first-person subject, use うれしい (い -adjective) instead.

りょうしんはよろこんでいます。	*My parents are happy／pleased.*
私はうれしいです。	*I'm happy／pleased.*

10　In 第四課, we studied the expression 楽しみにしています "I look forward (to it)". In order to specify the event, you need a nominalized clause with の, e.g. 会える "be able to meet" (cf. **13a**) ＋の. 楽しみ is the noun form derived from the adjective 楽しい.

14　～さま is a more respectful version of ～さん, e.g. おくさん／おくさま, お母さん／お母さま, お父さん／お父さま. The use of ～さま is the norm in letter writing.

<ruby>文法<rt>ぶんぽう</rt></ruby>

13a Verb Conjugation: Potential フォーム	
13b CLAUSE1 時に CLAUSE2	"When C1, C2"
13c VERBAL NOUN + に行く	"go for VERBAL NOUN"
13d Deriving Adverbs from Adjectives	
13e Relative Time	
13f Days of the Month	
13g Japanese Calendar	
13h <ruby>手紙<rt></rt></ruby>の書き<ruby>方<rt>かた</rt></ruby>	

13a　Verb Conjugation: Potential フォーム

In 第六課, **6f**, we studied the construction 「Dictionary フォーム ＋ ことができる」 "can／be able to do ~". In this lesson, we will learn the verb Potential フォーム, which is synonymous to, but more frequently used than, 〜ことができる.

A　る - **Verbs:** Attach られる to the stem (invariant part).

	Plain	Polite
い‐る	い‐られる	い‐られます
おき‐る	おき‐られる	おき‐られます
かり‐る	かり‐られる	かり‐られます
おぼえ‐る	おぼえ‐られる	おぼえ‐られます
かんがえ‐る	かんがえ‐られる	かんがえ‐られます
はじめ‐る	はじめ‐られる	はじめ‐られます

B　う - **Verbs:** Drop the final *u* of the Dictionary フォーム and add *eru*.

わ	ら	や	ま	は	な	た	さ	か	あ
	り		み	ひ	に	ち	し	き	い
	る	ゆ	む	ふ	ぬ	つ	す	く	う
	れ		め	へ	ね	て	せ	け	え
を	ろ	よ	も	ほ	の	と	そ	こ	お

a–u → a–eru
あう（会う）→ あえる（会える）
kak–u → kak–eru
かく（書く）→ かける（書ける）

	Plain	Polite
話す	話せる	話せます
待つ	待てる	待てます
しぬ	しねる	しねます
よぶ	よべる	よべます
飲む	飲める	飲めます
帰る	帰れる	帰れます

行く has two forms:

行く	行ける／行かれる	行けます／行かれます

C　Irregular Verbs

する	できる	できます
来る	来られる	来られます

(1)　今週は、早く家へ帰れます。

I can go home early this week.

(2)　何マイルはしれますか。

How many miles can you run?

(3)　私は来週、はたらけません。

I can't work next week.

(4)　春休みに日本へ来られますか。

Can you come to Japan during spring break?

春休みはみじかいですから行けませんが、夏に行けます。

Because spring break is short, I can't go (there) then, but I can go during the summer.

できる in 〜ことができる is the potential form of する. Like 好き, きらい, ほしい, etc., the direct object of the Potential フォーム is most frequently marked with が, rather than を.

(5)　古川さんはタンゴ が おどれます。

　　= 古川さんはタンゴをおどることができます。

Furukawa-san can dance the tango.

(6)　中山さんはうんてん が できます。

Nakayama-san can drive.

(7) 漢字 が おぼえられません。

I can't remember (memorize) kanji.

(8) 明日は、午前七時からしごと が できます。

Tomorrow, I can start working at 7 A.M.

(9) 山下さんはびょうきですから、来週しけん が うけられません。

Because Yamashita-san is ill, she can't take the exam next week.

In recent years, many people have begun to use a different potential form for certain frequently-occurring verbs. This new pattern drops ら from the potential form of some る -verbs as well as 来る , e.g.:

い ら れる	→	いれる	食べ ら れる	→	食べれる
おき ら れる	→	おきれる	ね ら れる	→	ねれる
見 ら れる	→	見れる	来 ら れる	→	来れる

Although this novel pattern is becoming legitimate (e.g., appearing in newspapers), not all る -verbs have this variation. For example, most people do not (yet) say かんがえれる for かんがえられる "can think" or はじめれる for はじめられる "can start". Because whether the potential form of a given る - verb can be used without ら is not easily predictable, and because not all speakers feel comfortable with this " ら-less" pattern, you are discouraged from using it.

13b CLAUSE1 時に CLAUSE2 "When C1, C2"

The forms of the predicate that can appear in C1 with 時に are restricted to the plain forms. Because C1 supplies the time frame for C2, C1 is called a *subordinate clause*, and C2 is called the *main clause*.

A Verb Dictionary フォーム

When the C1 verb is in its Dictionary フォーム , e.g. 日本へ 行く 時に ,

* the situation indicated by C1 has not been realized (or completed) when C2 occurs (when C2 is in the non-past tense), or

* C1 had not been realized (or completed) when C2 occurred (when C2 is in the past tense).

For example, in (1) and (2) below, C2 (buying whiskey) occurs before C1 (going to / leaving for Japan).

Event order	1	くうこうでウィスキーを買う。
	2	日本へ行く。

(1) 日本へ 行く 時に、くうこうでウィスキーを買います。

When I go to (leave for) Japan, I'll buy whiskey at the airport.

(2) 日本へ 行く 時に、くうこうでウィスキーを買いました。

When I went to (left for) Japan, I bought whiskey at the airport.

B   Verb たフォーム

When the たフォーム is used in C1, C1 occurs **before** C2 is realized or completed. In (3) and (4), C1 (going to / arriving in Japan) takes / took place first, and then C2 (buying a dictionary).

Event order	1 日本へ行く。
	2 日本語のじしょを買う。

(3) 日本へ 行った 時に、日本語のじしょを買います。

When I go to (arrive in) Japan, I'll buy a Japanese dictionary.

(4) 日本へ 行った 時に、日本語のじしょを買いました。

When I went to (arrived in) Japan, I bought a Japanese dictionary.

The Dictionary フォーム and たフォーム in a subordinate clause with 時に signal only event sequences with respect to the main-clause event. This fact indicates that these forms in C1 are **not** tense markers. The tense is expressed solely by the main-clause predicate.

C1: Dictionary フォーム

Event order   2   1

(5)   大学を そつぎょうする 時に、ゆびわを作ります。

I'll have a ring made when I graduate from college.

C1: たフォーム

Event order   1   2

(6) 大学を そつぎょうした 時に、中国へ行きます。

When I graduate from college, I'll go to China.

(7) 日本へ りょこうした 時に、しんかんせんにのります。

I'll take the Shinkansen when I travel to Japan.

(8) 日本へ りょこうした 時に、おてらやじんじゃを見ました。

I saw shrines and temples when I traveled to Japan.

(9) 友達に 会った 時に、日本語をれんしゅうしました。

I practiced Japanese when I saw (met) my friend.

C　い-Adjectives: Use the Plain フォーム.

Unlike typical verbs, adjectives and nominal predicates denote *states of affairs* (e.g. 頭がいたい, 私は
大学院生だ), rather than events or actions (e.g. 銀行が開く, 料理する). Therefore, the consider-
ation as to whether or not the C1 situation is completed before C2 is normally irrelevant. Sentences
(10)-(12) below indicate that the speaker's feeling lonely and calling a friend occur simultaneously.
Note that the tense is signaled solely by the C2 (main) predicate; the form of the C1 predicate **does not**
mark tense.

(10)　私は　さびしい　時に、友達にでんわをします。
　　　I call a friend when(ever) I feel lonely.

(11)　私は　さびしい　時に、友達にでんわをしました。
　　　I { called / used to call } a friend when I felt lonely.

(12)　私は　さびしかった　時に、友達にでんわをしました。
　　　I { called / used to call } a friend when I felt lonely.

(13)　りょうが*　うるさくない　時に、べんきょうします。
　　　When(ever) the dorm is not noisy, I study.
　　　*For this usage of が, see (**14b**).

(14)　りょうが　うるさくない　時に、べんきょうしました。
　　　When the dorm was not noisy, I { called / used to study }.

(15)　りょうが　うるさくなかった　時に、べんきょうしました。
　　　When the dorm was not noisy, I { called / used to study }.

Both 〜い時に and 〜かった時に can be used without changing the meaning of the sentence when the
C2 predicate is in the past tense, cf. (11)-(12) and (14)-(15) above. When the sentence is in the non-past
tense, e.g. (10) and (13), the use of 〜かった時に is anomalous.

D　な-Adjectives: Insert な (non-past) or だった (past) before 時に.

Because 時 is a noun, this process is the same as when a な-adjective modifies a noun. Like い-
adjectives, both 〜な時に and 〜だった時に can be used without changing the meaning of the sentence when the C2 predicate is in the past tense, cf. (17)-(18) and (20)-(21).

(16) さくらが きれいな 時に、日本へ行きます。

$\left\{ \begin{array}{c} \textit{When} \\ \textit{Whenever} \end{array} \right\}$ *the cherry blossoms are pretty (in bloom), I go to Japan.*

(17) さくらが きれいな 時に、日本へ行きました。

When the cherry blossoms were pretty (in bloom),
I $\left\{ \begin{array}{c} \textit{went} \\ \textit{used to go} \end{array} \right\}$ *to Japan.*

(18) さくらが きれいだった 時に、日本へ行きました。

When the cherry blossoms were pretty (in bloom), I $\left\{ \begin{array}{c} \textit{went} \\ \textit{used to go} \end{array} \right\}$ *to Japan.*

(19) りょうが 静かじゃない 時に、図書館へ行きます。

$\left\{ \begin{array}{c} \textit{When} \\ \textit{Whenever} \end{array} \right\}$ *the dorm is not quiet, I go to the library.*

(20) りょうが 静かじゃない 時に、図書館へ行きました。

When the dorm was not quiet, I $\left\{ \begin{array}{c} \textit{went} \\ \textit{used to go} \end{array} \right\}$ *to the library.*

(21) りょうが 静かじゃなかった 時に、図書館へ行きました。

When the dorm was not quiet, I $\left\{ \begin{array}{c} \textit{went} \\ \textit{used to go} \end{array} \right\}$ *to the library.*

(22) ひまな時に何をしたいですか。

What do you want to do when you have free time?

E   **Nominal Predicates:** Insert の (non-past) or だった (past) before 時に.

Both 〜の時に and 〜だった時に can be used without changing the meaning of the sentence when the C2 predicate is in the past tense (cf. (24)-(25)).

(23) 学生の 時に、たくさん本を読みます。

People read many books when they are students.

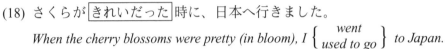

(24) 私は 学生の 時に、たくさん本を読みました。

I read many books when I was a student.

(25) 私は 学生だった 時に、たくさん本を読みました。

I read many books when I was a student.

(26) オフィスアワーの 時に、ぶんぽうのしつもんをします。

I ask grammar questions during office hours.

(27) 私は こどもの 時に、にんじんが食べられませんでした。

When I was a child, I couldn't eat carrots.

13c　VERBAL NOUN + に行く　　"go for VERBAL NOUN"

In 第六課, we studied「Pre-ますフォーム ＋ に ＋ 行く／来る／帰る」"go / come / return in order to do ~", e.g. 図書館へ本を返しに行く. When this pattern involves a verbal noun, you can omit the verb する. For example, ホームステイ is a verbal noun (ホームステイする). Thus, you can say either ホームステイしに行く or ホームステイに行く.

(1)　午後三時ごろ さんぽに 行きませんか。

　　　(Lit.) Wouldn't you go for a walk about 3 P.M.?

　　　Would you like to go for a walk about 3 P.M.?

(2)　先生、 おねがいに 来ました。

　　　Sensei, I've come to (make) a request.

(3)　夏休みに日本へ ホームステイに 行くつもりです。

　　　I plan to go to Japan for a homestay during summer vacation.

13d　Deriving Adverbs from Adjectives

While adjectives modify nouns, adverbs modify predicates. You can create an adverb from an adjective by applying the following:

い -adjectives:　Stem ＋ く　　　早 - い　*early*　　　　　→　早 - く　　　*early*

な -adjectives:　Stem ＋ に　　　きれい　*beautiful / clean*　→　きれい - に　*beautifully / neatly*

早い時間

early time

しけんがありますから、明日の朝、 早く おきるつもりです。

I plan to get up early tomorrow morning because I have a test.

春夏秋冬

春夏秋冬

大きい車

big car

漢字をもっと 大きく 書いて下さい。

Please write the kanji larger.

きれいな店

漢字を きれいに 書いて下さい。

beautiful shop

Please write the kanji neatly.

静かなへや

静かに あるいて下さい。

quiet room

Please walk quietly.

13e   Relative Time

As studied in 第四課, **4g**, relative time expressions are generally not marked with に.

← Past		Now		Future →
おととい day before yesterday	<ruby>昨日<rt>きのう</rt></ruby> yesterday	<ruby>今日<rt>きょう</rt></ruby> today	<ruby>明日<rt>あした</rt></ruby> tomorrow	あさって day after tomorrow
<ruby>先々週<rt>せんせんしゅう</rt></ruby> week before last	<ruby>先週<rt>せんしゅう</rt></ruby> last week	<ruby>今週<rt>こんしゅう</rt></ruby> this week	<ruby>来週<rt>らいしゅう</rt></ruby> next week	<ruby>さ来週<rt>らいしゅう</rt></ruby> week after next
<ruby>先々月<rt>せんせんげつ</rt></ruby> month before last	<ruby>先月<rt>せんげつ</rt></ruby> last month	<ruby>今月<rt>こんげつ</rt></ruby> this month	<ruby>来月<rt>らいげつ</rt></ruby> next month	<ruby>さ来月<rt>らいげつ</rt></ruby> month after next
おととし year before last	<ruby>去年<rt>きょねん</rt></ruby> last year	<ruby>今年<rt>ことし</rt></ruby> this year	<ruby>来年<rt>らいねん</rt></ruby> next year	<ruby>さ来年<rt>らいねん</rt></ruby> year after next

13f   Days of the Month

一日	ついたち	十一日	じゅういちにち	二十一日	にじゅういちにち
二日	ふつか	十二日	じゅうににち	二十二日	にじゅうににち
三日	みっか	十三日	じゅうさんにち	二十三日	にじゅうさんにち
四日	よっか	十四日	じゅうよっか	二十四日	にじゅうよっか
五日	いつか	十五日	じゅうごにち	二十五日	にじゅうごにち
六日	むいか	十六日	じゅうろくにち	二十六日	にじゅうろくにち
七日	なのか	十七日	じゅうしちにち	二十七日	にじゅうしちにち
八日	ようか	十八日	じゅうはちにち	二十八日	にじゅうはちにち
九日	ここのか	十九日	じゅうくにち	二十九日	にじゅうくにち
十日	とおか	二十日	はつか	三十日	さんじゅうにち
				三十一日	さんじゅういちにち

13g   Japanese Calendar

In addition to the Gregorian Calendar, the Japanese use the *Japanese Calendar*, based on the era of a emperor. The <ruby>昭和<rt>しょうわ</rt></ruby> era began in 1926, when Emperor Hirohito reigned, and ended with his death in 1989. The year 1989 was the start of Emperor Akihito's reign and was named <ruby>平成<rt>へいせい</rt></ruby>.

July 9, 1868	<ruby>明治<rt>めいじ</rt></ruby><ruby>元年<rt>がんねん</rt></ruby><ruby>七<rt>しち</rt></ruby>月<ruby>九日<rt>ここのか</rt></ruby>	Oct. 24, 1929	昭和四年十月<ruby>二十四<rt>よ</rt></ruby>日
Aug. 1, 1914	<ruby>大正<rt>たいしょう</rt></ruby>三年八月<ruby>一日<rt>ついたち</rt></ruby>	Dec. 7, 1941	昭和十六年十二月<ruby>七<rt>なのか</rt></ruby>日
Nov. 11, 1918	大正<ruby>七<rt>しち</rt></ruby>年十一月十一日	April 4, 1968	昭和四十三年<ruby>四<rt>し</rt></ruby>月<ruby>四<rt>よっか</rt></ruby>日

The first year of an era is commonly called 元年（がんねん）, e.g. 平成元年.

1868	明治	元年
1869		2 年
1870		3 年
・		・
・		・
・		・
1910		43 年
1911		44 年
1912	明治	45 年
	大正	元年
1913		2 年
1914		3 年
・		・
・		・
・		・
1924		13 年
1925		14 年
1926	大正	15 年
	昭和	元年
1927		2 年
1928		3 年
・		・
・		・
・		・
1950		25 年
・		・
・		・

・		・
1960		35 年
1961		36 年
1962		37 年
1963		38 年
1964		39 年
1965		40 年
1966		41 年
1967		42 年
1968		43 年
1969		44 年
1970		45 年
1971		46 年
1972		47 年
1973		48 年
1974		49 年
1975		50 年
1976		51 年
1977		52 年
1978		53 年
1979		54 年
1980		55 年
1981		56 年
1982		57 年
1983		58 年
1984		59 年
1985		60 年

1986		61 年
1987		62 年
1988		63 年
1989	昭和	64 年
	平成	元年
1990		2 年
1991		3 年
1992		4 年
1993		5 年
1994		6 年
1995		7 年
1996		8 年
1997		9 年
1998		10 年
1999		11 年
2000		12 年
2001		13 年
2002		14 年
2003		15 年
2004		16 年
2005		17 年
2006		18 年
2007		19 年
2008		20 年
2009		21 年
2010		22 年

13h　手紙の書き方

In 第九課, we learned 方（ほう） "direction / side / way". This 漢字 can co-occur with the Pre-ますフォーム of a verb and indicate "a way of ~ing", e.g. 書き方（かた）, 読み方, 作り方, つかい方.

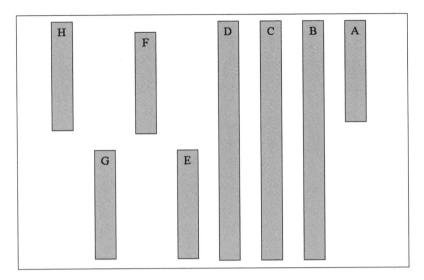

A　Opening words: ask about the addressee's health. New paragraphs begin with a one-space indentation.

例: こんにちは。〇〇さん、お元気ですか。

B　Seasonal greetings: talk about the weather.

例: こちらは今、秋です。まいにち、いいてんきです。

We're in autumn now. The weather is fine every day.

例: そちらは寒いですか。こちらはとても寒いです。

Is it cold over there? It's very cold here.

C　Main topic: e.g. an invitation

例: (ところで／さて、) 〇〇月××日 (△曜日) にパーティーをしますが、いらっしゃいませんか。

We'll have a party on＿＿＿＿＿＿. Would you like to come?

Both ところで and さて mean "by the way". While such a transition word makes the writing flow more naturally, its use is optional. ところで is commonly used both in speech and writing; さて is rarely used in speech.

D　Final greetings　　　　例: では、〜を楽しみにしています。

I look forward to ~.

E　Closing word　　　　例: さようなら

F　Date　　　　例: 平成十五年十一月二十四日

G　Your name

H　Addressee's name

練習問題
_{れんしゅうもんだい}

I.　　あなたは Employer です。三人のクラスメートにインタビューして下さい。

例

A:　　B さんは週まつもしごとができますか。

B:　　はい、もちろん、しごとができます。

　　　(or) いいえ、週まつはしごとはできません。

　　　(or) あのう、すみません。週まつはちょっと，，。

		さん	さん	さん
例	週まつ			
1.	日本語の ワープロ			
2.				
3.				
4.	日本語で E メール			
5.	8:00 A.M.			

II.　ビンゴの時間です。クラスメートに聞きましょう。

例　Q:　X さんは<u>ピアノがひけます</u>か。

　　A:　はい、(ピアノが) ひけます。(or) いいえ、(ピアノは) ひけません。

III.　クラスメートに聞きましょう。

例　A:　冬休みに何をするのを楽しみにしていますか。

　　B:　<u>友達とあそぶの</u>を楽しみにしています。

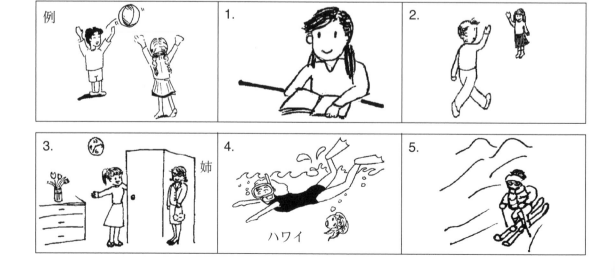

IV. Following the example, ask and answer questions with your partner.

例

A: いつひこうきにのりますか。

(or) どんな時に、ひこうきにのりますか。

B: りょこうする時に、ひこうきにのります。

例　ひこうきにのる。

1. 図書館でべんきょうする。

2. 友達にでんわする。

3. 先生と話したい。

4. 買い物をする。

V. Circle the correct form of the verb.

例　私は（ねる／ねた）時に、本を読みます。

1. でんしゃに（のる／のった）時に、新聞を買います。

2. 友達に（会う／会った）時に、いっしょにコーヒーを飲みます。

3. 日本へ（行く／行った）時に、すもうを見ます。

4. 朝、（おきる／おきた）時に、シャワーをあびます。

5. パーティーを（する／した）時に、おさけを買います。

VI. Following the example, interview your partner.

例

A: Bさんは高校の時に、どんなスポーツをしましたか。

B: 私は高校の時に、テニスをしました。

例	高校	どんなスポーツをしましたか。
1.	中学校	どんな音楽を聞きましたか。
2.		週まつに何をしましたか。
3.	小学校	どんな食べ物が好きでしたか。
4.		どんな食べ物がきらいでしたか。

VII.　Complete the following sentences.

1.　びょうきの時に、＿＿＿＿＿＿＿＿＿＿＿＿＿＿＿＿＿＿＿＿。

2.　寒い時に、＿＿＿＿＿＿＿＿＿＿＿＿＿＿＿＿＿＿＿＿＿＿。

3.　あつい時に、＿＿＿＿＿＿＿＿＿＿＿＿＿＿＿＿＿＿＿＿＿。

4.　しゅくだいが分からない時に、＿＿＿＿＿＿＿＿＿＿＿＿＿。

5.　さびしい時に、＿＿＿＿＿＿＿＿＿＿＿＿＿＿＿＿＿＿＿＿。

6.　ひまな時に、＿＿＿＿＿＿＿＿＿＿＿＿＿＿＿＿＿＿＿＿＿。

VIII.　Complete the following sentences.

1.　昨日、大学へ行く時に、＿＿＿＿＿＿＿＿＿＿＿＿＿＿＿＿。

2.　昨日、大学へ行った時に、＿＿＿＿＿＿＿＿＿＿＿＿＿＿＿＿。

3.　きむらさんは ＿＿＿＿＿＿＿＿＿＿＿ 時に、山本さんにお金をかりました。

4.　家へ帰る時に、＿＿＿＿＿＿＿＿＿＿＿＿＿＿＿＿＿＿＿＿。

5.　大学へ来た時に、＿＿＿＿＿＿＿＿＿＿＿＿＿＿＿＿＿＿＿。

6.　朝、＿＿＿＿＿＿＿＿＿＿＿＿＿＿＿＿時に、シャワーをあびます。

7.　＿＿＿＿＿＿＿＿＿＿＿＿＿＿＿＿＿＿＿時に、ひるねします。

IX.　読みましょう

私はリンです。私は来月、日本へ行きます。友達のほんださんが東京に住んでいるからです。

先週、スーツケースとひこうきのきっぷを買いました。そして、昨日、大学の店でトレーナーを買いました。トレーナーはおみやげです。

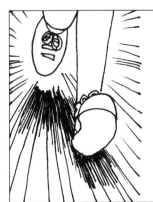

ほんださんはまいにち、朝早くジョギングをするからです。私も日本へ行った時に、ほんださんといっしょにジョギングをするつもりです。

私はまつりを見るのが好きです。それで、浅草へまつりを見に行くつもりです。

そして、まつりのしゃしんをたくさんとるつもりです。

カメラは秋葉原で買います。日本でカメラが安く買えるからです。

○ ですか。×ですか。

1. （　　）リンさんは友達のほんださんと日本へ行きます。
2. （　　）先週、リンさんはひこうきのきっぷを買いました。
3. （　　）リンさんは日本へ行った時に、大学の店で買ったトレーナーをきます。
4. （　　）リンさんはほんださんと日本でジョギングをします。
5. （　　）リンさんは秋葉原でまつりを見ます。
6. （　　）リンさんは浅草でしゃしんをたくさんとります。
7. （　　）リンさんは秋葉原でカメラを買います。

X.　Complete each sentence with a derived adverb.

1. ちょっとうるさいです。（静か　　　　　　）話して下さい。
2. その漢字は小さいです。（大きい　　　　　　）書いて下さい。
3. この字はちょっときたないです。（きれい　　　　　　）書いて下さい。
4. 週まつ、友達と（楽しい　　　　　　）あそびました。
5. 十一時はおそいです。（早い　　　　　　）来て下さい。
6. パーティーで友達は（にぎやか　　　　　　）話していました。
7. あまりべんきょうしていませんね。（まじめ　　　　　　）べんきょうして下さい。

8. プリンターを（安い　　　　　　）買うことができました。
9. スミスさんは日本に三年住んでいました。それで、日本語が（上手　　　　）話せます。
10. （早い　　　　　　）本を返して下さい。

新しい漢字

あき 秋	あきやま 秋山	かえ 返す	きょうと 京都	ごご 午後	ごぜん 午前	こんしゅう 今週
さむ 寒い	らいしゅう さ来週	しゅう 週まつ	せんしゅう 先週	せんせん しゅう 先々週	ともだち 友達	なつ 夏
はる 春	はるやす 春休み	ふゆ 冬	ふゆやす 冬休み	へんじ 返事	らいしゅう 来週	わたしたち 私達

新しい使い方 つか

か かた 書き方	こんげつ 今月	らいげつ さ来月	らいねん さ来年	しょうがっこう 小学校	せんげつ 先月	せん げせん 先々月
たの 楽しい	たの 楽しみ	ちゅうがっこう 中学校	とき 時	ぶん 文	らいげつ 来月	

Radicals: しんにょう（しんにゅう）

辶 in 返, 達, 週 is a にょう type radical and called しんにょう or しんにゅう. This radical has two variations: 辶 and 辶 (返・達・週). Although the latter is more common in printing, you are encouraged to use the former in writing. Most しんにょう 漢字 are related to some activity involving the feet: 返 "to return", 達 originally meant "to go through / arrive", 週 "to come around".

秋 あき	ノ	ニ	千	手	禾	禾	禾ノ	秒	秋
	autumn: (this 漢字 contains 火 (people burn branches in autumn?))								
返 ヘン・ かえ（す）	一	厂	反	反	返	返	返		
	to return: 返事 *reply*								
方 ホウ・かた	丶	亠	方	方					
	direction / side / way: 書き方 *way of writing,* 読み方 *way of reading*								

都	一	十	土	耂	耂	者	者	者	者ゝ	都
ト	都									
	capital: 京都 *Kyoto*									

| 午 | ノ | ← | 上 | 午 | | | | | | |
| ゴ | *horse; 7th sign in Chinese zodiac; used to refer to the interval 11 A.M. to 1 P.M.:* 午前 *A.M.,* 午後 *P.M. In modern times, the meaning of* 午 *is noon.* | | | | | | | | | |

| ☐ 後 | ノ | ク | 彳 | 彳 | 彳 | 彳 | 彳 | 佟 | 後 | |
| ゴ・うし(ろ) | *after / back:* 午後 *P.M.* | | | | | | | | | |

| 前 | 丶 | 丷 | 丷 | 广 | 计 | 計 | 計 | 前 | 前 | |
| ゼン・まえ | *before / in front of:* 前 *before / front,* 名前 *name,* 午前 *A.M.* | | | | | | | | | |

☐ 週	ノ	几	月	円	月	用	周	周	丶周	週
シュウ	週									
	week: 先週 *last week,* 今週 *this week,* 来週 *next week*									

寒	丶	丷	宀	宀	宇	宙	审	窜	実	寒
さむ(い)	寒	寒								
	cold									

| 小 | 亅 | 小 | 小 | | | | | | | |
| ショウ・こ・ちい(さい) | *small:* 小山さん *Koyama,* 小さい *small,* 小学校 *elementary school* | | | | | | | | | |

| 学 | 丶 | 丷 | 丷 | 灬 | 兴 | 学 | 学 | 学 | | |
| ガク・ガッ | *study:* 学生 *student (studying person),* 小学校 *elementary school* | | | | | | | | | |

楽	丶	亻	白	白	白	泊	泊	泊	浊	浊
ガク・たの(しい)・たの(しみ)	楽	楽	楽							
	comfort / ease: 音楽 *music*									

友	一	ナ	方	友						
とも	*friend:* 友達 *friend(s)*									

◾達	一	十	土	土	圭	幸	幸	圭	幸	`達
タチ・ダチ	達	達								
	plural marker: 私達 *we,* 友達 *friend(s),* (達 *generally makes the noun plural, but* 友達 *can be used as a singular noun, e.g.* 友達が一人あそびに来ました.)									

夏	一	一	广	币	冏	百	百	頁	夏	夏
なつ	*summer;* 夏休み *summer vacation*									

春	一	二	三	丰	夫	耒	春	春	春	
はる	*spring:* 春休み *spring break*									

冬	ノ	ク	夂	冬	冬					
ふゆ	*winter:* 冬休み *winter break*									

事	一	一	一	弖	马	写	写	事		
ジ	*matter:* 返事 *reply*									

◾休	ノ	イ	仁	什	付	休				
やす（み）	*to rest:* 夏休み *summer vacation,* 冬休み *winter break,* 春休み *spring break*									

漢字の復習

I.　読みましょう。

1.　昨日は午後十一時ごろ家に帰りました。
2.　先週、日本に留学している友達から手紙が来ました。
3.　石川先生は時々中国語の新聞を読んでいます。
4.　明日の朝、図書館へ本を返しに行くつもりです。
5.　水が少し飲みたいです。

II.　We have learned that 漢字 are fundamentally ideographic, representing ideas. The following words consists of 漢字 you already know. You may not be able to read them, but can you infer their meanings?

例	音楽家	•
1.	女友達	•
2.	開閉	•
3.	銀行員	•
4.	広大	•
5.	住人	•
6.	春夏秋冬	•
7.	小学生	•
8.	新年	•
9.	全員	•
10.	大小	•
11.	読書	•
12.	話好き	•
13.	父母	•
14.	待ち時間	•
15.	明暗	•
16.	来日	•
17.	料理店	•
18.	料理人	•

•	*bank clerk*
•	*cook*
•	*woman friend*
•	*musician*
•	*waiting time*
•	*new year*
•	*resident*
•	*restaurant*
•	*all members*
•	*coming to Japan*
•	*light and darkness*
•	*opening and closing*
•	*parents*
•	*reading*
•	*elementary-school pupil*
•	*size*
•	*talkative*
•	*four seasons*
•	*vast*

新しい語彙

〜さま		*suffix for an honored person*	おどる　ウ ⓘ	*to dance*
あさって		*day after tomorrow*	書き方	*way of writing*
(シャワーを) あびる　ル ⓣ		*to take (a shower)*	きっぷ	*ticket*
うける　ル ⓣ		*to take (an exam)*	くうこう	*airport*
うれしい　イ		*happy, pleased*	今月	*this month*
おととい		*day before yesterday*	さくら	*cherry blossom, tree*
おととし		*year before last*	さびしい　イ	*lonely*
			さ来月	*month after next*
			さ来週	*week after next*

さ来年	year after next	はたらく ウ i	to work
さんぽ（する）	stroll	春	spring
じつは	as a matter of fact	春休み	spring vacation
シャワー	shower	びょうき	illness
小学校	elementary school	ひるね（する）	nap
じんじゃ	Shinto shrine	プリンター	printer
スーツケース	suitcase	文	sentence
先月	last month	ぶんぽう	grammar
先々月	month before last	返事（する）	reply
先々週	week before last	ホームステイ（する）	homestay
そつぎょう（する）	graduation	ホストファミリー	host family
たすける ル t	to help	マイル	mile
中学校	middle school	（お）まつり	festival
つかい方	usage, way to use	（お）みやげ	gift
作り方	way of making	みんな	everyone (plain)
（お）てら	Buddhist temple	ゆき	snow
（お）てんき	weather	ゆきだるま	snowman
時	when	読み方	way of reading
夏	summer	よろこぶ ウ i	to be happy, pleased
のる ウ i	to ride	来月	next month
はしる ウ i	to run	りょこう（する）	trip, travel

名前

あきはばら（秋葉原）	Akihabara	タンゴ	Tango
秋山	Akiyama	ビートルズ	The Beatles
あさくさ（浅草）	Asakusa		

冬休みのけいかく
Winter-Break Plans

日本へ行くことにしました
I've decided to go to Japan

1

もうすぐ冬休みですね。山本さんは冬休みに何をしますか。

私は、車を買うために、仕事をします。大学のせいきょうで働くことにしました。

そうですか。大変ですね。ミラーさんは。

2

私は、ホームステイのプログラムで日本へ行くことにしました。日本のしゅうかんを知りたいからです。

ホストファミリーの秋山さんの家にとまります。

3

わあ、いいですね。

4

秋山さんのごしゅじんもおくさんも休みが一週間あるので、いっしょに奈良や京都へ行くことになっています。

5

いいですね。奈良や京都には有名なおてらやじんじゃがたくさんありますよ。

6

秋山さんの家はどこにあるんですか。

東京にあります。

7

そうですか。じゃあ、ディズニーランドへも行けますね。

ええ。ぜひ行ってみたいです。ところで、おみやげは何がいいでしょうか。

8

それから、チョコレートもいいですよ。

そうですねえ。大学のTシャツはどうですか。小さくて、かるくて、あまり高くないので、とても便利ですよ。

9

そうですね。じゃあ、Tシャツとチョコレートにします。

チョコレートはくうこうで買えますよ。

それは楽ですね。

会話

1　ソン　：もうすぐ冬休みですね。山本さんは冬休みに何をしますか。

It'll be winter break soon, you know? Yamamoto-san, what are you going to do during winter break?

山本　：私は、車を買うために、仕事をします。大学のせいきょうで働くことにしました。

In order to buy a car, I'm going to be working. I've decided to work at the Student Union Store.

ソン　：そうですか。大変ですね。ミラーさんは。

Really? That sounds tough. What about you, Miller-san?

2　ミラー：私は、ホームステイのプログラムで日本へ行くことにしました。日本のしゅうかんを知りたいからです。ホストファミリーの秋山さんの家にとまります。

I've decided to go to Japan on (Lit. by means of) a homestay program, because I want to learn about Japanese customs. I'll be staying at the house of Akiyamas, my host family.

3　ソン　：わあ、いいですね。

Wow, that's great.

4　ミラー：秋山さんのごしゅじんもおくさんも休みが一週間あるので、いっしょに奈良や京都へ行くことになっています。

(Lit.) Both Mr. and Mrs. Akiyama will have a week off, so it's been planned that we'll go to places like Nara and Kyoto.

Both Mr. and Mrs. Akiyama will have a week off, so it turns out they're planning to take me to places like Nara and Kyoto.

5　山本　：いいですね。奈良や京都には有名なおてらやじんじゃがたくさんありますよ。

That's wonderful. There are lots of famous temples and shrines in Nara and Kyoto.

6　ソン　：秋山さんの家はどこにあるんですか。

Where's Akiyama-san's house?

ミラー：東京にあります。

It's in Tokyo.

7　山本　：そうですか。じゃあ、ディズニーランドへも行けますね。

Well then, you can go to Disneyland too.

ミラー　：ええ。ぜひ行ってみたいです。ところで、おみやげは何がいいでしょうか。

Yes, I definitely want to go there. By the way, what's a good gift (for them)?

8　山本　：そうですねえ。大学のＴシャツはどうですか。小さくて、かるくて、あまり高くないので、とても便利ですよ。

Let's see. How about university T-shirts? Because they're small, light and not very expensive, they'd be very convenient.

ソン　：それから、チョコレートもいいですよ。

Chocolates would be nice, too.

9　ミラー　：そうですね。じゃあ、Ｔシャツとチョコレートにします。

You're right. Okay then, I'll decide on T-shirts and chocolates.

ソン　：チョコレートはくうこうで買えますよ。

You can buy the chocolates at the airport.

ミラー　：それは楽ですね。

That'll be easy, then.

使い方

1　せいきょう is an abbreviation of 生活協同組合 and written as 生協. This is a long compound word: せいかつ "life" + きょうどう "cooperative" + くみあい "association".

7　ぜひ originally meant "right and / or wrong", but in modern Japanese it is used as an emphatic adverb "by all means".

In Japan, when you visit someone, you bring a small gift, おみやげ, to show your thoughtfulness. Unlike American culture, おみやげ giving is almost mandatory, not optional.

でしょうか is equivalent to ですか, but the former is softer (thus politer) than the latter.

8, 9　そうですねえ is used to signal that you are thinking about an answer, "let's see …". そうですね with slight rising intonation indicates that you agree with the addressee. そうですね with significant rising intonation and emphasis on ね indicates that you are soliciting the addressee's confirmation, "I'm correct, aren't I?".

9　楽 means "ease / comfort". It can be used as a な -adjective, e.g. 楽なしゅくだい "easy homework assignment".

<ruby>文法<rt>ぶんぽう</rt></ruby>

14a	**CLAUSE1 ので CLAUSE2**	"Because C1, C2; C1, so C2"
14b	**Subject of a Subordinate Clause**	
14c	Dictionary フォーム ＋ ことにする	"I / We have decided to do ~"
	ないフォーム ＋ ことにする	"I / We have decided not to do ~"
14d	Dictionary フォーム ＋ ことになる	"It'll become that X does ~"
	ないフォーム ＋ ことになる	"It'll become that X does not do ~"
14e	Dictionary フォーム ＋ ことになった	"It was decided that X does ~"
	ないフォーム ＋ ことになった	"It was decided that X does not do ~"
	Dictionary フォーム ＋ ことになっている	"It's been decided that X does ~"
	ないフォーム ＋ ことになっている	"It's been decided that X does not do ~"
14f	てフォーム ＋ みる	"I'll try to do ~;
		I'll do ~ and see what it's like"
14g	Dictionary フォーム ＋ ために	"in order to do ~"

14a　CLAUSE1 ので CLAUSE2　　"Because C1, C2; C1, so C2"

This construction is similar to 「CLAUSE1 から CLAUSE2」, cf. 第五課, **5f**, which is also used to supply a reason for doing something or a cause of some event. With の で, **C1 is normally in a Plain フォーム**.

A　Verbs

(1)　一<ruby>週<rt>しゅう</rt></ruby><ruby>間<rt>かん</rt></ruby>休みが ある ので、タホへスキーをしに行くつもりです。

Because I have a one-week break, I plan to go to Tahoe for skiing.

(2)　来年、日本へ 留学する ので、今、日本語のじゅぎょうを<ruby>取<rt>と</rt></ruby>っています。

Because I'm going to study abroad in Japan next year, I'm taking a Japanese course now.

(3)　かぜを ひいた ので、学校を<ruby>休<rt>やす</rt></ruby>みました。

(Lit.) Because I caught a cold, I was absent from school.

Because I caught a cold, I didn't go to school.

(4)　<ruby>宿題<rt>しゅくだい</rt></ruby>がよく 分からない ので、<ruby>教<rt>おし</rt></ruby>えて下さいませんか。

(Lit.) I don't understand the assignment well, so wouldn't you teach it to me?

I don't understand the assignment well, so would you explain it to me?

(5)　きょうかしょを 読まなかった ので、今日のじゅぎょうはよく分かりませんでした。

Because I didn't read the textbook, I couldn't understand today's class well.

(6) ヤングさんが日本人のルームメートを さがしていた ので、よしださんをしょうかいし
ました。

Because Young-san was looking for a Japanese roommate, I introduced Yoshida-san (to her).

B　い -Adjectives

(7) あのモニターは おもい ので、はこべません。

Because that monitor is heavy, I can't carry it.

(8) このオートバイは 安かった ので、買えました。

Because this motorcycle was inexpensive, I could (afford to) buy it.

(9) あのレストランは おいしくない ので、行きません。

Because (the food at) that restaurant is not delicious, I $\left\{\begin{array}{l} won't \\ don't \end{array}\right\}$ go there.

(10) 先週のしけんは むずかしくなかった ので、いいてんが取れました。

Because last week's test was not difficult, I was able to get a good score.

C　な -Adjectives, Nominal Predicates

な -adjectives and nominal predicates (NOUN + です) behave irregularly in this construction. In affirmative sentences in the non-past tense, な is inserted before ので; in the affirmative past tense, だった is required.

(11) ひま な ので、えいがを見に行くつもりです。

Because I have free time, I plan to go see a movie.

(12) 弟はまだ十五さい な ので、うんてんすることができません。

Because my brother is still 15 years old, he can't drive.

(13) 昨日は雨〔あめ〕 だった ので、ピクニックに行きませんでした。

Because it was raining yesterday, we didn't go on a picnic.

When C1 is negative, 〜じゃないので／〜ではないので (non-past) or 〜じゃなかったので／〜
ではなかったので (past) is used.

(14) それは、私のせんもん じゃない ので、よく分かりません。

Because that's not my specialization, I don't understand it well.

(15) 静か じゃなかった ので、よくねむれませんでした。

Since it wasn't quiet, I couldn't sleep well.

| から vs. ので |

~から and ~ので are frequently interchangeable, but with ~から, you can use a polite form in C1, whereas with ~ので, you normally use a plain form.

| Polite フォーム + から、~ |
| Plain フォーム + ので、~ |

(16) ねぼう { しましたから / したので }、クラスにおくれました。

I overslept, so I was late for class.

(17) あまり人が { 来ませんから / 来ないので }、土曜日のピクニックはやめましょう。

Because not many people will come, let's cancel Saturday's picnic.

If you use a plain form with ~から, your speech will sound very casual.

(18) この漢字はむずかしいから、おぼえられない。

Since this kanji is difficult, I can't remember it.

On the other hand, if you use a polite form with ~ので, your speech will sound super polite.

(19) この漢字はとてもむずかしいですので、おぼえられません。

There are some restrictions on the ~ので construction. For example, with ~ので, C2 cannot be a command. (You will not learn command sentences in first year Japanese, however.)

With ので, ~ましょう and ~ましょうか normally do not occur in C2.

× とても寒いので、ヒーターをつけましょう。
○ とても寒いですから、ヒーターをつけましょう。

14b   Subject of a Subordinate Clause

When two clauses are connected (e.g. CLAUSE1 時に CLAUSE2, CLAUSE1 ので CLAUSE2), the subject of the two clauses may be different. In such a case, the subject of the subordinate clause (CLAUSE1) must be marked with が, not by は.

ルームメート 「が」 ねている時に、（私は）勉強します。

I study when my roommate is sleeping.

兄 「が」 あそびに来るので、（私は）すしを作りました。

Because my (older) brother is coming to visit me, I made sushi.

This restriction is reasonable because は is essentially the topic marker and the topic (what the sentence is about) appears in the main clause, rather than in the subordinate clause.

14c　Dictionary フォーム＋ことにする　　"I / We have decided to do ~"
　　　ないフォーム＋ことにする　　　"I / We have decided not to do ~"

〜ことにする／〜ないことにする indicates that you have just decided at the speech time to do or not to do something. It is the same as saying, with strong determination, that you will do / not do something. For this reason, the subject is normally the speaker, like 〜たいです and ほしいです.

〜ことにした means that you decided to do or not to do something; whether you have accomplished it or not is unspecified (cf. (2)-(3) below). 〜ことにしている means that you decided to do (or not to do) something and you have been doing so.

(1)　頭がいたいので、今日は仕事を休むことに します 。

I have a headache, so I've decided to take a day off from work.

I have a headache, so I'm taking a day off from work.

(2)　山本さんは冬休みに何をしますか。

Yamamoto-san, what are you going to do during winter break?

私は大学のせいきょうで働くことに しました 。

I decided to work at the Student Union Store.

(Yamamoto-san hasn't started working yet.)

(3)　中山さん、昨日、じゅぎょうに来ませんでしたね。

Nakayama-san, you didn't come to class yesterday, did you?

ええ 、友達があそびに来たので、行かないことに した んです。

No . *Since my friends came to visit me, I decided not to go to class.*

(Nakayama-san did cut class. Note that this exchange involves a negative Yes-No question, cf. 第六課, **6i**.)

(4)　毎朝、四マイルはしることに しています 。

I decided to run 4 miles every morning (and have been doing so).

(5)　つかれた時に、おふろに入ることに しています 。

I decided to take a bath when tired (and have been doing so).

I've made a practice of taking a bath when I get tired.

If you decide on something, use「Xにする」, cf. 第九課, **9g**.

(6)　おくり物は、日本のお茶にします。

As for the gift, I've decided on Japanese tea.

14d　**Dictionary** フォーム + ことになる　　　"It'll become that X does ~"
　　　　ないフォーム + ことになる　　　　　　"It'll become that X does not do ~"

 ～ことになる contrasts with ～ことにする. While ～ことにする implies strong control and determination of the person who does some action / activity, ～ことになる indicates that the person does something regardless of his / her will.

ルームメートはおさらをあらうのが
きらいなので、いつも私があらう
ことになります。

Because my roommate hates washing dishes,
$\left\{ \begin{array}{l} \textit{it always turns out that I do the washing.} \\ \textit{it's me that always ends up washing them.} \end{array} \right\}$

14e　**Dictionary** フォーム + ことになった　　　"It was decided that X does ~"
　　　　ないフォーム + ことになった　　　　　　"It was decided that X does not do ~"
　　　　Dictionary フォーム + ことになっている　"It's been decided that X does ~"
　　　　ないフォーム + ことになっている　　　　"It's been decided that X does not do ~"

 ～ことになった and ～ことになっている are significantly different from ～ことになる. ～ことになった and ～ことになっている imply that someone (or some people) has made the decision that X does something, whereas ～ことになる does not have this connotation. ～ことになった places more emphasis on the decision making, while ～ことになっている has more focus on the action or activity.

(1)　スミスさんは日本のかいしゃで働くことになりました。
　　　It was decided that Smith-san would work for a Japanese company.
　　　スミスさんは日本のかいしゃで働くことになっています。
　　　It's been decided that Smith-san will work for a Japanese company.

If the situation is specified, what X is doing is usually a common practice.

(2)　日本では、家に入る時、くつをぬぐことになっています。
　　　In Japan, it's customary for people to take off their shoes when they enter a house.

(3)　日本では、おしょうがつにおもちを食べることになっています。
　　　In Japan, people traditionally eat rice cakes during the New Year's holidays.

(4)　ぶんぽうが分からない時には、オフィスアワーに行って、先生に聞くことになっています。
　　　When we don't understand the grammar, we're supposed to go to office hours and ask our teachers.

(5) 教室では英語は話さないことになっています。

We (have the rule that we) don't speak English in the classroom.

(6) 日本語のクラスでは、毎週、新しい漢字を十三おぼえることになっています。

In Japanese class, (the students) are supposed to remember 13 new kanji each week.

Because 〜ことにする／した／している are highly assertive, many people prefer to use 〜ことになった to soften the statement (even when the decision is made by their own will).

(7a) 大学をやめることにしました。

*I've decided to leave college. (= I **will** leave college.)*

(7b) 大学をやめることになりました。

It turns out that I'll be leaving college.

14f　てフォーム＋みる　　　"I'll try to do ~; I'll do ~ and see what it's like"

(1) 来年、日本文学のクラスを取ってみます。

I'm going to take a course on Japanese literature next year (and see how it is).

(2) おすしを作ったので、食べてみて下さい。

(Lit.) I made sushi, so please eat it and see.

I made sushi, so please try some.

(3) 夏目そうせきのしょうせつを読んでみませんか。

(Lit.) Won't you try to read Soseki Natsume's novels (and see how they are)?

Why don't you try out Soseki Natsume's novels?

(4) 京都へも行ってみたいです。

I want to go to Kyoto too.

(5) できるだけやってみます。

I'll try as hard as I can.

(6) （お）さしみを食べてみませんか。

Won't you try some sashimi?

食べたことがありますが、あまり好きではありませんでした。

I've tried (Lit. eaten) it, but I didn't like it very much.

14g   Dictionary フォーム ＋ ために   "in order to do ~"

This pattern is similar to「Pre-ますフォーム＋に＋行きます／来ます／かえります」"go / come / return to do ~", cf. 第六課, **6e**. Both indicate that someone does X in order to accomplish something, e.g. (1) below. However, when the second (main) verb is not 行きます／来ます／かえります, you need to use「Dictionary フォーム＋ために」.

(1)   図書館へ本を返しに行きます。

I'm going to the library to return books.

本を返すために、図書館へ行きます。

In order to return books, I'm going to the library.

(2)   漢字をおぼえるために、フラッシュカードを作りました。

In order to memorize kanji, I've made flash cards.

(3)   日本へ留学するために、パスポートを取りました。

In order to study abroad in Japan, I got a passport.

(4)   プリンターをはこぶために、りょうしんに車をかりました。

In order to carry a printer, I borrowed a car from my parents.

れんしゅうもんだい
練習問題

I.   For each sentence in box A, choose an appropriate sentence from box B, and combine them to make a sentence with ～ので.

A	B
1.　私のアパートは静かです。	a.　じしょでしらべます。
2.　とても寒いです。	b.　おなかがすいています。
3.　ちょっとうるさいです。	c.　来年も取りたいです。
4.　たんごのいみが分かりません。	d.　ヒーターをつけます。
5.　雨がふっていました。	e.　よく勉強することができます。
6.　朝ごはんを食べませんでした。	f.　ラジオをけして下さいませんか。
7.　日本語のクラスはおもしろいです。	g.　昨日、テニスをすることはできませんでした。

II.　Complete the following sentences.

1.　よしゅうをしなかったので、＿＿＿＿＿＿＿＿＿＿＿＿＿＿＿＿＿＿＿＿＿＿。

2.　このレストランはひょうばんがいいので、＿＿＿＿＿＿＿＿＿＿＿＿＿＿＿＿＿。

3.　頭がいたいので、＿＿＿＿＿＿＿＿＿＿＿＿＿＿＿＿＿＿＿＿＿＿＿。

4.　ゆうべ＿＿＿＿＿＿＿＿＿＿＿＿＿＿＿＿＿＿＿＿＿ので、今ねむいです。

5.　＿＿＿＿＿＿＿＿＿＿＿＿＿＿＿＿＿＿＿ので、図書館へ行くつもりです。

6.　＿＿＿＿＿＿＿＿＿＿＿＿＿＿＿＿＿＿＿ので、どこかへ行きたいです。

III.　Ask your friends the following questions, and find out what they have been doing in various situations.

	（　　　　　　）さん	（　　　　　　）さん
1.　いいせいせきを取るために、何をすることにしていますか。		
2.　漢字をおぼえるために、何をすることにしていますか。		
3.　しけんがある時に、何をすることにしていますか。		
4.　お金がない時に、何をすることにしていますか。		

IV.　あなたの日本語のクラスで、学生は何をすることになっていますか。グループで話しましょう。

V.　あなたの国（くに）では、いろいろな時に、何をすることになっていますか。グループであなたの国のしゅうかんをしょうかいしましょう。

　　けっこんしき　　たんじょう日
　　おしょうがつ　　おそうしき

Other special occasions

あげる	to give
おいわい	congratulatory gift
おこうでん	obituary gift money

VI.　Ask your partner a question, and find out what s/he will try to do in each situation.

1.　せいせきがわるい時に、何をしてみますか。

2.　たんごがぜんぜんおぼえられない時に、何をしてみますか。

3.　宿題があります。でも、ねむい時に、何をしてみますか。

4.　ねむれない時に、何をしてみますか。

5.　新しい友達がほしい時に、何をしてみますか。

6.　日本へ行った時に、何をしてみたいですか。

VII.　ブラウンさん has problems. わたなべさん and やまださん make suggestions on how to solve them. Those suggestions are shown in the boxes below. Make up conversations between ブラウンさん, わたなべさん, and やまださん as shown in the example.

例1　ブラウン　：　私はさいきん、ふとりました。

　　　わたなべ　：　毎日ジョギングをしていますか。

　　　ブラウン　：　いいえ、していません。じゃあ、毎日ジョギングをすることにします。

例2　ブラウン　：　私はさいきん、ふとりました。

　　　やまだ　　：　チョコレートをたくさん食べるからですよ。

　　　ブラウン　：　そうですね。じゃあ、あまり食べないことにします。

Watanabe-san's suggestion	Brown-san's problem	Yamada-san's suggestion
 例1	 さいきん、ふとった。 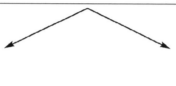	 例2
 1. 休みのひ	お金がない。 	 2.
 3.	日本語のせいせきがわるい。 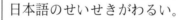	 4.
 5.	ルームメートがうるさいので、勉強ができない。 	 6. りょう

VIII. Make a dialog between A and B, using ～ことがあります and ～てみます as shown in the example.

例　A:　日本のおべんとうを食べたことがありますか。

B:　いいえ。まだ、<u>食べた</u>ことはありません。

A:　そうですか。<u>おいしいですよ</u>。

B:　じゃあ、<u>こんど買っ</u>てみます。

1　A:　けんどうをしたことがありますか。

B:　いいえ、＿＿＿＿＿＿＿＿＿＿＿＿＿＿＿
　　　ことはありません。

A:　そうですか。＿＿＿＿＿＿＿＿＿＿＿＿＿。

B:　じゃあ、＿＿＿＿＿＿＿＿＿＿＿＿＿＿＿
　　　てみます。

2　A:　日本のえいがを見たことがありますか。

B:　いいえ、＿＿＿＿＿＿＿＿＿＿＿＿＿＿＿
　　　ことはありません。

A:　そうですか。＿＿＿＿＿＿＿＿＿＿＿＿＿。

B:　じゃあ、＿＿＿＿＿＿＿＿＿＿＿てみます。

3　A:　うなぎを食べたことがありますか。

B:　いいえ、＿＿＿＿＿＿＿＿＿＿＿＿＿＿こ
　　　とはありません。

A:　そうですか。＿＿＿＿＿＿＿＿＿＿＿＿＿。

B:　じゃあ、＿＿＿＿＿＿＿＿＿＿＿てみます。

IX.　読みましょう

私はジョーンズです。日本語のプログラムの学生です。

高校生の時から日本語を勉強しています。でも、まだ、あまり上手じゃありません。

私はもっと日本語を勉強したいので、来年の夏休みに日本へ行くことにしました。そして、ホームステイをすることにしました。

私はまだ日本へ行ったことがありません。日本へ行った時に、おいしい日本料理が食べたいです。

そして、有名なこうえんや日本のにわが見たいので、京都へ行ってみたいです。

私は日本へ行くために、冬休みに本やで働くことにしました。仕事は午前十時から午後五時までです。

そして、六時から十時までレストランで働くつもりです。毎日いそがしくて、大変ですが、がんばります。

七月に日本へ行くのを楽しみにしています。

○ ですか。×ですか。

1. （　　）ジョーンズさんは日本語が上手です。
2. （　　）ジョーンズさんは日本語を勉強するために日本へ行くことにしました。
3. （　　）ジョーンズさんは日本でホストファミリーの家にとまります。
4. （　　）ジョーンズさんは京都へ有名なこうえんやにわを見に行きたがっています。
5. （　　）ジョーンズさんは日本へ行くために、冬休みに日本語を勉強することにしました。

新しい漢字

雨 (あめ)	教える (おし)	教室 (きょうしつ)	仕事 (しごと)	宿題 (しゅくだい)	大変 (たいへん)	取る (と)
働く (はたら)	勉強 (べんきょう)	毎朝 (まいあさ)	毎週 (まいしゅう)	毎日 (まいにち)	毎晩 (まいばん)	有名 (ゆうめい)

新しい使い方

国 (くに)	～週間 (しゅうかん)	夏目 (なつめ)	休み (やす)	休む (やす)	楽 (らく)

Radicals: ウかんむり

宀 in 家・安・字・寒・室・宿 is called ウかんむり because it looks like カタカナ「ウ」. Although it is rarely used, 宀 itself is a 漢字 meaning "roof". Most ウかんむり漢字 are related to the notion of "house".

雨	一	厂	冂	帀	雨	雨	雨	雨		
あめ	*rain*									

教	一	十	土	耂	耂	孝	孝	孝	教	教
キョウ・おし（える）	教									
	to teach: 教室 *classroom*									

| 室 | ` | ⸌ | 宀 | 宀 | 宏 | 宏 | 宰 | 宰 | 室 | |
| シツ | *room:* 教室 *classroom* | | | | | | | | | |

| 仕 | ノ | イ | 仁 | 什 | 仕 | | | | | |
| シ | *to serve / work:* 仕事 *work* | | | | | | | | | |

| 事 | 一 | 一 | 冖 | 口 | 写 | 写 | 写 | 事 | | |
| ジ・こと・ごと | *matter:* 返事 *reply,* 仕事 *work* | | | | | | | | | |

宿	`	⸌	宀	宀	宀	宁	宿	宿	宿	宿
シュク	宿									
	lodging: 宿題 *homework assignment (subject to do at home)*									

題	⟍	冂	日	日	旦	早	早	是	是	是
ダイ	是	題	題	題	題	題	題	題		
	subject / topic: 宿題 *homework assignment (subject to do at home)*									

| 変 | ` | 亠 | ナ | 亣 | 亦 | 亦 | 亦 | 変 | | |
| ヘン | *change:* 大変 *serious / difficult / awful (big change)* | | | | | | | | | |

取	一	厂	厂	F	耳	耳	取	取		
と（る）	*to take / get*									
勉	ノ	ク	ケ	兔	台	台	免	免	勉	勉
ベン	*to make efforts:* 勉強 *study (make efforts to become strong)*									
強	⊃	コ	弓	弓	弘	弘	弘	強	強	
キョウ	強									
	strong: 勉強 *study (make efforts to become strong)*									
▮働	ノ	イ	イ	ド	ケ	信	信	信	俥	俥
はたら（く）	俥	働	働							
	to work									
毎	ノ	ヒ	ヒ	勾	勾	毎				
マイ	*every:* 毎朝 *every morning,* 毎晩 *every evening,* 毎日 *every day,* 毎週 *every week*									
有	ノ	ナ	才	有	有	有				
ユウ	*to exist / own / have:* 有名 *famous (having a name)*									
名	ノ	ク	夕	夕	名	名				
メイ・な	*name:* 名前 *name,* 有名 *famous (owning a name)*									
楽	ヽ	㇀	白	白	白	白	泊	冰	淅	淅
ガク・ラク・たの（しみ）	楽	楽	楽							
	comfort / ease: 音楽 *music*									

漢字の復習

I.　読みましょう。

1.　ご兄弟はお元気ですか。
2.　来年、新しい車を買うつもりです。
3.　日本料理の作り方を教えて下さい。
4.　夏休みに京都へ行きます。とても楽しみにしています。
5.　私のめいは今年、小学校に入りました。

II.　Can you guess how to write the following words with 毎?

	every minute
	every month

	every hour

III.　Let's play しりとり. しりとり is a Japanese word game in which one player has to say a word starting with the last syllable of the word given by the previous player (しり "buttocks, rear-end" + とり < とる "to take"). Fill in each box with one of the 漢字 below so that the sequence of words makes しりとり.

しりとりの例　　あさ——さかな——なつ——つかれる

> 店　下　分　暗　東　英　月

1.　名前——☐ 文学——☐ い——石川——☐ かる
2.　教室——☐——聞く——☐ さい——妹——☐ 京
3.　手紙——☐——背

新しい語彙

X さい	X years old	オートバイ	motorcycle
X 週間	X week(s)	おくり物	a present
あげる ㋸ⓣ	to give	おくれる ㋸ⓘ	to be late
あらう ㋒ⓣ	to wash	おもい ㋑	heavy

かいしゃ		company	ねむい	イ		sleepy
かぜ		(to catch) a cold	ねむる	ウ i		to sleep
かるい	イ	light (weight)	はこぶ	ウ t		to carry
国		country	パスポート			passport
グループ		group	ヒーター			heater
けす	ウ t	to turn off	(かぜを) ひく	ウ t		to catch (a cold)
けっこんしき		wedding ceremony	ひょうばん			reputation
けんどう		kendo	ふとる	ウ i		to become fat
さいきん		recently	フラッシュカード			flash card
さがす	ウ t	to search for	(お) ふろ			bath
(お) さら		dish	(お) べんとう			box lunch
しゅうかん		custom	毎週			every week
しょうかい (する)		introduction	(お) もち			rice cake
(お) しょうがつ		New Year's Day	モニター			monitor
しらべる	ル t	to check	休み			day off
せいきょう		co-op	休む	ウ i		to rest, take a day off
せいせき		grade	やめる	ル t		to quit
ぜひ		by all means	やる	ウ t		to do, try
(お) そうしき		funeral ceremony	ゆうべ			last night
たんご		vocabulary, word	有名	ナ		famous
つける	ル t	to turn on	よしゅう (する)			preparatory study
できるだけ		as much as possible	楽	ナ		easy, simple, comfortable, relaxed
てん		points, score				
とまる	ウ i	to stay				
ぬぐ	ウ t	to take off (clothes / shoes)				

名前

ディズニーランド	*Disneyland*	夏目 （なつめ）	*Natsume*

一年生の漢字　by Stroke Count

In the following table, the 漢字 in dark black have been learned in Lessons 3-14.

①	一	②	二	七	八	九	十	人	入	③	三	千	土	上	小
山	下	川	大	女	々	子	口	夕	④	五	六	日	月	火	水
分	木	今	中	父	円	手	方	文	元	少	午	友	化	予	切
犬	心	天	内	介	不	反	⑤	四	本	半	生	石	広	古	目
兄	母	去	冬	仕	外	末	出	白	左	右	写	田	用	正	冊
⑥	百	行	先	会	安	早	好	年	多	字	気	名	米	全	休
毎	有	色	忙	自	当	両	耳	同	回	考	地	伝	肉	死	成
次	⑦	何	来	私	見	車	弟	男	作	住	図	花	利	返	村
言	赤	近	足	医	社	困	冷	初	対	⑧	金	明	学	英	長
姉	妹	東	京	国	知	物	店	事	雨	取	画	始	受	供	使
夜	青	歩	卒	法	味	所	者	門	枚	招	注	泣	泳	⑨	昨
食	茶	待	後	音	背	前	便	秋	春	室	変	映	飛	洗	屋
度	急	単	乗	思	科	専	相	故	計	送	持	昼	客	⑩	時
家	留	高	帰	校	書	紙	院	員	料	夏	勉	酒	病	降	真
眠	旅	配	借	個	案	弱	笑	⑪	閉	部	理	都	週	教	宿
強	習	雪	終	授	転	動	問	符	魚	紹	悪	族	婚	⑫	買
晩	間	飲	番	開	朝	寒	達	絵	覚	期	葉	晴	復	運	貯
答	痛	着	暑	最	短	貸	遊	然	落	結	⑬	新	暗	話	漢
楽	働	電	寝	試	業	意	遠	辞	鉄	数	⑭	語	読	銀	聞
静	歌	練	駅	説	様	⑮	質	熱	調	談	⑯	館	頭	機	親
薬	⑰	濯	績	⑱	曜	題	験	顔	難	⑲	願				

You have already learned different kanji!

155

Appendix A   Grammar Notes by Lesson

PART I

第一課

第二課

第三課

第四課

4a	Verb Conjugation: Pre- ますフォーム	
4b	Object Marker を	
4c	Beautifiers お and ご	
4d	で: Location Marker for Action Verbs	
4e	Instrument Marker で	"by means of"
4f	Direction / Goal Marker へ・に	
4g	Time Marker に	
4h	と "with"; ひとりで "by oneself"	
4i	A から B まで	"from A to B; from A as far as B"
4j	Pre- ますフォーム + ましょう	"Let's do ~"
	Pre- ますフォーム + ましょうか	"Shall we do ~?"
4k	Verbal Nouns	
4l	Final Particle ね	
4m	Days of the Week	
4n	Time	

第五課

5a	Object Marker に	
5b	Past Tense (Polite Speech)	
5c	Verb Conjugation: Dictionary フォーム	
5d	Dictionary フォーム + つもりです	"I intend / plan to do ~"
5e	X は Y があります	"X has Y"
5f	CLAUSE1 から CLAUSE2	"Because C1, C2; C1, so C2"
5g	どうしてですか	"Why is / was it so?"
5h	NOUN1 や NOUN2 など	"N1 and N2 among other things"
5i	もう "already"; まだ "yet"	
5j	Months of the Year	

第六課

6a	Verb Conjugation: Negative フォーム	
6b	Plain フォーム vs. Polite フォーム	
6c	ないフォーム + つもりです	"I intend / plan not to do ~"
6d	Pre- ますフォーム + ませんか	"Won't you do ~?; Would you like to do ~?"
6e	Pre- ますフォーム + に + 行く／来る／かえる	"go / come / return in order to do ~"
6f	Dictionary フォーム + ことができる	"can; be able to do ~"
6g	Plain フォーム + のです／んです	"It is the case that ~"
6h	Negative Scope Marker は	

第七課

第八課

第九課

第十課

10a	Verb Conjugation: たフォーム	
10b	たフォーム＋ことがある	"X has had the experience of VERB-ing"
10c	てフォーム＋いる	"X has VERB-ed"
10d	Transitive vs. Intransitive Verbs	
10e	Indirect Object Marker に	
10f	Verbs of Wearing Clothing	
10g	かかる	"It takes time / expense"
10h	NOUN ぐらい ; NOUN ごろ (に)	"about / approximately ~"

第十一課

11a	Noun Modification by Verbs	
11b	Past Tense of い -Adjectives	
11c	Past Tense of です	
11d	Noun Modification by Adjectives	
11e	Object Marker が	
11f	Sequential Voicing	

第十二課

12a	X がほしいです	"I / We want X"
	X はほしくありません	"I / We don't want X" (formal)
	X はほしくないです	"I / We don't want X" (less formal)
12b	X は Y をほしがっている	"X wants Y"
12c	Pre- ますフォーム＋たいです／	"I / We want to do ~"
	たくありません／たくないです	"I / We don't want to do ~"
12d	X は Pre- ますフォーム＋たがっている	"X wants to do ~"
12e	どうして／なぜ	"Why ~"
	Plain フォーム＋からだ	"It is because ~"
12f	Material Marker で	
12g	Quantifiers	

第十三課

13a	Verb Conjugation: Potential フォーム	
13b	CLAUSE1 時に CLAUSE2	"When C1, C2"
13c	VERBAL NOUN ＋ に行く	"go for VERBAL NOUN"
13d	Deriving Adverbs from Adjectives	
13e	Relative Time	
13f	Days of the Month	
13g	Japanese Calendar	
13h	手紙の書き方	

第十四課

14a	CLAUSE1 ので CLAUSE2	"Because C1, C2; C1, so C2"
14b	Subject of a Subordinate Clause	
14c	Dictionary フォーム + ことにする	"I / We have decided to do ~"
	ないフォーム + ことにする	"I / We have decided not to do ~"
14d	Dictionary フォーム + ことになる	"It'll become that X does ~"
	ないフォーム + ことになる	"It'll become that X does not do ~"
14e	Dictionary フォーム + ことになった	"It was decided that X does ~"
	ないフォーム + ことになった	"It was decided that X does not do ~"
	Dictionary フォーム + ことになっている	"It's been decided that X does ~"
	ないフォーム + ことになっている	"It's been decided that X does not do ~"
14f	てフォーム + みる	"I'll try to do ~; I'll do ~ and see what it's like"
14g	Dictionary フォーム + ために	"in order to do ~"

Appendix B   List of College Majors

Accounting	かいけいがく	kaikeigaku	会計学
Agriculture	のうがく	nōgaku	農学
Animal Husbandry	ちくさんがく	chikusangaku	畜産学
Anthropology	じんるいがく	jinruigaku	人類学
Archaeology	こうこがく	kōkogaku	考古学
Architecture	けんちくがく	kenchikugaku	建築学
Art	びじゅつ	bijutsu	美術
Art History	びじゅつし	bijutsushi	美術史
Astronomy	てんもんがく	tenmongaku	天文学
Astrophysics	てんたいぶつりがく	tentai-butsurigaku	天体物理学
Aviation	こうくうがく	kōkūgaku	航空学
Bacteriology	さいきんがく	saikingaku	細菌学
Biochemistry	せい（ぶつ）かがく	sei(butsu)-kagaku	生(物)化学
Biology	せいぶつがく	seibutsugaku	生物学
Biophysics	せい（ぶつ）ぶつりがく	sei(butsu)-butsurigaku	生(物)物理学
Botany	しょくぶつがく	shokubutsugaku	植物学
Business Administration	けいえいがく	keieigaku	経営学
Chemical Engineering	かがくこうがく	kagaku-kōgaku	化学工学
Chemistry	かがく	kagaku	化学
Chinese Literature	ちゅうごくぶんがく	chūgoku-bungaku	中国文学
Civil Engineering	どぼくこうがく	doboku-kōgaku	土木工学
Cognitive Science	にんちかがく	ninchi-kagaku	認知科学
Comparative Literature	ひかくぶんがく	hikaku-bungaku	比較文学
Computer Science	コンピューターサイエンス じょうほうこうがく	konpyūtā-saiensu jōhō-kōgaku	 情報工学
Criminology	はんざいがく	hanzaigaku	犯罪学
Dentistry	しがく	shigaku	歯学
Drama	えんげき	engeki	演劇
Earth Scince	ちがく	chigaku	地学
East Asian Studies	ひがしアジアけんきゅう	higashi-ajia kenkyū	東アジア研究
Ecology	せいたいがく	seitaigaku	生態学
Economics	けいざいがく	keizaigaku	経済学
Education	きょういくがく	kyōikugaku	教育学
Electrical Engineering	でんしこうがく でんきこうがく	denshi-kōgaku denki-kōgaku	電子工学 電気工学
Engineering	こうがく	kōgaku	工学

English Literature	えいぶんがく	ei-bungaku	英文学
Entomology	こんちゅうがく	konchūgaku	昆虫学
Environmental Sciences	かんきょうがく	kankyōgaku	環境学
Ethnic Studies	みんぞくがく	minzokugaku	民族学
Film Studies	えいががく	eigagaku	映画学
Fisheries	すいさんがく	suisangaku	水産学
Forestry	りんがく	ringaku	林学
French Literature	ふつぶん(がく)	futsu-bun(gaku)	仏文(学)
Gender Studies	ジェンダーけんきゅう	jendā kenkyū	ジェンダー研究
Genetics	いでんがく	idengaku	遺伝学
Geography	ちりがく	chirigaku	地理学
Geology	ちしつがく	chishitsugaku	地質学
Geophysics	ちきゅうぶつりがく	chikyū-butsurigaku	地球物理学
German Literature	ドイツぶんがく	doitsu-bungaku	ドイツ文学
Gerontology	ろうねんがく	rōnengaku	老年学
Health Science	けんこうがく	kenkōgaku	健康学
History	れきし・しがく	rekishi/shigaku	歴史・史学
Home Economics	かせいがく	kaseigaku	家政学
Horticulture	えんげいがく	engeigaku	園芸学
Humanities	じんぶんかがく	jinbun-kagaku	人文科学
Hygiene	えいせいがく	eiseigaku	衛生学
Information Sciences	じょうほう(か)がく	jōhō(ka)gaku	情報(科)学
International Relations	こくさいかんけい(ろん)	kokusai-kankei(ron)	国際関係(論)
Italian Literature	イタリアぶんがく	itaria-bungaku	イタリア文学
Japanese Literature	にほんぶんがく	nihon-bungaku	日本文学
Journalism	しんぶんがく	shinbungaku	新聞学
Korean Literature	かんこくぶんがく	kankoku-bungaku	韓国文学
Latin American Literature	ちゅうなんべいぶんがく	chūnanbei-bungaku	中南米文学
Law	ほうりつ(がく)・ほうがく	hōritsu(gaku)/hōgaku	法律(学)・法学
Library Science	としょかんがく	toshokangaku	図書館学
Linguistics	げんごがく	gengogaku	言語学
Literature	ぶんがく	bungaku	文学
Mathematics	すうがく	sūgaku	数学
Mechanical Engineering	きかいこうがく	kikai-kōgaku	機械工学
Medical Science	いがく	igaku	医学
Medieval Studies	ちゅうせいがく	chūseigaku	中世学
Meteorology	きしょうがく	kishōgaku	気象学
Middle Eastern Studies	ちゅうとうがく	chūtōgaku	中東学
Mining/Mineral Engineering	こうざんこうがく	kōzan-kōgaku	鉱山工学

Molecular Biology	ぶんしせいぶつがく	bunshi-seibutsugaku	分子生物学
Music	おんがく	ongaku	音楽
Neuroscience	のうかがく	nō-kagaku	脳科学
Nuclear Engineering	げんし(りょく)こうがく	genshi(ryoku)-kōgaku	原子(力)工学
Nutritional Science	えいようがく	eiyōgaku	栄養学
Nursing	かんごがく	kangogaku	看護学
Oceanography	かいようがく	kaiyōgaku	海洋学
Optometry	けんがんがく	kengangaku	検眼学
Pharmaceutical Sciences	やくがく	yakugaku	薬学
Philosophy	てつがく	tetsugaku	哲学
Physical Education	たいいくがく	taiikugaku	体育学
Physics	ぶつりがく	butsurigaku	物理学
Physiology	せいりがく	seirigaku	生理学
Political Science	せいじがく	seijigaku	政治学
Psychology	しんりがく	shinrigaku	心理学
Public Policy	こうきょうせいさく	kōkyō-seisaku	公共政策
Religious Studies	しゅうきょうがく	shūkyōgaku	宗教学
Rhetoric	しゅうじがく	shūjigaku	修辞学
Science	かがく	kagaku	科学
Seismology	じしんがく	jishingaku	地震学
Slavic Literature	ロシアぶんがく	roshia-bungaku	ロシア文学
Social Welfare	(しゃかい)ふくしがく	(shakai)fukushigaku	(社会)福祉学
Sociology	しゃかいがく	shakaigaku	社会学
Soil Science	どじょうがく	dojōgaku	土壌学
Spanish Literature	スペインぶんがく	supein-bungaku	スペイン文学
Statistics	とうけいがく	tōkeigaku	統計学
Theater	えんげき	engeki	演劇
Tourism	かんこうがく	kankōgaku	観光学
Toxicology	どくぶつがく	dokubutsugaku	毒物学
Urban Studies	としがく	toshigaku	都市学
Veterinary Medicine	じゅういがく	jūigaku	獣医学
Women's Studies	じょせいがく	joseigaku	女性学
Zoology	どうぶつがく	dōbutsugaku	動物学

Undeclared	まだわかりません。	*I still don't know.*
	mada wakarimasen.	
	まだきめていません。	*I haven't decided yet.*
	mada kimeteimasen.	

Appendix C   Verb/Adjective/Copula Conjugation

上: Plain フォーム   下: Polite フォーム

		う verb	る verb		Irregular Verb	
Non-Past	Affirmative	会う	いる	食べる	来る	する
		会います	います	食べます	来ます	します
	Negative	会わない	いない	食べない	来ない	しない
		会いません	いません	食べません	来ません	しません
Past	Affirmative	会った	いた	食べた	来た	した
		会いました	いました	食べました	来ました	しました
	Negative	会わなかった	いなかった	食べなかった	来なかった	しなかった
		会いませんでした	いませんでした	食べませんでした	来ませんでした	しませんでした
Other Verbs		開く　　買う 聞く　　知る 住む　　作る 飲む　　話す 待つ　　帰る	おきる かりる きる できる 見る	教える かんがえる しらべる ねる はじめる		

		う verb	る verb		Irregular Verb	
Negative フォーム	a	読ま (ない)	見 (ない)	食べ (ない)	来 (ない)	し (ない)
Passive フォーム	a	読まれる	見られる	食べられる	来られる	される
Causative フォーム	a	読ませる	見させる	食べさせる	来させる	させる
Pre- ますフォーム	i	読み (ます)	見 (ます)	食べ (ます)	来 (ます)	し (ます)
Dictionary フォーム	u	読む	見る	食べる	来る	する
Potential フォーム	e	読める	見られる	食べられる	来られる	できる
ばフォーム	e	読め (ば)	見れ (ば)	食べれ (ば)	来れ (ば)	すれ (ば)
Volitional フォーム	o	読もう	見よう	食べよう	来よう	しよう
てフォーム		読んで	見て	食べて	来て	して
たフォーム		読んだ	見た	食べた	来た	した

う verb Dictionary フォーム	Final Syllable	てフォーム	たフォーム
会う	う	会って	会った
書く	く	書いて	書いた
およぐ	ぐ	およいで	およいだ
話す	す	話して	話した
待つ	つ	待って	待った
しぬ	ぬ	しんで	しんだ
よぶ	ぶ	よんで	よんだ
飲む	む	飲んで	飲んだ
帰る	る	帰って	帰った

上: Plain フォーム   下: Polite フォーム

	い -adjective	な -adjective	Nominal Predicate
Non-past Affirmative	長い	元気だ	学生だ
	長いです	元気です	学生です
Non-past Negative	長くない	元気じゃない	学生じゃない
	長くないです	元気じゃないです	学生じゃないです
	長くありません	元気じゃありません	学生じゃありません
Past Affirmative	長かった	元気だった	学生だった
	長かったです	元気でした	学生でした
Past Negative	長くなかった	元気じゃなかった	学生じゃなかった
	長くなかったです	元気じゃなかったです	学生じゃなかったです
	長くありませんでした	元気じゃありませんでした	学生じゃありませんでした

Appendix D   Kanji by Lesson

3	いち	一
	きゅう・く	九
	ご	五
	さん	三
	し・よん	四
	しち・なな	七
	じゅう	十
	せん	千
	に	二
	はち	八
	ひゃく	百
	ろく	六
4	かようび	火曜日
	きんようび	金曜日
	げつようび	月曜日
	～じ	～時
	すいようび	水曜日
	どようび	土曜日
	なに・なん	何
	なにか・なんか	何か
	なにも	何も
	なんじ	何時
	なんぷん	何分
	なんようび	何曜日
	にちようび	日曜日
	にほん	日本
	はん	半
	～ふん・ぷん	～分
	もくようび	木曜日
5	あした	明日
	いく	行く
	いま	今
	うえ	上
	がくせい	学生
	～がつ	～月
	きのう	昨日
	きます	来ます
	きょう	今日
	くる	来る

	こやま	小山
	した	下
	せんせい	先生
	ほん	本
	わたし	私
6	あう	会う
	うち	家
	えいご	英語
	かう	買う
	～ご	～語
	こない	来ない
	こんばん	今晩
	～じん	～人
	たべる	食べる
	ちゅうかん	中間
	なにご	何語
	にほんご	日本語
	にほんじん	日本人
	のむ	飲む
	みる	見る
	やまもと	山本
	りゅうがくせい	留学生
7	あかるい	明るい
	あたらしい	新しい
	いしかわ	石川
	おおきい	大きい
	おかね	お金
	くらい	暗い
	くるま	車
	だいがく	大学
	たかい	高い
	ちいさい	小さい
	ながい	長い
	はいる	入る
	ひろい	広い
	ふるい	古い
	め	目
	やすい	安い
	やました	山下

8	あに	兄
	あね	姉
	いもうと	妹
	おかあさん	お母さん
	おとうさん	お父さん
	おとうと	弟
	おとこ	男
	おにいさん	お兄さん
	おねえさん	お姉さん
	おんな	女
	かえる	帰る
	きょうだい	兄弟
	ください	下さい
	こうこうせい	高校生
	だいがくせい	大学生
	ちち	父
	とうきょう	東京
	～にん	～人
	はは	母
	はやい	早い
	ひと	人
	ひとり	一人
	ふたり	二人
	ふるかわ	古川
9	いちばん	一番
	いつつ	五つ
	～えん	～円
	おちゃ	お茶
	かく	書く
	～かげつ	～か月
	ここのつ	九つ
	じかん	時間
	～じかん	～時間
	じょうず	上手
	すき	好き
	ちゅうごく	中国
	つくる	作る
	とお	十
	なか	中
	ななつ	七つ
	～ねん	～年
	はなし	話

	はなす	話す
	ひとつ	一つ
	ふたつ	二つ
	へた	下手
	ほう	方
	～ほん	～本
	まつ	待つ
	みっつ	三つ
	むっつ	六つ
	やすかわ	安川
	やっつ	八つ
	よっつ	四つ
	よむ	読む
10	あく	開く
	あさ	朝
	おおい	多い
	がっこう	学校
	かんじ	漢字
	ぎんこう	銀行
	ことし	今年
	しまる	閉まる
	しる	知る
	すむ	住む
	てがみ	手紙
	としょかん	図書館
	なかやま	中山
	はやかわ	早川
	ひがしアジア	東アジア
	まえ	前
	わかる	分かる
11	うしろ	後ろ
	えいぶんがく	英文学
	おおどおり	大どおり
	おんがく	音楽
	がくぶ	学部
	かた	方
	かみ	紙
	きく	聞く
	げんき	元気
	こづつみ	小づつみ
	しずか	静か
	しんぶん	新聞

	せ	背
	だいがくいんせい	大学院生
	つき	月
	て	手
	ときどき	時々
	なまえ	名前
	～ねんせい	～年生
	ひがしやま	東山
	ひとびと	人々
	ほんばこ	本ばこ
12	あたま	頭
	かいもの	買い物
	きょねん	去年
	けさ	今朝
	こめ	米
	すこし	少し
	ぜんぶ	全部
	だいすき	大好き
	たべもの	食べ物
	たんじょうび	たんじょう日
	てんいん	店員
	はな	花
	べんり	便利
	みず	水
	みせ	店
	よみもの	読み物
	らいねん	来年
	りょうり	料理
13	あき	秋
	あきやま	秋山
	かえす	返す
	かきかた	書き方
	きょうと	京都
	ごご	午後
	ごぜん	午前
	こんげつ	今月
	こんしゅう	今週
	さむい	寒い
	さらいげつ	さ来月
	さらいしゅう	さ来週
	さらいねん	さ来年
	しゅうまつ	週まつ

	しょうがっこう	小学校
	せんげつ	先月
	せんしゅう	先週
	せんせんげつ	先々月
	せんせんしゅう	先々週
	たのしい	楽しい
	たのしみ	楽しみ
	ちゅうがっこう	中学校
	とき	時
	ともだち	友達
	なつ	夏
	はる	春
	はるやすみ	春休み
	ふゆ	冬
	ふゆやすみ	冬休み
	ぶん	文
	へんじ	返事
	らいげつ	来月
	らいしゅう	来週
	わたしたち	私達
14	あめ	雨
	おしえる	教える
	きょうしつ	教室
	くに	国
	しごと	仕事
	～しゅうかん	～週間
	しゅくだい	宿題
	たいへん	大変
	とる	取る
	なつめ	夏目
	はたらく	働く
	べんきょう	勉強
	まいあさ	毎朝
	まいしゅう	毎週
	まいにち	毎日
	まいばん	毎晩
	やすみ	休み
	やすむ	休む
	ゆうめい	有名
	らく	楽

Appendix E　Kanji by あいうえお

あ	あう	会う	6	**か**	かいもの	買い物	12
	あかるい	明るい	7		かう	買う	6
	あき	秋	13		かえす	返す	13
	あきやま	秋山	13		かえる	帰る	8
	あく	開く	10		かきかた	書き方	13
	あさ	朝	10		かく	書く	9
	あした	明日	5		がくせい	学生	5
	あたま	頭	12		がくぶ	学部	11
	あたらしい	新しい	7		～かげつ	～か月	9
	あに	兄	8		かた	方	11
	あね	姉	8		～がつ	～月	5
	あめ	雨	14		がっこう	学校	10
い	いく	行く	5		かみ	紙	11
	いしかわ	石川	7		かようび	火曜日	4
	いち	一	3		かんじ	漢字	10
	いちばん	一番	9	**き**	きく	聞く	11
	いつつ	五つ	9		きのう	昨日	5
	いま	今	5		きます	来ます	5
	いもうと	妹	8		きゅう	九	3
う	うえ	上	5		きょう	今日	5
	うしろ	後ろ	11		きょうしつ	教室	14
	うち	家	6		きょうだい	兄弟	8
え	えいご	英語	6		きょうと	京都	13
	えいぶんがく	英文学	11		きょねん	去年	12
	～えん	～円	9		ぎんこう	銀行	10
お	おおい	多い	10		きんようび	金曜日	4
	おおきい	大きい	7	**く**	く	九	3
	おおどおり	大どおり	11		ください	下さい	8
	おかあさん	お母さん	8		くに	国	14
	おかね	お金	7		くらい	暗い	7
	おしえる	教える	14		くる	来る	5
	おちゃ	お茶	9		くるま	車	7
	おとうさん	お父さん	8	**け**	けさ	今朝	12
	おとうと	弟	8		げつようび	月曜日	4
	おとこ	男	8		げんき	元気	11
	おにいさん	お兄さん	8	**こ**	ご	五	3
	おねえさん	お姉さん	8		～ご	～語	6
	おんがく	音楽	11		こうこうせい	高校生	8
	おんな	女	8		ごご	午後	13

	ここのつ	九つ	9
	ごぜん	午前	13
	こづつみ	小づつみ	11
	ことし	今年	10
	こない	来ない	6
	こめ	米	12
	こやま	小山	5
	こんげつ	今月	13
	こんしゅう	今週	13
	こんばん	今晩	6
さ	さむい	寒い	13
	さらいげつ	さ来月	13
	さらいしゅう	さ来週	13
	さらいねん	さ来年	13
	さん	三	3
し	し	四	3
	～じ	～時	4
	じかん	時間	9
	～じかん	～時間	9
	しごと	仕事	14
	しずか	静か	11
	した	下	5
	しち	七	3
	しまる	閉まる	10
	じゅう	十	3
	～しゅうかん	～週間	14
	しゅうまつ	週まつ	13
	しゅくだい	宿題	14
	しょうがっこう	小学校	13
	じょうず	上手	9
	しる	知る	10
	～じん	～人	6
	しんぶん	新聞	11
す	すいようび	水曜日	4
	すき	好き	9
	すこし	少し	12
	すむ	住む	10
せ	せ	背	11
	せん	千	3
	せんげつ	先月	13
	せんしゅう	先週	13
	せんせい	先生	5

	せんせんげつ	先々月	13
	せんせんしゅう	先々週	13
	ぜんぶ	全部	12
た	だいがく	大学	7
	だいがくいんせい	大学院生	11
	だいがくせい	大学生	8
	だいすき	大好き	12
	たいへん	大変	14
	たかい	高い	7
	たのしい	楽しい	13
	たのしみ	楽しみ	13
	たべもの	食べ物	12
	たべる	食べる	6
	たんじょうび	たんじょう日	12
ち	ちいさい	小さい	7
	ちち	父	8
	ちゅうがっこう	中学校	13
	ちゅうかん	中間	6
	ちゅうごく	中国	9
つ	つき	月	11
	つくる	作る	9
て	て	手	11
	てがみ	手紙	10
	てんいん	店員	12
と	とうきょう	東京	8
	とお	十	9
	とき	時	13
	ときどき	時々	11
	としょかん	図書館	10
	ともだち	友達	13
	どようび	土曜日	4
	とる	取る	14
な	なか	中	9
	ながい	長い	7
	なかやま	中山	10
	なつ	夏	13
	なつめ	夏目	14
	なな	七	3
	ななつ	七つ	9
	なに	何	4
	なにか	何か	4
	なにご	何語	6

	なにも	何も	4
	なまえ	名前	11
	なん	何	4
	なんか	何か	4
	なんじ	何時	4
	なんぷん	何分	4
	なんようび	何曜日	4
に	に	二	3
	にちようび	日曜日	4
	にほん	日本	4
	にほんご	日本語	6
	にほんじん	日本人	6
	～にん	～人	8
ね	～ねん	～年	9
	～ねんせい	～年生	11
の	のむ	飲む	6
は	はいる	入る	7
	はたらく	働く	14
	はち	八	3
	はな	花	12
	はなし	話	9
	はなす	話す	9
	はは	母	8
	はやい	早い	8
	はやかわ	早川	10
	はる	春	13
	はるやすみ	春休み	13
	はん	半	4
ひ	ひがしアジア	東アジア	10
	ひがしやま	東山	11
	ひと	人	8
	ひとつ	一つ	9
	ひとびと	人々	11
	ひとり	一人	8
	ひゃく	百	3
	ひろい	広い	7
ふ	ふたつ	二つ	9
	ふたり	二人	8
	ふゆ	冬	13
	ふゆやすみ	冬休み	13
	ふるい	古い	7
	ふるかわ	古川	8

	～ふん・ぷん	～分	4
	ぶん	文	13
へ	へた	下手	9
	べんきょう	勉強	14
	へんじ	返事	13
	べんり	便利	12
ほ	ほう	方	9
	ほん	本	5
	～ほん	～本	9
	ほんばこ	本ばこ	11
ま	まいあさ	毎朝	14
	まいしゅう	毎週	14
	まいにち	毎日	14
	まいばん	毎晩	14
	まえ	前	10
	まつ	待つ	9
み	みず	水	12
	みせ	店	12
	みっつ	三つ	9
	みる	見る	6
む	むっつ	六つ	9
め	め	目	7
も	もくようび	木曜日	4
や	やすい	安い	7
	やすかわ	安川	9
	やすみ	休み	14
	やすむ	休む	14
	やっつ	八つ	9
	やました	山下	7
	やまもと	山本	6
ゆ	ゆうめい	有名	14
よ	よっつ	四つ	9
	よみもの	読み物	12
	よむ	読む	9
	よん	四	3
ら	らいげつ	来月	13
	らいしゅう	来週	13
	らいねん	来年	12
	らく	楽	14
り	りゅうがくせい	留学	6
	りょうり	料理	12
ろ	ろく	六	3

わ	わかる	分かる	10
	わたし	私	5
	わたしたち	私達	13

Appendix F Kanji by Stroke Count

Count	L3	L4	L5	L6	L7	L8	L9	L10	L11	L12	L13	L14
1	一											
2	九七十二八			人	入							
3	三千	土	上小山下		川大	女			々			
4	五六	火日月水分木	今	中		父	円手方		文元	少	午友	
5	四	本半	生		石広古目	兄母				去	冬	仕
6	百		行先	会	安	早	好年	多字	気名	米全	休	毎有
7		何	来私	見	車	弟男	作	住図		花利	返	
8		金	明学	英	長	姉妹東京	国	知		店物	事	雨取
9			昨	食			茶待	前	後音背	便	秋春	室変
10		時		家留	高	帰校	書	紙	院	員料	夏	勉
11								閉	部	理	都週	教宿強
12				買晩間飲			番	開朝			寒達	
13					新暗		話	漢	楽			働
14				語			読	銀	聞静			
15												
16								館		頭		
17												
18		曜										題
19												
Total	12	13	13	13	13	13	13	13	13	13	13	13

Appendix G Vocabulary List (Japanese to English)

品詞（ひんし） Parts of speech
漢字（かんじ） Kanji
反対語・対語（はんたいご・ついご） Antonym/A pair of words
X The kanji is used, but not taught.

単語課（たんごか） Lesson where the word is introduced
漢字課（かんじか） Lesson where the kanji is introduced

	English	
Adj irreg	Irregular adjective	N proper Proper noun
Conj	Conjunction	N verbal Verbal noun
Interject	Interjection	

日本語 Japanese	英語 English	品詞	単語課	漢字	漢字課	反対語・対語
CD プレーヤー	CD player	Noun	12			
E メール	email	Noun	9			
T シャツ	T-shirt	Noun	9			
あ アームストロング	Armstrong	N proper	11			
あう	meet	Verb う	4	会う	6	
あかるい	bright, cheerful	Adj い	7	明るい	7	くらい
あき	autumn	Noun	12	秋	13	
あきはばら	Akihabara	N proper	13	秋葉原	X	
あきやま	Akiyama	N proper	13	秋山	13	
あく	open (intransitive)	Verb う	10	開く	10	しまる
あげる	give	Verb る	14	上げる	18	
あさ	morning	Noun	5	朝	10	ばん
あさくさ	Asakusa	N proper	13	浅草	X	
あさごはん	breakfast	Noun	4	朝ごはん	10	ばんごはん
あさって	day after tomorrow	Noun	13			おととい
あし	foot, leg	Noun	7	足	21	
あした	tomorrow	Noun	4	明日	5	きのう
あそこ	place over there	Pronoun	2			ここ
あそぶ	play	Verb う	6	遊ぶ	24	
あたま	head	Noun	7	頭	12	
あたらしい	new	Adj い	7	新しい	7	ふるい
あちら	that direction	Pronoun	7			
あつい	hot	Adj い	11	暑い	22	さむい
あなた	you	Pronoun	2			
あに	elder brother (plain)	Noun	8	兄	8	おとうと

	あね	elder sister (plain)	Noun	8	姉	8	いもうと
	あの＋NOUN	that NOUN (over there)	Adj irreg	2			
	アパート	apartment	Noun	2			
	あびる	take (a shower)	Verb る	13			
	アフリカ	Africa	N proper	12			
	あまい	sweet	Adj い	11			からい
	あまり	(not) much	Adv	7			
	あめ	rain	Noun	8	雨	14	
	アメリカ	America	N proper	5			
	アメリカじん	American people	Noun	6	アメリカ人	6	
	あらう	wash	Verb う	14	洗う	16	よごす
	アラスカ	Alaska	N proper	11			
	ある	exist (things)	Verb う	3			ない
	あるいて	on foot	Phrase	4	歩いて	18	
	あるく	walk	Verb う	8	歩く	18	
	あれ	that one	Pronoun	2			これ
い	いい	good	Adj い	7			わるい
	いいえ	no	Adv	2			はい
	いう	say, speak, talk	Verb う	11	言う	16	
	いかが	how (respectful)	Adv	7			
	イギリス	England	N proper	9			
	いく	go	Verb う	4	行く	5	くる
	いくら	how much	Adv	10			
	いしかわ	Ishikawa	N proper	2	石川	7	
	いじわる（な）	mean	Adj な	7			しんせつ（な）、やさしい
	いす	chair	Noun	3			
	いそがしい	busy	Adj い	10	忙しい	19	ひま（な）
	いたい	painful	Adj い	12	痛い	21	
	いただく	receive (respectful)	Verb う	8			
	イタリアりょうり	Italian cuisine	Noun	9	料理	12	
	いち	one	Noun	3	一	3	
	いちがつ	January	N proper	5	一月	5	
	いちねんせい	first-year student	Noun	2	一年生	11	
	いちばん	first, best, number one	Noun	9	一番	9	
	いつ	when	Adv	4			
	いっしょに	together	Phrase	4			
	いつつ	five things	Counter	9	五つ	9	
	いつも	always	Adv	7			
	いぬ	dog	Noun	3	犬	21	
	いぬごや	doghouse	Noun	3	犬ごや	21	
	いま	now	Noun	4	今	5	

いみ	meaning	Noun	12	意味	20	
いもうと	younger sister (plain)	Noun	8	妹	8	あね
いもうとさん	younger sister (respect)	Noun	8	妹さん	8	おねえさん
イヤリング	earrings	Noun	10			
いらっしゃる	exist (respectful)	Verb う	3			
いる	exist (people, animals)	Verb る	3			
いろいろ (な)	various, many kinds of	Adj な	12	色々	18	
インタビュー (する)	interview	N verbal	10			
う ウィスキー	whiskey	Noun	9			
ウィルソン	Wilson	N proper	7			
ううん	no (casual)	Adv	6			うん
うえ	on, above	Noun	3	上	5	した
ウェイター	waiter	Noun	9			
ウォン	Wong	N proper	2			
(しけんを) うける	take (exam)	Verb る	13	受ける	16	
うしろ	back, behind	Noun	3	後ろ	11	まえ
うた	song	Noun	8	歌	15	
うたう	sing	Verb う	8	歌う	15	
うち	house, home	Noun	3	家	6	
うなぎ	eel	Noun	12			
うるさい	noisy	Adj い	7			しずか (な)
うれしい (1st person)	happy, pleased	Adj い	13			かなしい
うん	yes (casual)	Adv	5			ううん
うんてん (する)	drive	N verbal	11	運転	19	
うんどう (する)	exercise	N verbal	4	運動	19	
え え	picture, drawing	Noun	9	絵	15	
えいが	movie	Noun	4	映画	15	
えいご	English	Noun	2	英語	6	
えいぶんがく	English literature	Noun	11	英文学	11	
エイミー	Amy	N proper	2			
えき	station	Noun	4	駅	20	
エグザミナー	Examiner	N proper	2			
エッセー	essay	Noun	11			
エルビス	Elvis	N proper	11			
〜えん	X Yen	Counter	9	〜円	9	
えんぴつ	pencil	Noun	2			
お おい	nephew (plain)	Noun	8			めい
おいごさん	nephew (respectful)	Noun	8			めいごさん
おいしい	delicious	Adj い	7			まずい
おおい	many, plenty	Adj い	10	多い	10	すくない
おおきい	big, large	Adj い	7	大きい	7	ちいさい
オークランド	Oakland	N proper	5			

おおさか	Osaka	N proper	7	大阪	X	
オーダー（する）	order	N verbal	9			
おおどおり	boulevard	Noun	11	大どおり	11	
オートバイ	motorcycle	Noun	14			
おかあさん	mother (respectful)	Noun	8	お母さん	8	おとうさん
おかし	snack	Noun	11			
おかね	money	Noun	6	お金	7	
おかんじょう	check	Noun	9			
おきる	wake up, get up	Verb る	5			ねる
おくさん	wife (respectful)	Noun	8			ごしゅじん
おくりもの	present	Noun	14	おくり物	14	
おくる	send	Verb う	10	送る	24	
おくれる	be late	Verb る	14			まにあう
おこさん	child (respectful)	Noun	8	お子さん	16	
おこめ	uncooked rice	Noun	12	お米	12	
おさけ	liquor, Japanese sake	Noun	5	お酒	16	
おさしみ	raw fish	Noun	6			
おさとう	sugar	Noun	12			
おさら	dish	Noun	14			
おじ	uncle (plain)	Noun	8			おば
おじいさん	grandfather (respect)	Noun	8			おばあさん
おしえる	teach	Verb る	5	教える	14	ならう
おしお	salt	Noun	12			
おじさん	uncle (respectful)	Noun	8			おばさん
おしょうがつ	(1st month of) New Year	N proper	14	お正月	23	
おす	vinegar	Noun	11			
おすし	sushi	Noun	4			
おそい	slow, late	Adj い	11			はやい
おそうしき	funeral ceremony	Noun	14			
おちゃ	tea	Noun	4	お茶	9	
おつり	change	Noun	12			
おてあらい	toilet, lavatory	Noun	3	お手洗い	16	
おてら	Buddhist temple	Noun	13			
おてんき	weather	Noun	13	お天気	22	
おとうさん	father (respectful)	Noun	8	お父さん	8	おかあさん
おとうと	younger brother (plain)	Noun	8	弟	8	あに
おとうとさん	younger brother (resp)	Noun	8	弟さん	8	おにいさん
おとこ	male	Noun	2	男	8	おんな
おととい	day before yesterday	Noun	13			あさって
おととし	year before last	Noun	13			さらいねん
おどる	dance	Verb う	13			
おなか	stomach	Noun	9			

おなまえ	name (respectful)	Noun	1	お名前	11	
おにいさん	elder brother (respect)	Noun	8	お兄さん	8	おとうとさん
おねえさん	elder sister (respectful)	Noun	8	お姉さん	8	いもうとさん
おねがい (する)	favor, request	N verbal	9	お願い	25	
おば	aunt (plain)	Noun	8			おじ
おばあさん	grandmother (respect)	Noun	8			おじいさん
おばさん	aunt (respectful)	Noun	8			おじさん
おはし	chopsticks	Noun	4			
オフィス	office	Noun	3			
オフィスアワー	office hours	Noun	10			
おふろ	bath	Noun	14			
おべんとう	box lunch	Noun	14			
おぼえる	memorize	Verb る	12	覚える	15	わすれる
おまごさん	grandchild (respectful)	Noun	8			
おまつり	festival	Noun	13			
おみせ	store, shop	Noun	6	お店	12	
おみやげ	gift	Noun	13			
おもい	heavy	Adj い	14			かるい
おもしろい	interesting	Adj い	7			つまらない
おもち	rice cake	Noun	14			
およぐ	swim	Verb う	6	泳ぐ	25	
オレンジ	orange	Noun	9			
おんがく	music	Noun	9	音楽	11	
おんな	female	Noun	2	女	8	おとこ
がいこく	foreign country	Noun	11	外国	16	
かいしゃ	company	Noun	14	会社	23	
かいもの (する)	shopping	N verbal	4	買い物	12	
かう	buy	Verb う	5	買う	6	
かえす	return	Verb う	6	返す	13	かりる
かえる	go home	Verb う	4	帰る	8	でかける
かかる	take (time, expense)	Verb う	10			
かきかた	way of writing	Noun	13	書き方	13	
かく	write	Verb う	4	書く	9	けす
かく	draw	Verb う	9			けす
がくせい	student	Noun	1	学生	5	
がくぶ	academic department	Noun	11	学部	11	
〜かげつ	X month(s)	Counter	9	〜か月	9	
(めがねを) かける	wear (glasses)	Verb る	10			はずす
かさ	umbrella	Noun	6			
かす	lend	Verb う	8	貸す	23	かりる
かぜ	a cold	Noun	14			
かぞく	family (plain)	Noun	8	家族	26	

か

	かた	person (respectful)	Noun	2	方	11	
	かたい	tough, hard	Adj い	11			やわらかい
	カタカナ	katakana	Noun	2			ひらがな
	～がつ	Xth month	Suffix	5	～月	5	
	がっこう	school	Noun	10	学校	10	
	かない	wife (plain)	Noun	8			しゅじん
	カナダ	Canada	N proper	6			
	カナダじん	Canadian people	Noun	6	カナダ人	6	
	かね	money	Noun	6	金	7	
	かばん	briefcase	Noun	3			
	カフェテリア	cafeteria	Noun	4			
	かぶる	wear (hat, cap)	Verb う	10			とる
	かみ	hair	Noun	7			
	かみ	paper	Noun	11	紙	11	
	カメラ	camera	Noun	3			
	かようび	Tuesday	N proper	4	火曜日	4	
	から	from	Particle	4			
	から	because	Conj	5			
	カラオケ	karaoke	Noun	12			
	カリフォルニア	California	N proper	3			
	かりる	borrow	Verb る	6	借りる	23	かえす、かす
	かるい	light (weight)	Adj い	14			おもい
	カレーライス	curry rice	Noun	9			
	かわいい	cute	Adj い	9			
	かんがえる	think	Verb る	11	考える	24	
	かんこくご	Korean language	Noun	6	かんこく語	6	
	かんこくじん	Korean people	Noun	6	かんこく人	6	
	かんじ	Chinese characters	Noun	10	漢字	10	
	かんたん（な）	easy	Adj な	9			むずかしい
	がんばる	do one's best	Verb う	6			
き	きえる	turn off (intransitive)	Verb る	10			つく
	きく	listen, ask	Verb う	5	聞く	11	
	ギター	guitar	Noun	9			
	きたない	dirty	Adj い	7			きれい（な）
	きっぷ	ticket	Noun	13	切符	22	
	きのう	yesterday	Noun	5	昨日	5	あした
	キム	Kim	N proper	4			
	きむら	Kimura	N proper	3	木村	15	
	キャンパス	campus	Noun	6			
	きゅう	nine	Noun	3	九	3	
	ぎゅうにく	beef	Noun	12	ぎゅう肉	24	
	きょう	today	Noun	4	今日	5	

きょうかしょ	textbook	Noun	9	教科書	20	
きょうしつ	classroom	Noun	3	教室	14	
きょうだい	siblings	Noun	8	兄弟	8	
きょうと	Kyoto	N proper	2	京都	13	
きょねん	last year	Noun	8	去年	12	らいねん
きらい (な)	dislike	Adj な	9			すき (な)
きる	wear (dress, shirt, suit)	Verb る	10	着る	21	ぬぐ
きれい (な)	clean, beautiful	Adj な	7			きたない
ぎんこう	bank	Noun	3	銀行	10	
きんようび	Friday	N proper	4	金曜日	4	
く く	nine	Noun	3	九	3	
くうこう	airport	Noun	13			
くがつ	September	N proper	5	九月	5	
ください	please give	Phrase	8	下さい	8	
くだもの	fruit	Noun	9			
くち	mouth	Noun	7	口	21	
くつ	shoes	Noun	6			
クッキー	cookie	Noun	11			
くに	country	Noun	14	国	14	
くらい	dark	Adj い	7	暗い	7	あかるい
〜ぐらい	about, approximately	Suffix	10			
クラシック	classical music	Noun	9			
クラス	class	Noun	2			
クラスメート	classmate	Noun	9			
クラブ	club	Noun	11			
くる	come	V irreg	4	来る	5	いく
グループ	group	Noun	14			
くるま	car	Noun	2	車	7	
くれる	give	Verb る	14			もらう
け けいざいがく	economics	Noun	2	けいざい学	11	
ケーキ	cake	Noun	7			
けさ	this morning	Noun	12	今朝	12	こんばん
けす	turn off	Verb う	14			つける
けっこう (な)	fine, nice, wonderful	Adj な	8			だめ (な)
けっこんしき	wedding ceremony	Noun	14	結婚しき	26	
げつようび	Monday	N proper	4	月曜日	4	
げんき (な)	energetic	Adj な	7	元気	11	
けんどう	kendo	Noun	14			
こ 〜こ	X unit(s)	Counter	9	〜個	23	
ご	five	Noun	3	五	3	
〜ご	suffix (language)	Suffix	6	〜語	6	
こうえん	park	Noun	6			

こうこう	high school	Noun	8	高校	8	
こうこうせい	high school student	Noun	8	高校生	8	
コース	course	Noun	7			
コーヒー	coffee	Noun	4			
コーラ	cola	Noun	4			
ごかぞく	family (respectful)	Noun	8	ご家族	26	
ごがつ	May	N proper	5	五月	5	
ごきょうだい	siblings (respectful)	Noun	8	ご兄弟	8	
ここ	here	Pronoun	2			そこ、あそこ
ごご	afternoon, P.M.	Noun	4	午後	13	ごぜん
ここのつ	nine things	Noun	9	九つ	9	
ごしゅじん	husband (respectful)	Noun	8			おくさん
ごぜん	morning, A.M.	Noun	4	午前	13	ごご
ごせんもん	major, speciality (resp)	Noun	1	ご専門	22	
こちら	this direction	Pronoun	7			そちら、あちら
こづつみ	parcel	Noun	11	小づつみ	11	
ことし	this year	Noun	8	今年	10	
こども	child (plain)	Noun	8	子供	16	おとな
この + NOUN	this NOUN	Adj irreg	2			その、あの
このあいだ	some time ago, the other day	Phrase	12	この間	23	
ごはん	(cooked) rice, meal	Noun	4			
コピー（する）	copy	N verbal	4			
こむぎこ	wheat flour	Noun	12			
こめ	uncooked rice	Noun	12	米	12	
こやま	Koyama	N proper	3	小山	5	
ごりょうしん	parents (respectful)	Noun	8	ご両親	20	
ゴルフ	golf	Noun	6			
これ	this one	Pronoun	2			それ、あれ
これから	now, from now on	Phrase	4			
〜ごろ	about, approximately	Suffix	10			
コロンブス	Columbus	N proper	11			
こんげつ	this month	Noun	13	今月	13	
こんしゅう	this week	Noun	12	今週	13	
こんど	next time	Noun	6	今度	18	
こんばん	this evening	Noun	5	今晩	6	けさ
コンピューター	computer	Noun	2			
さ サービス（する）	service	N verbal	11			
〜さい	X year(s) old	Counter	14			
サイエンス	science	Noun	2			
さいきん	recently	Noun	14	最近	22	むかし
さがす	search for	Verb う	14			

さかな	fish	Noun	6	魚	24	
さくら	cherry blossom/tree	Noun	13			
さけ	liquor, Japanese sake	Noun	5	酒	16	
さけ	salmon	Noun	12			
さしみ	raw fish	Noun	6			
～さつ	counter (bound things)	Counter	9	～冊	23	
ざっし	magazine	Noun	2			
さとう	sugar	Noun	12			
さびしい	lonely	Adj い	13			
～さま	suffix (honored person)	Suffix	13	～様	26	
さむい	cold	Adj い	11	寒い	13	あつい
さら	dish	Noun	14			
さらいげつ	month after next	Noun	13	さ来月	13	せんせんげつ
さらいしゅう	week after next	Noun	13	さ来週	13	せんせんしゅう
さらいねん	year after next	Noun	13	さ来年	13	おととし
サラリーマン	company employee	Noun	14			
さん	three	Noun	3	三	3	
さんがつ	March	N proper	5	三月	5	
サングラス	sunglasses	Noun	10			
さんにん	three persons	Noun	8	三人	8	
ざんねん (な)	regrettable, regret	Adj な	6			
さんねんせい	third-year student	Noun	2	三年生	11	
サンフランシスコ	San Francisco	N proper	2			
さんぽ (する)	stroll	N verbal	13			
し	four	Noun	3	四	3	
～じ	X o'clock	Suffix	4	～時	4	
ジーンズ	jeans	Noun	10			
シェークスピア	Shakespeare	N proper	11			
しお	salt	Noun	12			
シカゴ	Chicago	N proper	3			
しがつ	April	N proper	5	四月	5	
～じかん	X hour(s)	Counter	9	～時間	9	
じかん	time	Noun	10	時間	10	
しけん	test, examination	Noun	6	試験	17	
しごと (する)	job	N verbal	8	仕事	14	
じしょ	dictionary	Noun	2	辞書	23	
しずか (な)	quiet	Adj な	7	静か	11	うるさい
した	under, below	Noun	3	下	5	うえ
しち	seven	Noun	3	七	3	
しちがつ	July	N proper	5	七月	5	
じつは	to tell the truth	Phrase	13			
しつもん (する)	question	N verbal	6	質問	19	こたえる

し

しつれい（な）	impolite	Adj な	7			
じてんしゃ	bicycle	Noun	4	自転車	19	
しぬ	die	Verb う	8	死ぬ	25	うまれる
しまる	close (intransitive)	Verb う	10	閉まる	10	あく
ジミー	Jimmy	N proper	2			
ジム	gymnasium	Noun	4			
じゃ	well then	Conj	5			
じゃがいも	potato	Noun	12			
しゃしん	photograph	Noun	2	写真	19	
ジャズ	Jazz	Noun	9			
ジャック	Jack	N proper	10			
ジャパン	Japan	N proper	11			
シャワー	shower	Noun	13			
じゅう	ten	Noun	3	十	3	
じゅういちがつ	November	N proper	5	十一月	5	
じゅうがつ	October	N proper	5	十月	5	
〜しゅうかん	X week(s)	Counter	14	〜週間	14	
しゅうかん	custom	Noun	14			
ジュース	juice	Noun	8			
じゅうにがつ	December	N proper	5	十二月	5	
しゅうまつ	weekend	Noun	4	週末	16	
じゅぎょう	class	Noun	12	授業	18	
しゅくだい	homework	Noun	4	宿題	14	
しゅじん	husband (plain)	Noun	8			かない
シュミット	Schmidt	N proper	8			
しょうかい（する）	introduction	N verbal	14	紹介	24	
しょうがつ	(1st month of) New Year	N proper	14	正月	23	
しょうがっこう	elementary school	Noun	13	小学校	13	
じょうず（な）	good at	Adj な	9	上手	9	へた（な）
しょうせつ	novel	Noun	11	小説	22	
しょうゆ	soy sauce	Noun	12			
ショートパンツ	shorts	Noun	10			
ジョーンズ	Jones	N proper	4			
ジョギング（する）	jogging	N verbal	5			
ジョン	John	N proper	11			
しらべる	check	Verb る	14	調べる	23	
しる	get to know	Verb う	10	知る	10	
シン	Singh	N proper	7			
〜じん	suffix (nationality)	Suffix	6	〜人	6	
しんおおさか	Shin-Osaka	N proper	10	新大阪	X	
しんかんせん	Japanese bullet train	N proper	4			
じんじゃ	Shinto shrine	Noun	13			

	しんせつ (な)	kind	Adj な	7	親切	20	いじわる (な)
	しんぶん	newspaper	Noun	2	新聞	11	
す	す	vinegar	Noun	11			
	すいようび	Wednesday	N proper	4	水曜日	4	
	すうがく	mathematics	Noun	6	数学	26	
	スーツ	suit	Noun	10			
	スーツケース	suitcase	Noun	13			
	スーパー	supermarket	Noun	4			
	スカート	skirt	Noun	10			
	すき (な)	like	Adj な	9	好き	9	きらい (な)
	スキー	ski	Noun	6			
	スキット	skit	Noun	13			
	すきやき	Sukiyaki	Noun	9			
	すく	become empty	Verb う	9			こむ
	すぐ	immediately, soon	Adv	5			
	すごい	teriffic	Adj い	11			
	すこし	a little	Adv	6	少し	11	たくさん
	すし	sushi	Noun	4			
	すずしい	cool	Adj い	11			あたたかい
	ステーキ	steak	Noun	5			
	ステレオ	stereo (set)	Noun	11			
	スニーカー	sneakers	Noun	10			
	スパゲティ	spaghetti	Noun	6			
	スペインご	Spanish language	Noun	6	スペイン語	6	
	スポーツ	sport	Noun	9			
	ズボン	trousers, pants	Noun	10			
	スミス	Smith	N proper	7			
	すむ	start living somewhere	Verb う	10	住む	10	
	すもう	sumo wrestling	Noun	10			
	する	do	V irreg	4			
	する	wear (accessory)	V irreg	10			とる、はずす
	すわる	sit down	Verb う	10			たつ
せ	せ	body height	Noun	7	背	11	
	せいきょう	co-op	Noun	14			
	せいせき	grade	Noun	14	成績	25	
	せいぶつがく	biology	Noun	11	生物学	21	
	セーター	sweater	Noun	10			
	セール	sale	Noun	7			
	ぜひ	by all means	Adv	14			
	せまい	narrow, small	Adj い	7			ひろい
	せん	thousand	Noun	3	千	3	
	せんげつ	last month	Noun	13	先月	13	らいげつ

せんしゅ	sports player	Noun	11				
せんしゅう	last week	Noun	5	先週	13	らいしゅう	
せんせい	teacher	Noun	1	先生	5		
ぜんぜん	(not) at all	Adv	7	全然	25		
せんせんげつ	month before last	Noun	13	先々月	13	さらいげつ	
せんせんしゅう	week before last	Noun	13	先々週	13	さらいしゅう	
せんたく (する)	laundry	N verbal	12	洗濯	16		
セント	cent(s)	Noun	9				
ぜんぶ	all	Adv	12	全部	12		
せんもん	major, speciality	Noun	1	専門	22		
そ そうじ (する)	clean	N verbal	9				
そうしき	funeral ceremony	Noun	14				
そこ	there	Pronoun	2			ここ	
そこ	bottom	Noun	11				
そして	and then	Conj	4				
そちら	that direction	Pronoun	7			こちら	
そつぎょう (する)	graduation	N verbal	13	卒業	18	にゅうがく (する)	
ソックス	socks	Noun	10				
そと	outside	Noun	3	外	16	なか	
その + NOUN	that NOUN	Adj irreg	2			この	
そふ	grandfather (plain)	Noun	8			そぼ	
ソファー	sofa	Noun	3				
そぼ	grandmother (plain)	Noun	8			そふ	
それ	that one	Pronoun	2			これ	
それから	after that	Conj	4				
それじゃ	well then (casual)	Conj	6				
それで	therefore, so that	Conj	8				
ソン	Son	N proper	2				
た タイ	Thailand	N proper	11				
〜だい	counter (cars, TV, etc.)	Counter	9				
ダイエット (する)	diet	N verbal	12				
だいがく	college, university	Noun	2	大学	7		
だいがくいんせい	graduate student	Noun	2	大学院生	11		
だいがくせい	undergraduate student	Noun	2	大学生	8		
だいじょうぶ (な)	alright, okay	Adj な	12			だめ (な)	
だいすき (な)	like very much	Adj な	12	大好き	12		
たいへん (な)	tough	Adj な	5	大変	14	らく (な)	
タイムズ	Times	N proper	2				
ダウンタウン	downtown	Noun	4				
たかい	expensive, high	Adj い	7	高い	7	やすい、ひくい	
たくさん	a lot, many	Adv	5			すこし、ちょっと	

タクシー	taxi	Noun	8				
たすける	help	Verb る	13				
～たち	plural marker (people)	Suffix	2	～達	13		
たつ	stand up	Verb う	10			すわる	
たなか	Tanaka	N proper	3	田中	19		
たのしい	enjoyable, pleasant	Adj い	9	楽しい	13		
たのしみにする	look forward to	Phrase	4	楽しみ	13		
たべもの	food	Noun	9	食べ物	12		
たべる	eat	Verb る	4	食べる	6		
タホ	Tahoe	N proper	5				
たまご	egg	Noun	12				
たまねぎ	onion	Noun	12				
だめ (な)	no good	Adj な	11			いい、 けっこう (な)	
だれ	who	Pronoun	2				
だれか	someone	Pronoun	3			だれも	
だれも	anyone	Pronoun	3			だれか	
タンゴ	Tango	N proper	13				
たんご	vocabulary, word	Noun	14	単語	18		
たんじょうび	birthday	Noun	12	たんじょう日	12		
ダンス (する)	dance	N verbal	11				
ち	blood	Noun	11				
ちいさい	small	Adj い	7	小さい	7	おおきい	
チーム	team	Noun	11				
ちえ	wisdom, intelligence	Noun	11				
チェン	Chen	N proper	5				
ちかい	near	Adj い	7	近い	20	とおい	
ちかく	vicinity	Noun	3	近く	20		
ちから	power	Noun	11				
ちず	map	Noun	9	地図	24		
ちち	father (plain)	Noun	8	父	8	はは	
チャイナタウン	Chinatown	Noun	5				
ちゅうがっこう	junior high school	Noun	13	中学校	13		
ちゅうかりょうり	Chinese cuisine	Noun	9	料理	12		
ちゅうかん	midterm	Noun	6	中間	6		
ちゅうごく	China	N proper	9	中国	9		
ちゅうごくご	Chinese language	Noun	6	中国語	9		
ちゅうごくじん	Chinese people	Noun	6	中国人	9		
チョコレート	chocolate	Noun	12				
ちょっと	a little	Adv	7			たくさん	
～つ	X unit(s)	Counter	9				
つえ	cane	Noun	11				

Row labels in left margin: **ち** (beside ち／blood row), **つ** (beside ～つ row)

つかいかた	usage, way to use	Noun	13	使い方	16		
つかう	use	Verb う	6	使う	16		
つかれる	get tired	Verb る	5				
つき	moon	Noun	11	月	11		
つく	turn on (intransitive)	Verb う	10			きえる	
つくえ	desk	Noun	3				
つくりかた	way of making	Noun	13	作り方	13		
つくる	make	Verb う	5	作る	9	こわす	
つける	turn on (transitive)	Verb る	14			けす	
つまらない	trivial, trifle, boring	Adj い	7			おもしろい	
つもり	intention	Noun	5				
て	て	hand, arm	Noun	7	手	11	
	ディズニー	Disney	N proper	11			
	ディズニーランド	Disneyland	N proper	14			
	テープ	tape	Noun	6			
	テーブル	table	Noun	3			
	てがみ	letter	Noun	3	手紙	10	
	テキスト	textbook	Noun	2			
	できる	be able to	Verb る	6			
	できるだけ	as much as possible	Phrase	14			
	デザート	dessert	Noun	9			
	ですから	therefore, so	Conj	6			
	テスト（する）	quiz, examination	N verbal	5			
	デトロイト	Detroit	N proper	11			
	テニス	tennis	Noun	4			
	デパート	department store	Noun	4			
	でも	but	Conj	4			
	デモ	demonstration	Noun	7			
	てら	Buddhist temple	Noun	13			
	（〜に）でる	attend, enter (a contest)	Verb る	12	出る	17	やすむ
	テレビ	TV	Noun	4			
	てん	points, score	Noun	14			
	てんいん	store clerk	Noun	12	店員	12	
	てんき	weather	Noun	13	天気	22	
	でんき	electricity, electric light	Noun	10	電気	15	
	でんしゃ	train	Noun	4	電車	15	
	でんしレンジ	microwave oven	Noun	12			
	てんぷら	tempura	Noun	5			
	でんわ（する）	telephone	N verbal	10	電話	15	
と	ドア	door	Noun	10			
	ドイツご	German language	Noun	6	ドイツ語	6	
	ドイツじん	German people	Noun	6	ドイツ人	6	

ドイル	Doyle	N proper	3			
どう	how	Adv	7			
とうきょう	Tokyo	N proper	7	東京	8	
どうして	why	Adv	5			
どうぞ	please	Adv	9			
とうふ	tofu	Noun	12			
とお	ten things	Noun	9	十	9	
とおい	far	Adj い	7	遠い	20	ちかい
とおり	street	Noun	11			
とき	time, when	Noun	13	時	13	
ときどき	sometimes	Adv	11	時々	11	
とくい（な）	good at	Adj な	9			
とけい	watch, clock	Noun	3	時計	23	
どこ	where	Pronoun	2			
どこかに	somewhere	Adv	3			どこにも
どこにも	anywhere	Adv	3			どこかに
ところで	by the way	Conj	8			
としょかん	library	Noun	2	図書館	10	
とても	very	Adv	7			
どなた	who (respectful)	Pronoun	2			
どなたか	someone (respectful)	Pronoun	3			どなたも
どなたも	anyone (respectful)	Pronoun	3			どなたか
となり	next to	Noun	3			
どの + NOUN	which NOUN	Adj irreg	2			
どのぐらい	how long, how much	Adv	10			
とまる	stay over night	Verb う	14			
ともだち	friend	Noun	4	友達	13	
どようび	Saturday	N proper	4	土曜日	4	
とりにく	chicken	Noun	12	とり肉	24	
とる	take	Verb う	5	取る	14	
（しゃしんを）とる	take (a picture)	Verb う	8			
ドル	dollar	Noun	5			
どれ	which one	Pronoun	2			
トレーナー	sweatshirt	Noun	10			
とんかつ	pork cutlet	Noun	5			
どんな + NOUN	what kind of	Adj irreg	7			
な　なか	inside	Noun	3	中	9	そと
ながい	long	Adj い	7	長い	7	みじかい
なかやま	Nakayama	N proper	10	中山	10	
なごや	Nagoya	N proper	10	名古屋	X	
なさる	do (respectful)	Verb う	9			
なぜ	why	Adv	12			

なつ	summer	Noun	13	夏	13	
なつめ	Natsume	N proper	14	夏目	14	
なつやすみ	summer vacation	Noun	6	夏休み	13	
など	etc.	Particle	5			
なな	seven	Noun	3	七	3	
ななつ	seven things	Counter	9	七つ	9	
なに	what	Pronoun	3	何	4	
なにか	something	Pronoun	3	何か	4	なにも
なにご	what language	Pronoun	6	何語	6	
なにも	anything	Pronoun	3	何も	4	なにか
なまえ	name	Noun	1	名前	11	
なら	Nara	N proper	13	奈良	X	
ならう	learn	Verb う	12	習う	15	
なん	what	Pronoun	2	何	4	
なんか	something	Pronoun	4	何か	4	なにも
なんがつ	which month	Pronoun	5	何月	5	
なんじ	what hour	Pronoun	4	何時	4	
なんにん	how many people	Pronoun	8	何人	8	
なんねんせい	what-year student	Pronoun	2	何年生	11	
なんぷん	what minute	Pronoun	4	何分	4	
なんようび	which day of the week	Pronoun	4	何曜日	4	
に に	two	Noun	3	二	3	
ニール	Neil	N proper	11			
にがつ	February	N proper	5	二月	5	
にぎやか（な）	lively	Adj な	7			しずか（な）
にく	meat	Noun	11	肉	24	
にちようび	Sunday	N proper	4	日曜日	4	
にっけい	of Japanese ancestry	Noun	11	日系	X	
にねんせい	second-year student	Noun	2	二年生	11	
にほん	Japan	N proper	2	日本	4	
にほんご	Japanese language	Noun	1	日本語	6	
にほんじん	Japanese people	Noun	6	日本人	6	
にほんまち	Japantown	Noun	4	日本まち	4	
にほんりょうり	Japanese cuisine	Noun	5	日本料理	12	
ニューヨーク	New York	N proper	2			
にわ	garden	Noun	12			
～にん	counter (people)	Counter	8	～人	8	
にんじん	carrot	Noun	12			
ぬ ヌエン	Nguyen	N proper	10			
ぬぐ	take off (clothes, shoes)	Verb う	14			きる、はく
ね ねぎ	green onion	Noun	12			
ネクタイ	necktie	Noun	10			

ねこ	cat	Noun	3			
ネックレス	necklace	Noun	10			
ねぼうする	oversleep	V irreg	12	寝ぼうする	18	
ねむい	sleepy	Adj い	14	眠い	19	
ねむる	sleep	Verb う	14	眠る	19	おきる
ねる	go to bed, lie down	Verb る	5	寝る	15	おきる
～ねん	X year(s)	Counter	9	～年	9	
ノート	notebook	Noun	3			
のみもの	drinks	Noun	9	飲み物	12	
のむ	drink	Verb う	4	飲む	6	
のり	laver	Noun	12			
のりまき	norimaki	Noun	12			
のる	ride, get on	Verb う	13	乗る	18	おりる
バークレー	Berkeley	N proper	2			
パーティー	party	Noun	6			
パートナー	partner	Noun	10			
はい	yes	Adv	2			いいえ
～はい	counter (cup(s), bowl(s), glass(es))	Counter	9			
ハイヒール	high heeled shoes	Noun	10			
はいる	enter	Verb う	7	入る	7	でる
はかた	Hakata	N proper	10	博多	X	
はく	wear (shoes, socks, trousers)	Verb う	10			ぬぐ
パク	Pak	N proper	3			
はこ	box	Noun	11			
はこぶ	carry	Verb う	14	運ぶ	24	
はし	chopsticks	Noun	4			
はじめて	for the first time	Adv	10	始めて	15	
はじめる	start (transitive)	Verb る	10	始める	15	おえる、やめる
ばしょ	location, place	Noun	12			
はしる	run	Verb う	13			
バス	bus	Noun	4			
バスケットボール	basketball	Noun	9			
パスポート	passport	Noun	14			
バター	butter	Noun	12			
はたらく	work	Verb う	13	働く	14	
はち	eight	Noun	3	八	3	
はちがつ	August	N proper	5	八月	5	
はな	flower	Noun	6	花	12	
はな	nose	Noun	7			
はなし	talk, story	Noun	9	話	9	

の

は

はなす	speak, chat	Verb う	6	話す	9	
はは	mother (plain)	Noun	8	母	8	ちち
ハムレット	Hamlet	N proper	11			
はやい	early	Adj い	8	早い	8	おそい
はやい	fast	Adj い	9			おそい
はやかわ	Hayakawa	N proper	3	早川	10	
はる	spring	Noun	13	春	13	
はるやすみ	spring vacation	Noun	13	春休み	13	
ハワイ	Hawaii	N proper	11			
はん	half	Noun	4	半	4	
パン	bread	Noun	12			
ばん	evening	Noun	5	晩	6	あさ
ばんごはん	dinner, supper	Noun	4	晩ごはん	6	あさごはん
ハンサム	handsome	Adj な	9			
ハンドアウト	handout	Noun	9			
ハンバーガー	hamberger	Noun	5			
ピアノ	piano	Noun	6			
ヒーター	heater	Noun	14			
ビートルズ	The Beatles	N proper	13			
ビール	beer	Noun	4			
ひがしアジア	East Asia	N proper	10	東アジア	10	
ひがしやま	Higashiyama	N proper	11	東山	11	
ひく	play (string instrument)	Verb う	6			
(かぜを) ひく	catch (cold)	Verb う	14			
ひくい	low, short (height)	Adj い	7			たかい
ピクニック	picnic	Noun	6			
ひこうき	airplane	Noun	4	飛行機	15	
ピザ	pizza	Noun	11			
ビデオ	video	Noun	11			
ひと	person	Noun	2	人	8	
ひとつ	one thing	Noun	9	一つ	9	
ひとびと	people	Noun	11	人々	11	
ひとり	one person	Noun	8	一人	8	
ひとりで	by oneself	Phrase	4	一人で	8	
ひま (な)	leisure, not busy	Adj な	12			いそがしい
ひゃく	hundred	Noun	3	百	3	
ひよう	expense	Noun	10			
びょうき	illness	Noun	13	病気	17	
ひょうばん	reputation	Noun	14			
ひらがな	hiragana	Noun	1			カタカナ
ビル	building	Noun	2			
ひるごはん	lunch	Noun	4	昼ごはん	25	

ひ

ひるね（する）	nap	N verbal	13	昼寝	25	
ひろい	spacious, wide	Adj い	7	広い	7	せまい
ひろしま	Hiroshima	N proper	10	広島	X	
ふ	ふくしゅう（する）	review	N verbal	6	復習	18	よしゅう（する）
	ふじさん	Mt. Fuji	N proper	12	富士山	X	
	ふたつ	two things	Counter	9	二つ	9	
	ふたり	two persons	Counter	8	二人	8	
	ふとる	become fat	Verb う	14			
	ふね	boat, ship	Noun	11			
	ふべん（な）	inconvenient	Adj な	7	不便	26	べんり（な）
	ふまじめ（な）	not serious	Adj な	7			まじめ（な）
	ふゆ	winter	Noun	8	冬	13	
	ふゆやすみ	winter vacation	Noun	6	冬休み	13	
	ブラウス	blouse	Noun	10			
	ブラウン	Brown	N proper	2			
	フラッシュカード	flash card	Noun	14			
	プラン	plan	Noun	4			
	フランスご	French language	Noun	6	フランス語	6	
	フランスじん	French people	Noun	6	フランス人	6	
	プリンター	printer	Noun	13			
	ふる	fall	Verb う	8	降る	17	やむ、はれる
	ふるい	old	Adj い	7	古い	7	あたらしい
	ブルース	blues	Noun	11			
	ふるかわ	Furukawa	N proper	8	古川	8	
	プレスリー	Presley	N proper	11			
	プレゼント（する）	present	N verbal	10			
	ふろ	bath	Noun	14			
	プログラム	program	Noun	3			
	〜ふん	X minute(s)	Suffix	4	〜分	4	
	ぶん	sentence	Noun	13	文	13	
	〜ぷん	X minute(s)	Suffix	4	〜分	4	
	ぶんがく	literature	Noun	5	文学	11	
	ぶんぽう	grammar	Noun	13	文法	18	
へ	へえ	Oh	Interject	4			
	へた（な）	bad at	Adj な	9	下手	9	じょうず（な）
	ベッド	bed	Noun	3			
	へや	room	Noun	3	部屋	17	
	ペレス	Perez	N proper	11			
	ペン	pen	Noun	2			
	べんきょう（する）	study	N verbal	4	勉強	14	
	へんじ（する）	reply	N verbal	13	返事	13	
	べんとう	box lunch	Noun	14			

	べんり（な）	convenient	Adj な	7	便利	12	ふべん（な）
ほ	ほう	direction, side, way	Noun	9	方	9	
	ぼうし	hat, cap	Noun	10			
	ホームズ	Holmes	N proper	3			
	ホームステイ（する）	homestay	N verbal	13			
	ボールペン	ballpoint pen	Noun	2			
	ほか	other (than something)	Noun	10			
	ほしい	want, desire	Adj い	12			
	ほしがる	show signs of desire	Verb う	12			
	ホストファミリー	host family	Noun	13			
	ボストン	Boston	N proper	9			
	ポップコーン	popcorn	Noun	12			
	ホノルル	Honolulu	N proper	10			
	ほん	book	Noun	2	本	5	
	〜ほん	counter (long things)	Counter	9	〜本	9	
	ほんばこ	bookshelf	Noun	11	本ばこ	11	
	ほんや	bookstore	Noun	3	本屋	17	
ま	〜まい	counter (flat things)	Counter	9	〜枚	23	
	まいあさ	every morning	Noun	11	毎朝	14	まいばん
	まいしゅう	every week	Noun	14	毎週	14	
	まいにち	everyday	Noun	11	毎日	14	
	まいばん	every evening	Noun	11	毎晩	14	まいあさ
	マイル	mile	Noun	13			
	まえ	front	Noun	3	前	10	うしろ
	まえだ	Maeda	N proper	7	前田	25	
	マグカップ	mug	Noun	9			
	マクドナルド	McDonald's	N proper	5			
	まご	grandchild (plain)	Noun	8			
	まじめ（な）	serious	Adj な	7			ふまじめ（な）
	まずい	not tasty, yucky	Adj い	7			おいしい
	また	again	Adv	6			
	まだ	yet	Adv	5			もう
	まだ	still	Adv	8			もう
	まち	town, city	Noun	4			
	まつ	wait	Verb う	8	待つ	9	
	まつり	festival	Noun	13			
	まで	to, up to	Particle	4			から
	まど	window	Noun	10			
み	みじかい	short (length)	Adj い	7	短い	22	ながい
	みず	water	Noun	12	水	12	
	みせ	shop	Noun	6	店	12	
	ミッキーマウス	Mickey Mouse	N proper	11			

	みっつ	three things	Noun	9	三つ	9	
	みなさん	everyone (respectful)	Noun	12			
	みみ	ear	Noun	7	耳	21	
	みやげ	gift	Noun	13			
	ミラー	Miller	N proper	2			
	みる	see, watch	Verb る	4	見る	6	
	みんな	everyone (plain)	Noun	13			
む	むずかしい	difficult	Adj い	7	難しい	22	やさしい
	むっつ	six things	Noun	9	六つ	9	
め	め	eye	Noun	7	目	7	
	めい	niece (plain)	Noun	8			おい
	めいごさん	niece (respectful)	Noun	8			おいごさん
	めがね	glasses	Noun	10			
	メキシコじん	Mexican people	Noun	6	メキシコ人	6	
も	も	also	Particle	2			
	もう	already	Adv	5			まだ
	もうすぐ	soon	Phrase	5			
	もくようび	Thursday	N proper	4	木曜日	4	
	もしもし	hello (on the phone)	Interject	10			
	もち	rice cake	Noun	14			
	もちろん	of course	Adv	6			
	もつ	have, hold	Verb う	8	持つ	24	
	モニター	monitor	Noun	14			
	もらう	receive	Verb う	11			あげる
や	や	and	Particle	5			
	やさい	vegetable	Noun	12			
	やさしい	easy, gentle	Adj い	7			むずかしい
	やすい	cheap, inexpensive	Adj い	7	安い	7	たかい
	やすかわ	Yasukawa	N proper	8	安川	9	
	やすみ	day off	Noun	14	休み	14	
	やすむ	take a day off, rest	Verb う	14	休む	14	
	やっつ	eight things	Noun	9	八つ	9	
	やました	Yamashita	N proper	7	山下	7	
	やまだ	Yamada	N proper	3	山田	19	
	やまもと	Yamamoto	N proper	6	山本	6	
	やめる	quit doing something	Verb る	14			はじめる
	やる	do, try	Verb う	14			
	やわらかい	soft	Adj い	11			かたい
	ヤング	Young	N proper	3			
ゆ	ゆうびんきょく	post office	Noun	3			
	ゆうべ	last evening	Noun	14	夕べ	22	
	ゆうめい（な）	famous	Adj な	14	有名	14	

	ゆき	snow	Noun	13	雪	17	
	ゆきだるま	snowman	Noun	13	雪だるま	17	
	ゆびわ	ring	Noun	10			
よ	ようかん	sweet adzukibean paste	Noun	12			
	ヨーロッパ	Europe	N proper	10			
	よく	well	Adv	10			
	よこ	side	Noun	3			
	よこはま	Yokohama	N proper	8	横浜	X	
	よしゅう（する）	preparatory study	N verbal	14	予習	18	ふくしゅう（する）
	ヨセミテ	Yosemite	N proper	3			
	よっつ	four things	Noun	9	四つ	9	
	よねんせい	fouth-year student	Noun	2	四年生	11	
	よぶ	call, summon	Verb う	8			
	よぶ	invite	Verb う	12			
	よみかた	way of reading	Noun	13	読み方	13	
	よみもの	readings	Noun	12	読み物	12	
	よむ	read	Verb う	4	読む	9	
	よろこぶ (3rd person)	be happy, pleased	Verb う	13			
	よん	four	Noun	3	四	3	
ら	らいげつ	next month	Noun	13	来月	13	せんげつ
	らいしゅう	next week	Noun	11	来週	13	せんしゅう
	ライトきょうだい	Wright Brothers	N proper	11	ライト兄弟	11	
	らいねん	next year	Noun	12	来年	12	きょねん
	ラウール	Raoul	N proper	4			
	らく（な）	easy, simple, comfortable, relaxed	Adj な	14	楽	14	たいへん（な）
	ラジオ	radio	Noun	3			
	ラップトップ	laptop	Noun	12			
	ラボ	laboratory	Noun	7			
り	りゅうがく（する）	studying abroad	N verbal	12	留学	12	
	りゅうがくせい	foreign student	Noun	6	留学生	6	
	りょう	dormitory	Noun	2			
	りょうしん	parents (plain)	Noun	8	両親	20	
	りょうり（する）	cuisine, cooking	N verbal	5	料理	12	
	りょこう（する）	trip, travel	N verbal	13	旅行	19	
	リン	Lin	N proper	3			
	リンカーン	Lincoln	N proper	11			
	りんご	apple	Noun	9			
る	ルイス	Lewis	N proper	7			
	ルームメート	roommate	Noun	3			
れ	れい	example	Noun	4	例	X	

	れいぞうこ	refrigerator	Noun	12				
	レジ	cash register	Noun	12				
	レストラン	restaurant	Noun	5				
	レノン	Lennon	N proper	11				
	れんしゅう（する）	practice	N verbal	9	練習	18		
ろ	ろく	six	Noun	3	六	3		
	ろくがつ	June	N proper	5	六月	5		
	ロサンゼルス	Los Angeles	N proper	9				
	ロシアご	Russian language	Noun	6	ロシア語	6		
	ロス	Los Angeles	N proper	9				
	ロック	rock	Noun	9				
わ	わあ	Wow	Interject	4				
	ワイシャツ	dress shirt	Noun	10				
	ワイン	wine	Noun	5				
	わかる	understand	Verb う	10	分かる	10		
	わたし	I, me	Pronoun	1	私	5		
	わたしたち	we	Pronoun	2	私達	13		
	ワトソン	Watson	N proper	3				
	わるい	bad	Adj い	11	悪い	24	いい	
	ワンピース	dress	Noun	10				

Appendix H   Vocabulary List (English to Japanese)

品詞 (ひんし)	Parts of speech	単語課 (たんごか)	Lesson where the word is introduced
漢字 (かんじ)	Kanji	漢字課 (かんじか)	Lesson where the kanji is introduced
反対語・対語 (はんたいご・ついご)	Antonym/A pair of words		
X	The kanji is used, but not taught.		
Adj irreg	Irregular adjective	N proper	Proper noun
Conj	Conjunction	N verbal	Verbal noun
Interject	Interjection		

	英語 English	日本語 Japanese	品詞	単語課	漢字	漢字課	反対語・対語
A	a little	すこし	Adv	6	少し	11	たくさん
	a little	ちょっと	Adv	7			たくさん
	a lot	たくさん	Adv	5			すこし、 ちょっと
	A.M.	ごぜん	Noun	4	午前	13	ごご
	able to (to be)	できる	Verb る	6			
	about	～ぐらい	Suffix	10			
	about (time)	～ごろ	Suffix	10			
	above	うえ	Noun	3	上	5	した
	academic department	がくぶ	Noun	11	学部	11	
	Africa	アフリカ	N proper	12			
	after that	それから	Conj	4			
	afternoon	ごご	Noun	4	午後	13	ごぜん
	again	また	Adv	6			
	airplane	ひこうき	Noun	4	飛行機	15	
	airport	くうこう	Noun	13			
	Akihabara	あきはばら	N proper	13	秋葉原	X	
	Akiyama	あきやま	N proper	13	秋山	13	
	Alaska	アラスカ	N proper	11			
	all	ぜんぶ	Adv	12	全部	12	
	already	もう	Adv	5			まだ
	alright	だいじょうぶ（な）	Adj な	12			
	also	も	Particle	2			
	always	いつも	Adv	7			
	America	アメリカ	N proper	5			

American people	アメリカじん	Noun	6	アメリカ人	6	
Amy	エイミー	N proper	2			
and	や	Particle	5			
and then	そして	Conj	4			
anyone	だれも	Pronoun	3			
anyone (respectful)	どなたも	Pronoun	3			
anything	なにも	Pronoun	3	何も	4	
anywhere	どこにも	Adv	3			
apartment	アパート	Noun	2			
apple	りんご	Noun	9			
approximately	～ぐらい	Suffix	10			
approximately (time)	～ごろ	Suffix	10			
April	しがつ	N proper	5	四月	5	
arm	て	Noun	7	手	11	
Armstrong	アームストロング	N proper	11			
as much as possible	できるだけ	Phrase	14			
Asakusa	あさくさ	N proper	13	浅草	X	
ask	きく	Verb う	5	聞く	11	
(not) at all	ぜんぜん	Adv	7	全然	25	
attend	でる (～に)	Verb る	12	出る	17	やすむ
August	はちがつ	N proper	5	八月	5	
aunt (plain)	おば	Noun	8			
aunt (respectful)	おばさん	Noun	8			
autumn	あき	Noun	12	秋	13	はる
back	うしろ	Noun	3	後ろ	11	まえ
bad	わるい	Adj い	11	悪い	24	いい
bad at	へた (な)	Adj な	9	下手	9	じょうず (な)
ballpoint pen	ボールペン	Noun	2			
bank	ぎんこう	Noun	3	銀行	10	
basketball	バスケットボール	Noun	9			
bath	(お) ふろ	Noun	14			
(The) Beatles	ビートルズ	N proper	13			
beautiful	きれい (な)	Adj な	7			きたない
because	から	Conj	5			
become empty	すく	Verb う	9			こむ
become fat	ふとる	Verb う	14			
bed	ベッド	Noun	3			
beef	ぎゅうにく	Noun	12	ぎゅう肉	24	
beer	ビール	Noun	4			
behind	うしろ	Noun	3	後ろ	11	まえ
below	した	Noun	3	下	5	うえ
Berkeley	バークレー	N proper	2			

B

best	いちばん	Noun	9	一番	9	
bicycle	じてんしゃ	Noun	4	自転車	19	
big	おおきい	Adj い	7	大きい	7	ちいさい
biology	せいぶつがく	Noun	11	生物学	21	
birthday	たんじょうび	Noun	12	たんじょう日	12	
blood	ち	Noun	11			
blouse	ブラウス	Noun	10			
blues	ブルース	Noun	11			
boat	ふね	Noun	11			
body height	せ	Noun	7	背	11	
book	ほん	Noun	2	本	5	
bookshelf	ほんばこ	Noun	11	本ばこ	11	
bookstore	ほんや	Noun	3	本屋	17	
boring	つまらない	Adj い	7			おもしろい
borrow	かりる	Verb る	6	借りる	23	かえす、かす
Boston	ボストン	N proper	9			
bottom	そこ	Noun	11			
boulevard	おおどおり	Noun	11	大どおり	11	
(X) bound thing(s)	～さつ	Counter	9			
box	はこ	Noun	11			
box lunch	(お)べんとう	Noun	14			
bread	パン	Noun	12			
breakfast	あさごはん	Noun	4	朝ごはん	10	
briefcase	かばん	Noun	3			
bright	あかるい	Adj い	7	明るい	7	くらい
Brown	ブラウン	N proper	2			
Buddhist temple	(お)てら	Noun	13			
building	ビル	Noun	2			
bus	バス	Noun	4			
busy	いそがしい	Adj い	10	忙しい	19	ひま(な)
but	でも	Conj	4			
butter	バター	Noun	12			
buy	かう	Verb う	5	買う	6	
by all means	ぜひ	Adv	14			
by oneself	ひとりで	Phrase	4	一人で	8	
by the way	ところで	Conj	8			
C cafeteria	カフェテリア	Noun	4			
cake	ケーキ	Noun	7			
California	カリフォルニア	N proper	3			
call	よぶ	Verb う	8			
camera	カメラ	Noun	3			
campus	キャンパス	Noun	6			

Canada	カナダ	N proper	6			
Canadian people	カナダじん	Noun	6	カナダ人	6	
cane	つえ	Noun	11			
cap	ぼうし	Noun	10			
car	くるま	Noun	2	車	7	
carrot	にんじん	Noun	12			
carry	はこぶ	Verb う	14	運ぶ	24	
cash register	レジ	Noun	12			
cat	ねこ	Noun	3			
catch (cold)	ひく	Verb う	14			
CD player	CD プレーヤー	Noun	12			
(X) cent(s)	～セント	Counter	9			
chair	いす	Noun	3			
change	おつり	Noun	12			
chat	はなす	Verb う	6	話す	9	
cheap	やすい	Adj い	7	安い	7	たかい
check	おかんじょう	Noun	9			
check	しらべる	Verb る	14	調べる	23	
cheerful	あかるい	Adj い	7	明るい	7	くらい
Chen	チェン	N proper	5			
cherry blossom /tree	さくら	Noun	13			
Chicago	シカゴ	N proper	3			
chicken	とりにく	Noun	12	とり肉	24	
child (plain)	こども	Noun	8	子供	16	おとな
child (respectful)	おこさん	Noun	8	お子さん	16	
China	ちゅうごく	N proper	9	中国	9	
Chinatown	チャイナタウン	Noun	5			
Chinese characters	かんじ	Noun	10	漢字	10	
Chinese cuisine	ちゅうかりょうり	Noun	9	料理	12	
Chinese language	ちゅうごくご	Noun	6	中国語	9	
Chinese people	ちゅうごくじん	Noun	6	中国人	9	
chocolate	チョコレート	Noun	12			
chopsticks	（お）はし	Noun	4			
city	まち	Noun	4			
class	クラス	Noun	2			
class	じゅぎょう	Noun	12	授業	18	
classical music	クラシック	Noun	9			
classmate	クラスメート	Noun	9			
classroom	きょうしつ	Noun	3	教室	14	
clean	きれい（な）	Adj な	7			きたない
clean	そうじ（する）	N verbal	9			
clock	とけい	Noun	3			

	close (intransitive)	しまる	Verb う	10	閉まる	10	あく
	club	クラブ	Noun	11			
	coffee	コーヒー	Noun	4			
	cola	コーラ	Noun	4			
	cold	かぜ	Noun	14			
	cold	さむい	Adj い	11	寒い	13	あつい
	college	だいがく	Noun	2	大学	7	
	Columbus	コロンブス	N proper	11			
	come	くる	V irreg	4	来る	5	いく
	comfortable	らく（な）	Adj な	14	楽	14	たいへん（な）
	company	かいしゃ	Noun	14	会社	23	
	computer	コンピューター	Noun	2			
	convenient	べんり（な）	Adj な	7	便利	12	ふべん（な）
	cooked rice	ごはん	Noun	4			
	cookie	クッキー	Noun	11			
	cooking	りょうり（する）	N verbal	5	料理	12	
	cool	すずしい	Adj い	11			あたたかい
	co-op	せいきょう	Noun	14			
	copy	コピー（する）	N verbal	4			
	country	くに	Noun	14	国	14	
	course	コース	Noun	7			
	cuisine	りょうり（する）	N verbal	5	料理	12	
	curry rice	カレーライス	Noun	9			
	custom	しゅうかん	Noun	14			
	cute	かわいい	Adj い	9			
D	dance	ダンス（する）	N verbal	11			
	dance	おどる	Verb う	13			
	dark	くらい	Adj い	7	暗い	7	あかるい
	day after tomorrow	あさって	Noun	13			おととい
	day before yesterday	おととい	Noun	13			あさって
	day off	やすみ	Noun	14	休み	14	
	December	じゅうにがつ	N proper	5	十二月	5	
	delicious	おいしい	Adj い	7			まずい
	demonstration	デモ	Noun	7			
	(academic) department	がくぶ	Noun	11	学部	11	
	department store	デパート	Noun	4			
	desire	ほしい	Adj い	12			
	desk	つくえ	Noun	3			
	dessert	デザート	Noun	9			
	Detroit	デトロイト	N proper	11			
	dictionary	じしょ	Noun	2	辞書	23	
	die	しぬ	Verb う	8	死ぬ	25	うまれる

diet	ダイエット（する）	N verbal	12			
difficult	むずかしい	Adj い	7	難しい	22	やさしい
dinner	ばんごはん	Noun	4	晩ごはん	6	あさごはん
direction	ほう	Noun	9	方	9	
dirty	きたない	Adj い	7			きれい（な）
dish	（お）さら	Noun	14			
dislike	きらい（な）	Adj な	9			すき（な）
Disney	ディズニー	N proper	11			
Disneyland	ディズニーランド	N proper	14			
do	する	V irreg	4			
do	やる	Verb う	14			
do (respectful)	なさる	Verb う	9			
do one's best	がんばる	Verb う	6			
dog	いぬ	Noun	3	犬	21	
doghouse	いぬごや	Noun	3	犬ごや	21	
dollar	ドル	Noun	5			
door	ドア	Noun	10			
dormitory	りょう	Noun	2			
downtown	ダウンタウン	Noun	4			
Doyle	ドイル	N proper	3			
draw	かく	Verb う	9			けす
drawing	え	Noun	9	絵	15	
dress	ワンピース	Noun	10			
dress shirt	ワイシャツ	Noun	10			
drink	のむ	Verb う	4	飲む	6	
drinks	のみもの	Noun	9	飲み物	12	
drive	うんてん（する）	N verbal	11	運転	19	
E ear	みみ	Noun	7	耳	21	
early	はやい	Adj い	8	早い	8	おそい
earrings	イヤリング	Noun	10			
East Asia	ひがしアジア	N proper	10	東アジア	10	
easy	やさしい	Adj い	7			むずかしい
easy	かんたん（な）	Adj な	9			むずかしい
easy	らく（な）	Adj な	14	楽	14	たいへん（な）
eat	たべる	Verb る	4	食べる	6	
economics	けいざいがく	Noun	2	けいざい学	11	
eel	うなぎ	Noun	12			
egg	たまご	Noun	12			
eight	はち	Noun	3	八	3	
eight things	やっつ	Noun	9	八つ	9	
elder brother (plain)	あに	Noun	8	兄	8	おとうと
elder brother (resp)	おにいさん	Noun	8	お兄さん	8	おとうとさん

elder sister (plain)	あね	Noun	8	姉	8	いもうと
elder sister (respect)	おねえさん	Noun	8	お姉さん	8	いもうとさん
electric light	でんき	Noun	10	電気	15	
electricity	でんき	Noun	10	電気	15	
elementary school	しょうがっこう	Noun	13	小学校	13	
Elvis	エルビス	N proper	11			
email	E メール	Noun	9			
(become) empty	すく	Verb う	9			こむ
energetic	げんき (な)	Adj な	7	元気	11	
England	イギリス	N proper	9			
English	えいご	Noun	2	英語	6	
English literature	えいぶんがく	Noun	11	英文学	11	
enjoyable	たのしい	Adj い	9	楽しい	13	
enter	はいる	Verb う	7	入る	7	でる
enter (a contest)	(〜に) でる	Verb る	12	出る	17	
essay	エッセー	Noun	11			
etc.	など	Particle	5			
Europe	ヨーロッパ	N proper	10			
evening	ばん	Noun	5	晩	6	あさ
every evening	まいばん	Noun	11	毎晩	14	まいあさ
every morning	まいあさ	Noun	11	毎朝	14	まいばん
every week	まいしゅう	Noun	14	毎週	14	
everyday	まいにち	Noun	11	毎日	14	
everyone (respectful)	みなさん	Noun	12			
everyone (plain)	みんな	Noun	13			
examination	テスト (する)	N verbal	5			
examination	しけん	Noun	6	試験	17	
Examiner	エグザミナー	N proper	2			
example	れい	Noun	4	例	X	
exercise	うんどう (する)	N verbal	4	運動	19	
exist (people, animals)	いる	Verb る	3			
exist (respectful)	いらっしゃる	Verb う	3			
exist (things)	ある	Verb う	3			ない
expense	ひよう	Noun	10			
expensive	たかい	Adj い	7	高い	7	やすい
eye	め	Noun	7	目	7	
F fall	ふる	Verb う	8	降る	17	やむ、はれる
family (plain)	かぞく	Noun	8	家族	26	
family (respectful)	ごかぞく	Noun	8	ご家族	26	
famous	ゆうめい (な)	Adj な	14	有名	14	
far	とおい	Adj い	7	遠い	20	ちかい
fast	はやい	Adj い	9			おそい

(become) fat	ふとる	Verb う	14			
father (plain)	ちち	Noun	8	父	8	
father (respectful)	おとうさん	Noun	8	お父さん	8	
favor	おねがい（する）	N verbal	9	お願い	25	
February	にがつ	N proper	5	二月	5	
female	おんな	Noun	2	女	8	おとこ
festival	（お）まつり	Noun	13			
fine	けっこう（な）	Adj な	8			だめ（な）
first	いちばん	Noun	9	一番	9	
first-year student	いちねんせい	Noun	2	一年生	11	
fish	さかな	Noun	6	魚	24	
five	ご	Noun	3	五	3	
five things	いつつ	Noun	9	五つ	9	
flash card	フラッシュカード	Noun	14			
flower	はな	Noun	6	花	12	
food	たべもの	Noun	9	食べ物	12	
foot	あし	Noun	7	足	21	
for the first time	はじめて	Adv	10	始めて	15	
foreign country	がいこく	Noun	11	外国	16	
foreign student	りゅうがくせい	Noun	6	留学生	6	
four	し・よん	Noun	3	四	3	
four things	よっつ	Noun	9	四つ	9	
fourth-year student	よねんせい	Noun	2	四年生	11	
French language	フランスご	Noun	6	フランス語	6	
French people	フランスじん	Noun	6	フランス人	6	
Friday	きんようび	N proper	4	金曜日	4	
friend	ともだち	Noun	4	友達	13	
from	から	Particle	4			
from now on	これから	Phrase	4			
front	まえ	Noun	3	前	10	うしろ
fruit	くだもの	Noun	9			
funeral ceremony	（お）そうしき	Noun	14			
Furukawa	ふるかわ	N proper	8	古川	8	
G garden	にわ	Noun	12			
gentle	やさしい	Adj い	7			むずかしい
German language	ドイツご	Noun	6	ドイツ語	6	
German people	ドイツじん	Noun	6	ドイツ人	6	
get on	のる	Verb う	13			おりる
get tired	つかれる	Verb る	5			
get to know	しる	Verb う	10	知る	10	
get up	おきる	Verb る	5			ねる
gift	（お）みやげ	Noun	13			

give	あげる	Verb る	14	上げる	18	もらう
glasses	めがね	Noun	10			
go	いく	Verb う	4	行く	5	くる
go home	かえる	Verb う	4	帰る	8	でかける
go to bed	ねる	Verb る	5	寝る	15	おきる
golf	ゴルフ	Noun	6			
good	いい	Adj い	7			わるい
good at	じょうず (な)	Adj な	9	上手	9	へた (な)
good at	とくい (な)	Adj な	9			
grade	せいせき	Noun	14	成績	25	
graduate student	だいがくいんせい	Noun	2	大学院生	11	
graduation	そつぎょう (する)	N verbal	13	卒業	18	にゅうがく (する)
grammar	ぶんぽう	Noun	13	文法	18	
grandchild (plain)	まご	Noun	8			
grandchild (respect)	おまごさん	Noun	8			
grandfather (plain)	そふ	Noun	8			そぼ
grandfather (respect)	おじいさん	Noun	8			おばあさん
grandmother (plain)	そぼ	Noun	8			そふ
grandmother (resp)	おばあさん	Noun	8			おじいさん
green onion	ねぎ	Noun	12			
group	グループ	Noun	14			
guitar	ギター	Noun	9			
gymnasium	ジム	Noun	4			
H hair	かみ	Noun	7			
Hakata	はかた	N proper	10	博多	X	
half	はん	Noun	4	半	4	
hamburger	ハンバーガー	Noun	5			
Hamlet	ハムレット	N proper	11			
hand	て	Noun	7	手	11	
handout	ハンドアウト	Noun	9			
handsome	ハンサム	Adj な	9			
happy	うれしい (1st person)	Adj い	13			かなしい
(be) happy	よろこぶ (3rd person)	Verb う	13			
hard	かたい	Adj い	11			やわらかい
hat	ぼうし	Noun	10			
have	もつ	Verb う	8			
Hawaii	ハワイ	N proper	11			
Hayakawa	はやかわ	N proper	3	早川	10	
head	あたま	Noun	7	頭	12	
heater	ヒーター	Noun	14			
heavy	おもい	Adj い	14			かるい

(body) height	せ	Noun	7	背	11	
hello (on the phone)	もしもし	Interject	10			
help	たすける	Verb る	13			
here	ここ	Pronoun	2			そこ、あそこ
Higashiyama	ひがしやま	N proper	11	東山	11	
high	たかい	Adj い	7	高い	7	ひくい
high heeled shoes	ハイヒール	Noun	10			
high school	こうこう	Noun	8	高校	8	
high school student	こうこうせい	Noun	8	高校生	8	
Hiroshima	ひろしま	N proper	10	広島	X	
hold	もつ	Verb う	8			
Holmes	ホームズ	N proper	3			
home	うち	Noun	3	家	6	
homestay	ホームステイ（する）	N verbal	13			
homework	しゅくだい	Noun	4	宿題	14	
Honolulu	ホノルル	N proper	10			
host family	ホストファミリー	Noun	13			
hot	あつい	Adj い	11	暑い	22	さむい
house	うち	Noun	3	家	6	
how	どう	Adv	7			
how (respectful)	いかが	Adv	7			
how long	どのぐらい	Adv	10			
how many people	なんにん	Pronoun	8	何人	8	
how much	いくら、どのぐらい	Adv	10			
hundred	ひゃく	Noun	3	百	3	
husband (plain)	しゅじん	Noun	8			かない
husband (respectful)	ごしゅじん	Noun	8			おくさん
I I	わたし	Pronoun	1	私	5	
illness	びょうき	Noun	13	病気	17	
impolite	しつれい（な）	Adj な	7			
inconvenient	ふべん（な）	Adj な	7	不便	26	べんり（な）
inexpensive	やすい	Adj い	7	安い	7	たかい
inside	なか	Noun	3	中	9	そと
intelligence	ちえ	Noun	11			
intention	つもり	Noun	5			
interesting	おもしろい	Adj い	7			つまらない
interview	インタビュー（する）	N verbal	10			
introduction	しょうかい（する）	N verbal	14	紹介	24	
invite	よぶ	Verb う	12			
Ishikawa	いしかわ	N proper	2	石川	7	
Italian cuisine	イタリアりょうり	Noun	9	料理	12	
J Jack	ジャック	N proper	10			

	January	いちがつ	N proper	5	一月	5	
	Japan	にほん	N proper	2	日本	4	
	Japan	ジャパン	N proper	11			
	(of) Japanese ancestry	にっけい	Noun	11	日系	X	
	Japanese bullet train	しんかんせん	N proper	4			
	Japanese cuisine	にほんりょうり	Noun	5	日本料理	12	
	Japanese language	にほんご	Noun	1	日本語	6	
	Japanese people	にほんじん	Noun	6	日本人	6	
	Japantown	にほんまち	Noun	4	日本まち	4	
	Jazz	ジャズ	Noun	9			
	jeans	ジーンズ	Noun	10			
	Jimmy	ジミー	N proper	2			
	job	しごと（する）	N verbal	8	仕事	14	
	jogging	ジョギング（する）	N verbal	5			
	John	ジョン	N proper	11			
	Jones	ジョーンズ	N proper	4			
	juice	ジュース	Noun	8			
	July	しちがつ	N proper	5	七月	5	
	June	ろくがつ	N proper	5	六月	5	
	junior high school	ちゅうがっこう	Noun	13	中学校	13	
K	Kim	キム	N proper	4			
	Kimura	きむら	N proper	3	木村	15	
	kind	しんせつ（な）	Adj な	7	親切	20	いじわる（な）
	Korean language	かんこくご	Noun	6	かんこく語	6	
	Korean people	かんこくじん	Noun	6	かんこく人	6	
	Koyama	こやま	N proper	3	小山	5	
	Kyoto	きょうと	N proper	2	京都	13	
L	laboratory	ラボ	Noun	7			
	laptop	ラップトップ	Noun	12			
	large	おおきい	Adj い	7	大きい	7	ちいさい
	last evening	ゆうべ	Noun	14	夕べ	22	
	last month	せんげつ	Noun	13	先月	13	らいげつ
	last week	せんしゅう	Noun	5	先週	13	らいしゅう
	last year	きょねん	Noun	8	去年	12	らいねん
	late	おそい	Adj い	11			はやい
	(be) late	おくれる	Verb る	14			まにあう
	laundry	せんたく（する）	N verbal	12	洗濯	16	
	lavatory	おてあらい	Noun	3	お手洗い	16	
	laver	のり	Noun	12			
	learn	ならう	Verb う	12	習う	15	
	leg	あし	Noun	7			
	leisure	ひま（な）	Adj な	12			いそがしい

lend	かす	Verb う	8	貸す	23	かりる
Lennon	レノン	N proper	11			
letter	てがみ	Noun	3	手紙	10	
Lewis	ルイス	N proper	7			
library	としょかん	Noun	2	図書館	10	
lie down	ねる	Verb る	5	寝る	15	おきる
light (weight)	かるい	Adj い	14			おもい
like	すき (な)	Adj な	9	好き	9	きらい (な)
like very much	だいすき (な)	Adj な	12	大好き	12	
Lin	リン	N proper	3			
Lincoln	リンカーン	N proper	11			
liquor	(お) さけ	Noun	5	(お) 酒	16	
listen	きく	Verb う	5	聞く	11	
literature	ぶんがく	Noun	5	文学	11	
(a) little	すこし	Adv	6	少し	12	たくさん
(a) little	ちょっと	Adv	7			たくさん
lively	にぎやか (な)	Adj な	7			しずか (な)
location	ばしょ	Noun	12			
lonely	さびしい	Adj い	13			
long	ながい	Adj い	7	長い	7	みじかい
look forward to	たのしみにする	Phrase	4	楽しみ	13	
Los Angeles	ロサンゼルス／ロス	N proper	9			
(a) lot	たくさん	Adv	5			すこし、ちょっと
low (height)	ひくい	Adj い	7			たかい
lunch	ひるごはん	Noun	4	昼ごはん	25	
M Maeda	まえだ	N proper	7	前田	25	
magazine	ざっし	Noun	2			
major	せんもん	Noun	1	専門	22	
major (respectful)	ごせんもん	Noun	1	ご専門	22	
make	つくる	Verb う	5	作る	9	こわす
male	おとこ	Noun	2	男	8	おんな
many	おおい	Adj い	10	多い	10	すくない
many	たくさん	Adv	5			すこし、ちょっと
many kinds of	いろいろ (な)	Adj な	12			
map	ちず	Noun	9	地図	24	
March	さんがつ	N proper	5	三月	5	
mathematics	すうがく	Noun	6	数学	26	
May	ごがつ	N proper	5	五月	5	
McDonald's	マクドナルド	N proper	5			
me	わたし	Pronoun	1	私	5	

meal	ごはん	Noun	4			
mean	いじわる (な)	Adj な	7			しんせつ (な)、やさしい
meaning	いみ	Noun	12	意味	20	
meat	にく	Noun	11	肉	24	
meet	あう	Verb う	4	会う	6	
memorize	おぼえる	Verb る	12	覚える	15	わすれる
Mexican people	メキシコじん	Noun	6	メキシコ人	6	
Mickey Mouse	ミッキーマウス	N proper	11			
microwave oven	でんしレンジ	Noun	12			
midterm	ちゅうかん	Noun	6	中間	6	
mile	マイル	Noun	13			
Miller	ミラー	N proper	2			
Monday	げつようび	N proper	4	月曜日	4	
money	(お) かね	Noun	6	お金	7	
monitor	モニター	Noun	14			
(X) month(s)	〜かげつ	Counter	9	〜か月	9	
month after next	さらいげつ	Noun	13	さ来月	13	せんせんげつ
month before last	せんせんげつ	Noun	13	先々月	13	さらいげつ
moon	つき	Noun	11	月	11	
morning	ごぜん	Noun	4	午前	13	ごご
morning	あさ	Noun	5	朝	10	ばん
mother (plain)	はは	Noun	8	母	8	ちち
mother (respectful)	おかあさん	Noun	8	お母さん	8	おとうさん
motorcycle	オートバイ	Noun	14			
mouth	くち	Noun	7	口	21	
movie	えいが	Noun	4	映画	15	
Mt. Fuji	ふじさん	N proper	12	富士山	X	
mug	マグカップ	Noun	9			
music	おんがく	Noun	9	音楽	11	
N Nagoya	なごや	N proper	10	名古屋	X	
Nakayama	なかやま	N proper	10	中山	10	
name	なまえ	Noun	1	名前	11	
name (respectful)	おなまえ	Noun	1	お名前	11	
nap	ひるね (する)	N verbal	13	昼寝	25	
Nara	なら	N proper	11	奈良	X	
narrow	せまい	Adj い	7			ひろい
Natsume	なつめ	N proper	14	夏目	14	
near	ちかい	Adj い	7	近い	20	とおい
necklace	ネックレス	Noun	10			
necktie	ネクタイ	Noun	10			
Neil	ニール	N proper	11			

	nephew (plain)	おい	Noun	8			めい
	nephew (respectful)	おいごさん	Noun	8			めいごさん
	new	あたらしい	Adj い	7	新しい	7	ふるい
	(1st month of) New Year	(お) しょうがつ	N proper	14	(お) 正月	23	
	New York	ニューヨーク	N proper	2			
	newspaper	しんぶん	Noun	2	新聞	11	
	next month	らいげつ	Noun	13	来月	13	せんげつ
	next time	こんど	Noun	6	今度	18	
	next to	となり	Noun	3			
	next week	らいしゅう	Noun	11	来週	13	せんしゅう
	next year	らいねん	Noun	12	来年	12	きょねん
	Nguyen	ヌエン	N proper	10			
	nice	けっこう (な)	Adj な	8			だめ (な)
	niece (plain)	めい	Noun	8			おい
	niece (respectful)	めいごさん	Noun	8			おいごさん
	nine	きゅう・く	Noun	3	九	3	
	nine things	ここのつ	Noun	9	九つ	9	
	no	いいえ	Adv	2			はい
	no (casual)	ううん	Adv	6			うん
	no good	だめ (な)	Adj な	11			いい、 けっこう (な)
	noisy	うるさい	Adj い	7			しずか (な)
	nose	はな	Noun	7			
	(not) at all	ぜんぜん	Adv	7			
	not busy	ひま (な)	Adj な	12			いそがしい
	(not) much	あまり	Adv	7			
	not serious	ふまじめ (な)	Adj な	7			まじめ (な)
	notebook	ノート	Noun	3			
	novel	しょうせつ	Noun	11	小説	22	
	November	じゅういちがつ	N proper	5	十一月	5	
	now	いま	Noun	4	今	5	
	now	これから	Phrase	4			
	number one	いちばん	Noun	9	一番	9	
O	Oakland	オークランド	N proper	5			
	October	じゅうがつ	N proper	5	十月	5	
	of course	もちろん	Adv	6			
	office	オフィス	Noun	3			
	office hours	オフィスアワー	Noun	10			
	oh	へえ	Interject	4			
	okay	だいじょうぶ (な)	Adj な	12			だめ (な)
	old	ふるい	Adj い	7	古い	7	あたらしい
	on	うえ	Noun	3	上	5	した

on foot	あるいて	Phrase	4	歩いて	18	
one	いち	Noun	3	一	3	
one person	ひとり	Noun	8	一人	8	
one thing	ひとつ	Noun	9	一つ	9	
onion	たまねぎ	Noun	12			
open (intransitive)	あく	Verb う	10	開く	10	しまる
orange	オレンジ	Noun	9			
order	オーダー（する）	N verbal	9			
Osaka	おおさか	N proper	7	大阪	X	
other (than something)	ほか	Noun	10			
outside	そと	Noun	3	外	16	なか
oversleep	ねぼうする	V irreg	12	寝ぼうする	18	
P.M.	ごご	Noun	4	午後	13	ごぜん
painful	いたい	Adj い	12	痛い	21	
Pak	パク	N proper	3			
pants	ズボン	Noun	10			
paper	かみ	Noun	11	紙	11	
parcel	こづつみ	Noun	11	小づつみ	11	
parents (plain)	りょうしん	Noun	8	両親	20	
parents (respectful)	ごりょうしん	Noun	8	ご両親	20	
park	こうえん	Noun	6			
partner	パートナー	Noun	10			
party	パーティー	Noun	6			
passport	パスポート	Noun	14			
pen	ペン	Noun	2			
pencil	えんぴつ	Noun	2			
people	ひとびと	Noun	11	人々	11	
Perez	ペレス	N proper	11			
person	ひと	Noun	2	人	8	
person (respectful)	かた	Noun	2	方	11	
photograph	しゃしん	Noun	2	写真	19	
piano	ピアノ	Noun	6			
picnic	ピクニック	Noun	6			
picture	え	Noun	9	絵	15	
pizza	ピザ	Noun	11			
place	ばしょ	Noun	12			
place over there	あそこ	Pronoun	2			ここ
plan	プラン	Noun	4			
play	あそぶ	Verb う	6	遊ぶ	24	
play (string instrument)	ひく	Verb う	6			
pleasant	たのしい	Adj い	9	楽しい	13	
please	どうぞ	Adv	9			

The letter **P** appears in a box to the left of the "P.M." row.

	please give	ください	Phrase	8	下さい	8	
	(to be) pleased	うれしい (1st person)	Adj い	13			かなしい
	(to be) pleased	よろこぶ (3rd person)	Verb う	13			
	plenty	おおい	Adj い	10	多い	10	すくない
	plural marker (people)	～たち	Suffix	2	～達	13	
	points	てん	Noun	14			
	popcorn	ポップコーン	Noun	12			
	pork cutlet	とんかつ	Noun	5			
	post office	ゆうびんきょく	Noun	3			
	potato	じゃがいも	Noun	12			
	power	ちから	Noun	11			
	practice	れんしゅう (する)	N verbal	9	練習	18	
	preparatory study	よしゅう (する)	N verbal	14	予習	18	ふくしゅう (する)
	present	プレゼント (する)	N verbal	10			
	present	おくりもの	Noun	14	おくり物	14	
	Presley	プレスリー	N proper	11			
	printer	プリンター	Noun	13			
	program	プログラム	Noun	3			
Q	question	しつもん (する)	N verbal	6	質問	19	こたえる
	quiet	しずか (な)	Adj な	7	静か	11	うるさい
	quit doing something	やめる	Verb る	14			はじめる
R	radio	ラジオ	Noun	3			
	rain	あめ	Noun	8	雨	14	
	Raoul	ラウール	N proper	4			
	raw fish	(お) さしみ	Noun	6			
	read	よむ	Verb う	4	読む	9	
	readings	よみもの	Noun	12	読み物	12	
	receive	もらう	Verb う	11			あげる
	receive (respectful)	いただく	Verb う	8			さしあげる
	recently	さいきん	Noun	14	最近	22	むかし
	refrigerator	れいぞうこ	Noun	12			
	regret	ざんねん (な)	Adj な	6			
	regrettable	ざんねん (な)	Adj な	6			
	relaxed	らく (な)	Adj な	14	楽	14	
	reply	へんじ (する)	N verbal	13	返事	13	
	reputation	ひょうばん	Noun	14			
	request	おねがい (する)	N verbal	9			
	rest	やすむ	Verb う	14	休む	14	
	restaurant	レストラン	Noun	5			
	return	かえす	Verb う	6	返す	13	かりる
	review	ふくしゅう (する)	N verbal	6	復習	18	よしゅう(する)

(cooked) rice	ごはん	Noun	4			
(uncooked) rice	（お）こめ	Noun	12	お米	12	
rice cake	（お）もち	Noun	14			
ride	のる	Verb う	13	乗る	18	おりる
ring	ゆびわ	Noun	10			
rock	ロック	Noun	9			
room	へや	Noun	3	部屋	17	
roommate	ルームメート	Noun	3			
run	はしる	Verb う	13			
Russian language	ロシアご	Noun	6	ロシア語	6	
sake	（お）さけ	Noun	5	酒	16	
sale	セール	Noun	7			
salmon	さけ	Noun	12			
salt	（お）しお	Noun	12			
San Francisco	サンフランシスコ	N proper	2			
Saturday	どようび	N proper	4	土曜日	4	
say	いう	Verb う	11	言う	16	
Schmidt	シュミット	N proper	8			
school	がっこう	Noun	10	学校	10	
science	サイエンス	Noun	2			
score	てん	Noun	14			
search for	さがす	Verb う	14			
second-year student	にねんせい	Noun	2	二年生	11	
see	みる	Verb る	4	見る	6	
send	おくる	Verb う	10	送る	24	
sentence	ぶん	Noun	13	文	13	
September	くがつ	N proper	5	九月	5	
serious	まじめ（な）	Adj な	7			ふまじめ（な）
service	サービス（する）	N verbal	11			
seven	しち・なな	Noun	3	七	3	
seven things	ななつ	Counter	9	七つ	9	
Shakespeare	シェークスピア	N proper	11			
Shin-Osaka	しんおおさか	N proper	10	新大阪	X	
Shinto shrine	じんじゃ	Noun	13			
ship	ふね	Noun	11			
shoes	くつ	Noun	6			
shop	（お）みせ	Noun	6	（お）店	12	
shopping	かいもの（する）	N verbal	4	買い物	12	
short (height)	ひくい	Adj い	7			たかい
short (length)	みじかい	Adj い	7	短い	22	ながい
shorts	ショートパンツ	Noun	10			
show signs of desire	ほしがる	Verb う	12			

S

shower	シャワー	Noun	13			
siblings	きょうだい	Noun	8	兄弟	8	
siblings (respectful)	ごきょうだい	Noun	8	ご兄弟	8	
side	よこ	Noun	3			
side	ほう	Noun	9	方	9	
simple	らく（な）	Adj な	14	楽	14	たいへん（な）
sing	うたう	Verb う	8	歌う	15	
Singh	シン	N proper	7			
sit down	すわる	Verb う	10			たつ
six	ろく	Noun	3	六	3	
six things	むっつ	Noun	9	六つ	9	
ski	スキー	Noun	6			
skirt	スカート	Noun	10			
skit	スキット	Noun	13			
sleep	ねむる	Verb う	14	眠る	19	おきる
sleepy	ねむい	Adj い	14	眠い	19	
slow	おそい	Adj い	11			はやい
small	せまい	Adj い	7			ひろい
small	ちいさい	Adj い	7	小さい	7	おおきい
Smith	スミス	N proper	7			
snack	おかし	Noun	11			
sneakers	スニーカー	Noun	10			
snow	ゆき	Noun	13	雪	17	
snowman	ゆきだるま	Noun	13	雪だるま	17	
so	ですから	Conj	6			
so that	それで	Conj	8			
socks	ソックス	Noun	10			
sofa	ソファー	Noun	3			
soft	やわらかい	Adj い	11			かたい
some time ago	このあいだ	Phrase	12	この間	23	
someone	だれか	Pronoun	3			だれも
someone (respectful)	どなたか	Pronoun	3			どなたも
something	なにか・なんか	Pronoun	3	何か	4	なにも
sometimes	ときどき	Adv	11	時々	11	いつも
somewhere	どこかに	Adv	3			どこにも
Son	ソン	N proper	2			
song	うた	Noun	8	歌	15	
soon	すぐ・もうすぐ	Adv	5			
soy sauce	（お）しょうゆ	Noun	12			
spacious	ひろい	Adj い	7	広い	7	せまい
spaghetti	スパゲティ	Noun	6			
Spanish language	スペインご	Noun	6	スペイン語	6	

speak	はなす	Verb う	6	話す	9	
speak	いう	Verb う	11	言う	16	
speciality	せんもん	Noun	1	専門	22	
speciality (respectful)	ごせんもん	Noun	1	ご専門	22	
sport	スポーツ	Noun	9			
sports player	せんしゅ	Noun	11			
spring	はる	Noun	13	春	13	
spring vacation	はるやすみ	Noun	13	春休み	13	
stand up	たつ	Verb う	10			すわる
start (transitive)	はじめる	Verb る	10	始める	15	おえる、やめる
start living somewhere	すむ	Verb う	10	住む	10	
station	えき	Noun	4	駅	20	
stay over night	とまる	Verb う	14			
steak	ステーキ	Noun	5			
stereo (set)	ステレオ	Noun	11			
still	まだ	Adv	8			もう
stomach	おなか	Noun	9			
store	(お) みせ	Noun	6	(お) 店	12	
store clerk	てんいん	Noun	12	店員	12	
story	はなし	Noun	9	話	9	
street	とおり	Noun	11			
stroll	さんぽ (する)	N verbal	13			
student	がくせい	Noun	1	学生	5	
study	べんきょう (する)	N verbal	4	勉強	14	
studying abroad	りゅうがく (する)	N verbal	12	留学	12	
sugar	(お) さとう	Noun	12			
suit	スーツ	Noun	10			
suitcase	スーツケース	Noun	13			
summer	なつ	Noun	13	夏	13	
summer vacation	なつやすみ	Noun	6	夏休み	13	
summon	よぶ	Verb う	8			
Sunday	にちようび	N proper	4	日曜日	4	
sunglasses	サングラス	Noun	10			
supermarket	スーパー	Noun	4			
supper	ばんごはん	Noun	4	晩ごはん	6	あさごはん
sweater	セーター	Noun	10			
sweatshirt	トレーナー	Noun	10			
sweet	あまい	Adj い	11			からい
swim	およぐ	Verb う	6	泳ぐ	25	
T table	テーブル	Noun	3			
Tahoe	タホ	N proper	5			
take	とる	Verb う	5	取る	14	

take (picture)	（しゃしんを）とる	Verb う	8			
take (shower)	（シャワーを）あびる	Verb る	13			
take (exam)	（しけんを）うける	Verb る	13	受ける	16	
take (time, expense)	かかる	Verb う	10			
take a day off	やすむ	Verb う	14	休む	14	
take off (clothes, shoes)	ぬぐ	Verb う	14			きる、はく
talk	はなし	Noun	9	話	9	
talk	いう	Verb う	11	言う	16	
Tanaka	たなか	N proper	3	田中	19	
Tango	タンゴ	N proper	13			
tape	テープ	Noun	6			
taxi	タクシー	Noun	8			
tea	おちゃ	Noun	4	お茶	9	
teach	おしえる	Verb る	5	教える	14	ならう
teacher	せんせい	Noun	1	先生	5	
team	チーム	Noun	11			
telephone	でんわ（する）	N verbal	10	電話	15	
ten	じゅう	Noun	3	十	3	
ten things	とお	Noun	9	十	9	
tennis	テニス	Noun	4			
teriffic	すごい	Adj い	11			
test	しけん	Noun	6	試験	17	
textbook	テキスト	Noun	2			
textbook	きょうかしょ	Noun	9	教科書	20	
Thailand	タイ	N proper	11			
that direction	あちら	Pronoun	7			こちら
that direction	そちら	Pronoun	7			こちら
that NOUN	その + NOUN	Adj irreg	2			この
that NOUN (over there)	あの + NOUN	Adj irreg	2			この
that one	あれ	Pronoun	2			これ
that one	それ	Pronoun	2			これ
the other day	このあいだ	Phrase	12	この間	23	
there	そこ	Pronoun	2			ここ
therefore	ですから	Conj	6			
therefore	それで	Conj	8			
think	かんがえる	Verb る	11	考える	24	
third-year student	さんねんせい	Noun	2	三年生	11	
this direction	こちら	Pronoun	7			あちら
this evening	こんばん	Noun	5	今晩	6	けさ
this month	こんげつ	Noun	13	今月	13	
this morning	けさ	Noun	12	今朝	12	こんばん
this NOUN	この + NOUN	Adj irreg	2			その、あの

this one	これ	Pronoun	2			それ、あれ
this week	こんしゅう	Noun	12	今週	13	
this year	ことし	Noun	8	今年	10	
thousand	せん	Noun	3	千	3	
three	さん	Noun	3	三	3	
three persons	さんにん	Noun	8	三人	8	
three things	みっつ	Noun	9	三つ	9	
Thursday	もくようび	N proper	4	木曜日	4	
ticket	きっぷ	Noun	13	切符	22	
time	じかん	Noun	10	時間	10	
time	とき	Noun	13	時	13	
Times	タイムズ	N proper	2			
to	まで	Particle	4			から
to tell the truth	じつは	Phrase	13			
today	きょう	Noun	4	今日	5	
together	いっしょに	Phrase	4			
toilet	おてあらい	Noun	3	お手洗い	16	
Tokyo	とうきょう	N proper	7	東京	8	
tomorrow	あした	Noun	4	明日	5	きのう
tough	たいへん（な）	Adj な	5	大変	14	らく（な）
tough	かたい	Adj い	11			やわらかい
town	まち	Noun	4			
train	でんしゃ	Noun	4	電車	15	
travel	りょこう（する）	N verbal	13	旅行	19	
trifle	つまらない	Adj い	7			おもしろい
trip	りょこう（する）	N verbal	13	旅行	19	
trivial	つまらない	Adj い	7			おもしろい
trousers	ズボン	Noun	10			
try	やる	Verb う	14			
T-shirt	Tシャツ	Noun	9			
Tuesday	かようび	N proper	4	火曜日	4	
turn off (transitive)	けす	Verb う	14			つける
turn off (intransitive)	きえる	Verb る	10			つく
turn on (intransitive)	つく	Verb う	10			きえる
turn on (transitive)	つける	Verb る	14			けす
TV	テレビ	Noun	4			
two	に	Noun	3	二	3	
two persons	ふたり	Noun	8	二人	8	
two things	ふたつ	Counter	9	二つ	9	
U umbrella	かさ	Noun	6			
uncle (plain)	おじ	Noun	8			おば
uncle (respectful)	おじさん	Noun	8			おばさん

	English	Japanese	Type		Kanji		Related
	uncooked rice	（お）こめ	Noun	12	（お）米	12	
	under	した	Noun	3	下	5	うえ
	undergraduate	だいがくせい	Noun	2	大学生	8	
	understand	わかる	Verb う	10	分かる	10	
	(X) unit(s)	～こ	Counter	9			
	university	だいがく	Noun	2	大学	7	
	untasty	まずい	Adj い	7			おいしい
	up to	まで	Particle	4			から
	usage	つかいかた	Noun	13	使い方	16	
	use	つかう	Verb う	6	使う	16	
V	various	いろいろ（な）	Adj な	12	色々	18	
	vegetable	やさい	Noun	12			
	very	とても	Adv	7			
	vicinity	ちかく	Noun	3	近く	20	
	video	ビデオ	Noun	11			
	vinegar	（お）す	Noun	11			
	vocabulary	たんご	Noun	14	単語	18	
W	wait	まつ	Verb う	8	待つ	9	
	waiter	ウェイター	Noun	9			
	wake up (intransitive)	おきる	Verb る	5			ねる
	walk	あるく	Verb う	8	歩く	18	
	want	ほしい	Adj い	12			
	wash	あらう	Verb う	14	洗う	16	よごす
	watch	とけい	Noun	3	時計	23	
	watch	みる	Verb る	4	見る	6	
	water	みず	Noun	12	水	12	
	Watson	ワトソン	N proper	3			
	way	ほう	Noun	9	方	9	
	way of making	つくりかた	Noun	13	作り方	13	
	way of reading	よみかた	Noun	13	読み方	13	
	way of writing	かきかた	Noun	13	書き方	13	
	way to use	つかいかた	Noun	13	使い方	16	
	we	わたしたち	Pronoun	2	私達	13	
	wear (accessory)	する	V irreg	10			とる、はずす
	wear (dress, shirt, suit)	きる	Verb る	10	着る	21	ぬぐ
	wear (glasses)	（めがねを）かける	Verb る	10			はずす
	wear (hat, cap)	かぶる	Verb う	10			とる
	wear (shoes, socks, trousers)	はく	Verb う	10			ぬぐ
	weather	（お）てんき	Noun	13	（お）天気	22	
	wedding ceremony	けっこんしき	Noun	14	結婚しき	26	
	Wednesday	すいようび	N proper	4	水曜日	4	

week after next	さらいしゅう	Noun	13	さ来週	13	せんせんしゅう
week before last	せんせんしゅう	Noun	13	先々週	13	さらいしゅう
weekend	しゅうまつ	Noun	4	週まつ	13	
well	よく	Adv	10			
well then (casual)	じゃ	Conj	5			
well then (casual)	それじゃ	Conj	6			
what	なに・なん	Pronoun	2	何	4	
what hour	なんじ	Pronoun	4	何時	4	
what kind of	どんな＋NOUN	Adj irreg	7			
what language	なにご	Pronoun	6	何語	6	
what minute	なんぷん	Pronoun	4	何分	4	
what-year student	なんねんせい	Pronoun	2	何年生	11	
wheat flour	こむぎこ	Noun	12			
when	いつ	Adv	4			
when	とき	Noun	13	時	13	
where	どこ	Pronoun	2			
which day of the week	なんようび	Pronoun	4	何曜日	4	
which month	なんがつ	Pronoun	5	何月	5	
which NOUN	どの＋NOUN	Adj irreg	2			
which one	どれ	Pronoun	2			
whiskey	ウィスキー	Noun	9			
who	だれ	Pronoun	2			
who (respectful)	どなた	Pronoun	2			
why	どうして	Adv	5			
why	なぜ	Adv	12			
wide	ひろい	Adj い	7	広い	7	せまい
wife (plain)	かない	Noun	8			しゅじん
wife (respectful)	おくさん	Noun	8			ごしゅじん
Wilson	ウィルソン	N proper	7			
window	まど	Noun	10			
wine	ワイン	Noun	5			
winter	ふゆ	Noun	8	冬	13	
winter vacation	ふゆやすみ	Noun	6	冬休み	13	
wisdom	ちえ	Noun	11			
wonderful	けっこう（な）	Adj な	8			だめ（な）
Wong	ウォン	N proper	2			
word	たんご	Noun	14	単語	18	
work	はたらく	Verb う	13	働く	14	
wow	わあ	Interject	4			
Wright Brothers	ライトきょうだい	N proper	11	ライト兄弟	11	
write	かく	Verb う	4	書く	9	けす

Y	Yamada	やまだ	N proper	3	山田	19	
	Yamamoto	やまもと	N proper	6	山本	6	
	Yamashita	やました	N proper	7	山下	7	
	Yasukawa	やすかわ	N proper	8	安川	9	
	year after next	さらいねん	Noun	13	さ来年	13	おととし
	year before last	おととし	Noun	13			さらいねん
	yes	はい	Adv	2			いいえ
	yes (casual)	うん	Adv	5			ううん
	yesterday	きのう	Noun	5	昨日	5	あした
	yet	まだ	Adv	5			もう
	Yokohama	よこはま	N proper	8	横浜	X	
	Yosemite	ヨセミテ	N proper	3			
	you	あなた	Pronoun	2			
	Young	ヤング	N proper	3			
	younger brother (plain)	おとうと	Noun	8	弟	8	あに
	younger brother (resp)	おとうとさん	Noun	8	弟さん	8	おにいさん
	younger sister (plain)	いもうと	Noun	8	妹	8	あね
	younger sister (resp)	いもうとさん	Noun	8	妹さん	8	おねえさん
	yucky	まずい	Adj い	7			おいしい

Appendix I   Predicates by Category

い -Adjectives

7	あかるい	bright, cheerful
7	あたらしい	new
11	あつい	hot
11	あまい	sweet
7	いい	good
10	いそがしい	busy
12	いたい	painful
7	うるさい	noisy
13	うれしい (1st person)	happy, pleased
7	おいしい	delicious
10	おおい	many, plenty
7	おおきい	big, large
11	おそい	slow
14	おもい	heavy
7	おもしろい	interesting
11	かたい	tough, hard
14	かるい	light (weight)
9	かわいい	cute
7	きたない	dirty
7	くらい	dark
13	さびしい	lonely
11	さむい	cold
11	すごい	teriffic
11	すずしい	cool
7	せまい	narrow, small
7	たかい	expensive, high
9	たのしい	enjoyable, pleasant
7	ちいさい	small
7	ちかい	near
7	つまらない	trivial, trifle, boring
7	とおい	far
7	ながい	long
14	ねむい	sleepy
8	はやい	early
9	はやい	fast
7	ひくい	low, short (height)

7	ひろい	spacious, wide
7	ふるい	old
12	ほしい	want, desire
7	まずい	not tasty, yucky
7	みじかい	short (length)
7	むずかしい	difficult
7	やさしい	easy, gentle
7	やすい	cheap, inexpensive
11	やわらかい	soft
11	わるい	bad

な -Adjectives

7	いじわる	mean
12	いろいろ	various, many kinds of
9	かんたん	easy
9	きらい	dislike
7	きれい	clean, beautiful
8	けっこう	fine, nice, wonderful
7	げんき	energetic
6	ざんねん	regrettable, regret
7	しずか	quiet
7	しつれい	impolite
9	じょうず	good at
7	しんせつ	kind
9	すき	like
12	だいじょうぶ	alright, okay
12	だいすき	like very much
5	たいへん	tough
11	だめ	no good
9	とくい	good at
7	にぎやか	lively
9	ハンサム	handsome
12	ひま	leisure, not busy
7	ふべん	inconvenient
7	ふまじめ	not serious
9	へた	bad at
7	べんり	convenient

7	まじめ	serious
14	ゆうめい	famous
14	らく	easy, simple, comfortable, relaxed

Verbal Nouns

10	インタビュー	interview
11	うんてん	drive
4	うんどう	exercise
9	オーダー	order
9	おねがい	favor, request
4	かいもの	shopping
4	コピー	copy
11	サービス	service
13	さんぽ	stroll
8	しごと	job
6	しつもん	question
14	しょうかい	introduction
5	ジョギング	jogging
12	せんたく	laundry
9	そうじ	clean
13	そつぎょう	graduation
12	ダイエット	diet
11	ダンス	dance
5	テスト	test, examination
10	でんわ	telephone
13	ひるね	nap
6	ふくしゅう	review
10	プレゼント	present
4	べんきょう	study
13	へんじ	reply
13	ホームステイ	homestay
14	よしゅう	preparatory study
12	りゅうがく	studying abroad
5	りょうり	cuisine, cooking
13	りょこう	trip, travel
9	れんしゅう	practice

う Verbs

4	あう	meet
10	あく	open
6	あそぶ	play
14	あらう	wash
3	ある	exist (things)
8	あるく	walk
11	いう	say, speak, talk
4	いく	go
8	いただく	receive
3	いらっしゃる	exist
8	うたう	sing
10	おくる	send
13	おどる	dance
6	およぐ	swim
5	かう	buy
6	かえす	return
4	かえる	go home
10	かかる	take (time, expense)
4	かく	write
9	かく	draw
8	かす	lend
10	かぶる	wear (hat, cap)
6	がんばる	do one's best
5	きく	listen, ask
14	けす	turn off
14	さがす	search for
8	しぬ	die
10	しまる	close (intransitive)
10	しる	get to know
9	すく	become empty
10	すむ	start living somewhere
10	すわる	sit down
10	たつ	stand up
6	つかう	use
10	つく	turn on
5	つくる	make
14	とまる	stay over night
5	とる	take
8	（しゃしんを）とる	take (a picture)
9	なさる	do

12	ならう	learn
14	ぬぐ	take off
14	ねむる	sleep
4	のむ	drink
13	のる	ride, get on
7	はいる	enter
10	はく	wear (shoes, socks, trousers)
14	はこぶ	carry, transport
13	はしる	run
13	はたらく	work
6	はなす	speak, chat
6	ひく	play (string instrument)
14	(かぜを) ひく	catch (cold)
14	ふとる	become fat
8	ふる	fall
12	ほしがる	show signs of desire
8	まつ	wait
8	もつ	have, hold
11	もらう	receive
14	やすむ	take a day off
14	やる	do, try
8	よぶ	call, summon
12	よぶ	invite
4	よむ	read
13	よろこぶ	(3rd person) be happy, pleased
10	わかる	understand

10	(めがねを) かける	wear (glasses)
6	かりる	borrow
11	かんがえる	think
10	きえる	turn off
10	きる	wear (dress, shirt, suit)
14	しらべる	check
13	たすける	help
4	たべる	eat
5	つかれる	get tired
14	つける	turn on
6	できる	able to (to be)
12	(〜に) でる	attend, enter (a contest)
5	ねる	go to bed, lie down
10	はじめる	start
4	みる	see, watch
14	やめる	quit doing something

Irregular Verbs

4	くる	come
4	する	do
10	する	wear (accessory)
12	ねぼうする	oversleep

る Verbs

14	あげる	raise
13	(シャワーを) あびる	take (a shower)
3	いる	exist (people, animals)
13	(しけんを) うける	take (an exam)
5	おきる	wake up, get up
14	おくれる	late (to be)
5	おしえる	teach
12	おぼえる	memorize

Appendix J   Subject Index

（〜て）ください　*please do ~*	8b
（〜ないで）ください *please don't do ~*	8c
（X を）ください・くださいませんか　*please give me X*	9e
（〜て）くださいませんか *would you please do ~?*	8b
（〜ないで）くださいませんか *would you please not do ~?*	8c
くにがまえ　kanji radical	10KN
〜ぐらい　*about/approximately ~*	10h
くんよみ　explanatory/ instructional reading	5KN

け	けっこう　*fine*	8UN
こ	ご -NOUN　beautifier	4c
	こ demonstratives	2f
	こ・そ・あ demonstratives	2f
	こちら　*this direction*	7k
	（〜た）ことがある　*have had the experience of Verb-ing*	10b
	（Dictionary フォーム +）ことが できる　*can, be able to*	6f
	（Dictionary フォーム +）ことに する　*have decided to do ~*	14c
	（Dictionary フォーム +） ことになった　*it was decided that X does ~*	14e
	（Dictionary フォーム +） ことになっている *it's been decided that X does ~*	14e
	（Dictionary フォーム +）ことに なる　*it'll become that X does ~*	14d
	〜ごろ（に）　*about / approximately ~*	10h
	ごんべん　kanji radical	9KN

し	（X は Y）じゃありません *X is not Y*	2b
	（X は Y が）じょうずだ *X is good at Y*	9a
	しょうわ	13g
	しんにゅう・しんにょう kanji radical	13KN

す	（X は Y が）すきだ　*X likes Y*	9a
	すこし　*a little*	7g
	（X に）する　*decide on X / make something X*	9g
せ	ぜんぜん　negative adverb	7g
そ	そ demonstratives	2f
	そちら　*that direction*	7k

た	〜たことがある　*have had the experience of Verb-ing*	10b
	たいしょう	13g
	（Pre- ますフォーム +） たいです　*want to do ~*	12c
	（Pre- ますフォーム +）たがっ ている　*want to do ~*	12d
	（Pre- ますフォーム +）たくない *don't want to do ~*	12c
	たフォーム	10a
	（Dictionary フォーム +）ために *in order to do ~*	14g
	たれ　kanji radical	8KN
	だれか　*someone*	3d
	だれも　*anyone*	3d

ち	ちょっと　*a little*	7g
つ	つくり　kanji radical	8KN
	（Dictionary フォーム +） つもりだ　*intend / plan to do ~*	5d
	（ないフォーム +）つもりだ *intend / plan not to do ~*	6c

て	で　instrument marker	4e
	で　location marker for action verbs	4d
	で　material marker	12f
	〜ている　*be Verb-ing*	8d
	〜ている　*have Verb-ed*	10c
	てがみのかきかた　letter format	13h
	〜てください　*please do ~*	8b
	〜てくださいませんか *would you please do ~?*	8b
	（past tense of）です	11c
	〜てみる　*try to do ~ ; do ~ and see what it is like*	14f
	です：X は Y です　*X is Y*	2a

(X は Y) ではありません *X is not Y*		2b
てフォーム		8a
てフォームソング		8a
と	と: X と Y *and*	3e
	と *with*	4h
	ど interrogatives	2f
	どうして *why*	12e
	どうしてですか *why is / was it so?*	5g
	(X は) どうですか *how about X?*	8f
	(X は) どうですか *how is X?*	7i
	〜ときに *when*	13b
	(X は Y が) とくいだ *X is good at Y*	9a
	どこかに *somewhere*	3d
	どこにも *anywhere*	3d
	どなたか *someone* (respectful)	3d
	どなたも *anyone* (respectful)	3d
	となり *next to*	3c
	どんな *what kind of*	7j
な	な -Adjectives	7b
	(Negative フォーム of) な -Adjectives	7b
	〜ないことにする *have decided not to do ~*	14c
	〜ないことになった *it was decided that X does not do ~*	14e
	〜ないことになっている *it's been decided that X does not do ~*	14e
	〜ないことになる *it'll become that X does not do ~*	14d
	〜ないつもりだ *intend / plan not to do ~*	6c
	〜ないでください *please don't do ~*	8c
	〜ないでくださいませんか *would you please not do ~?*	8c
	ないフォーム	6a
	なかったフォーム	10a
	なぜ *why*	12e

など: X や Y など *X and Y among other things*		5h
なに interrogative pronoun		2d
なにか *something*		3d
なにも *anything*		3d
なべぶた kanji radical		9KN
に	に direction / goal marker	4f
	に indirect object marker	10e
	に location marker	3c
	に object marker	5a
	に time marker	4g
	(Pre- ますフォーム +) に＋いく・くる・かえる *go / come / return in order to do ~*	6e
	にょう kanji radical	8KN
	にんべん kanji radical	11KN
	(NOUN +) に＋いく *go for NOUN*	13c
ね	ね	4l
の	の: NOUN の NOUN	2e
	ので *because*	14a
	(Plain フォーム +) のです・んです *it is the case that ~*	6g
は	は negative scope marker	6h
	は topic marker	3b
	は - が construction	7e
ひ	ひとりで *by oneself*	4h
	ひへん kanji radical	8KN
へ	へ direction / goal marker	4f
	へいせい	13g
	(X は Y が) へただ *X is bad at Y*	9a
	へん kanji radical	8KN
ほ	(X が) ほしい *want X*	12a
	(X は Y を) ほしがっている *X wants Y*	12b
	(X は) ほしくありません・ないです *don't want X*	12a
ま	(Pre- ますフォーム +) ましょう *let's do*	4j
	(Pre- ますフォーム +) ましょうか *shall we do ~?*	4j

(Pre- ますフォーム +) ませんか *won't you do ~?;* *would you like to do ~?*		6d
まだ *still*		8e
まだ *yet*		5i
まだれ kanji radical		12KN
まで: A から B まで *from A to B; from A as far as B*		4i
み	(〜て) みる *try to do ~;* *do ~ and see what it is like*	14f
め	めいじ	13g

も	も *also*	2g
	もう *already*	5i
	もうすぐ *soon*	5UN
	もんがまえ kanji radical	10KN
や	や: X や Y など *X and Y among other things*	5h
よ	よ final particle	3f
	ようび days of the week	4m
	よこ *beside*	3c
を	を object marker	4b
ん	ん moraic consonant	1f